PLAY RECONSIDERED

THOMAS S. HENRICKS

Play Reconsidered

SOCIOLOGICAL PERSPECTIVES
ON HUMAN EXPRESSION

UNIVERSITY OF ILLINOIS PRESS

URBANA AND CHICAGO

© 2006 by the Board of Trustees
of the University of Illinois
Manufactured in the United States of America
1 2 3 4 5 C P 5 4 3 2 1

∞ This book is printed on acid-free paper.

Library of Congress Cataloging-in-Publication Data
Henricks, Thomas S.
Play reconsidered : sociological perspectives on human
expression / Thomas S. Henricks.
p.   cm.
Includes bibliographical references and index.
ISBN-13: 978-0-252-03078-9 (cloth : alk. paper)
ISBN-10: 0-252-03078-8 (cloth : alk. paper)
ISBN-13: 978-0-252-07318-2 (pbk. : alk. paper)
ISBN-10: 0-252-07318-5 (pbk. : alk. paper)
1. Play—Sociological aspects.
I. Title.
GV14.45H466   2006
306.4'81—dc22   2005031443

Contents

Acknowledgments

Like the expressive behaviors that are the subject of this book, scholarly activities are shaped by many different forces and forms. Some of these influences—people, ideas, and circumstances—establish topics and lines of thought. Others operate in more distant and mysterious ways. The capabilities, character, and style of expression of writers are ultimately the results of their upbringing. And writers can only work because others provide the resources and freedom for them to do so. As will be seen, much of what follows is a kind of dialogue with the dead, an attempt to understand what was said—and not said—by the classic sociologists. Other people, however, have been more proximate, and continuing, sources of support.

Within this latter category, I would thank first my colleagues at TASP, the Association for the Study of Play. By welcoming and responding thoughtfully to scholarly work of all types, the members of that organization have provided the playful space for my theoretical reckonings to take shape and grow. Special thanks goes to Brian Sutton-Smith, who is, to my mind at least, the modern authority on the nature and significance of play. Because this book focuses on the contributions of sociologists—and because Professor Sutton-Smith is a folklorist and cross-cultural psychologist—his work is not featured in its own chapter. However, he has steadfastly encouraged the development of this project; and the perceptive reader will note his influence in much of what follows. I would also thank John Loy for his support, including his identification of significant themes and theorists. I have long admired Professor Loy's sociological treatments of sport; my own analyses of play try to incorporate some of his sensibility.

Like other professors, I am indebted to institutional friends and co-workers. Elon University has provided me with periods for concentrated study, and university librarians have helped me obtain needed resources. More generally, Elon colleagues promote an institutional culture that blends teaching and research and that honors different forms of scholarly expression. I would also thank here Laurie Matheson at the University of Illinois Press. Her shepherding of this project through its various phases—including her attempts to sharpen the focus and appeal of the work—are reflected in the pages that follow. Special thanks also to Angela Burton for her oversight of the final stages of the manuscript preparation process and to copyeditor Louis Simon for his thorough and perceptive reading. The final version of the text presented here has been much improved because of their recommendations.

At a greater distance are some professors who have shaped my intellectual style and commitments. My interest in theoretical sociology was encouraged and directed by Donald Levine, Victor Lidz, and Barry Schwartz. Two other teachers, Mihaly Csikszentmihalyi and Victor Turner, pushed forward my curiosities about play. Even farther back, Professors Richard Thurston and John Reist set forth the challenges of scholarly writing. Beyond this, they bear no responsibilities for what appears here.

Most people are products of their family connections, past and present. Like many other spouses and partners, my wife, Judy, has supported—and otherwise made possible—this long undertaking. I thank her, my parents, and my children for making tangible the boundaries of a life.

PLAY RECONSIDERED

1 Johan Huizinga's Challenge to Play Studies

Human beings, it is sometimes said, long for both the contradictory and the impossible. We want a world filled with fresh and stimulating experiences, but we also want the comforts and stability of home. We desire to be unbound, to wander freely, and to take what we please. But we also want to be needed, to have others hold us down and make our lives worthwhile. We fancy ourselves to be distinctive, never-to-be-repeated beings whose destiny is to rise above others. Yet we crave the support and companionship of those very others, and we would never rise so far that we cannot sense their approbation. Part of us seeks creativity and rebellion; the other part, shelter and direction. Security and stimulation, permanence and change, innocence and knowledge, love and hate—it is in our nature to contemplate the oppositions of life. As Boorstin (1962, pp. 3–6) once framed the matter, we want more than the world can hold.

Perhaps no academic field confronts these contradictions and ambiguities quite as directly as the study of human play. For play is the laboratory of the possible. To play fully and imaginatively is to step sideways into another reality, between the cracks of ordinary life. Although that ordinary world, so full of cumbersome routines and responsibilities, is still visible to us, its images, strangely, are robbed of their powers. Selectively, players take the objects and ideas of routine life and hold them aloft. Like willful children, they unscrew reality or rub it on their bodies or toss it across the room. Things are dismantled and built anew.

Such reckless manipulation is customary only for kings and gods. But in play, all of us are granted a certain dispensation from the normal consequences of action. Players hit and shout and run about as if possessed. Bedclothes become royal garments; heroic personalities are fashioned; boundary lines are drawn between rocks and trees. New purposes—seemingly of the most artificial or trivial character—are adopted and then pursued with a fascinated intensity. Likewise, relationships feel fresh and alive. People become parents and children, deadly enemies, blood brothers, firefighters, and lovers in new ways. To play deeply is to cut oneself off from the continuities and complexities of life. Reality, at that point, becomes a kid and a ball. Eventfulness reigns.

If play is indeed the triumph of present over past and future, it should be noted that this present can quickly take the shape of a fully developed world. Like Lewis Carroll's Alice, we find ourselves suddenly in a place where customary logic no longer applies. Space and time take on radically new meanings. Language confounds us. People—and ideas—scurry about. We are surprised at every turn. In such ways, the play world is a kind of puzzlement. Like Alice, we are drawn in deeper and deeper, at each moment learning something curious about the universe and about ourselves.

Play and the Modern Social Sciences

Like other portions of contemporary society, the academic world is compartmentalized. Consistent with the division of labor in other fields, knowledge making has been apportioned to a growing number of disciplines and subdisciplines, each with its own fiercely guarded set of claims, commitments, and traditions. Typically, scholars are trained within these disciplines and receive academic appointments inside their boundaries. Not surprisingly, scholarly creativity tends to be evaluated in these terms as well. "Solid" or substantial scholarship is that which comprehends and contributes to the ever-changing discourse within these fields. With dozens of studies produced each year in even the narrowest of disciplines, scholars race to keep up. Under such terms, it is fitting that academia should be dominated by a cult of expertise, that scholars should know more and more about less and less.

Of course, some topics are too broad or important to be contained by any one discipline. Subjects like war, racism, poverty, crime, and so forth, pose challenges for every aspect of human experience. However, such topics tend to be approached as "interdisciplinary" or "multi-disciplinary" ventures. That is, the different dimensions of the issue in question are commonly divided up among the specialists at hand. These specialists are expected to concentrate on aspects of the general problem that reflect the concerns and capabilities of their respective disciplines. Through some undefined integrative process, these different studies are gathered together. Knowledge marches forward.

Understood in this context, the study of human play has been doubly burdened. On the one hand, no discipline has moved this topic to the center of its theoretical or research tradition or otherwise claimed its ownership. Perhaps play, like those other topics listed above, is simply too broad and evanescent a concept to be contained by any one field. However, it would also be difficult to claim that play has been a subject of great interdisciplinary interest. Despite—as I will try to show—the wide-ranging implications of play for human experience, other matters within the social sciences have been felt generally to be much more "serious" or consequential. In the past, this reticence of scholars to focus intensively on play was traced to the lingering effects of Protestantism, or at least its morally reproving versions, on the academy. However, in our purportedly post-industrial world—where cultural innovation, leisure, and personal experience have taken center stage—this reticence is more difficult to understand.

To argue that studies of play have been much less prominent within the social sciences than studies of work, religion, family life, inequality, and so on, is not to claim that play has been without its scholarly proponents. Certainly some of the more notable observers in the social and behavioral sciences (e.g., Erikson, 1950; Freud, 1958; Piaget, 1962; Csikszentmihalyi, 1990) have emphasized the importance of play in human experience; and within the last thirty years, play studies has emerged as a matter for coordinated interdisciplinary interest. National and international play studies associations have been founded; advocacy organizations have articulated the value of certain kinds of play, playgrounds, and toys for child development and community life. Nevertheless, the future development of play studies seems limited by the deficiencies of the multi-disciplinary model used within academia as a whole and by the interests of the specialists who heretofore have gathered at the table.

In what is probably the most important work on the nature of play in recent years, Sutton-Smith (1997) has argued that the play studies literature can be organized in terms of seven major "rhetorics" or "ideologies," each with its own characteristic way of approaching the subject. For example, certain researchers have focused on play as "progress," as creative or recreational activity that promotes the personal growth of players. Other researchers, he argues, have focused on play as "power," emphasizing forms of social contest or confrontation that may be functional for society as whole. Still other scholars have seen play as an exploration of chance or fate, as an occasion for social bonding, as imaginative manipulation, as a special pattern of personal experience or selfhood, and as a pattern of foolery and status inversion. Scholars focusing on ancient and traditional societies frequently highlight the rhetorics of power, community identity, frivolity, and fate. Students of the modern world tend to favor the rhetorics of progress, imagination, and the self.

On the one hand, Sutton-Smith celebrates this diversity of play research. However, he is also critical of the extent to which play studies reflects the compartmentalization found in other portions of academic life. That is, the prevailing traditions of play research must be considered rhetorics or ideologies in the sense that scholars seem trapped within their own narrow, but strongly defended, conceptions of play. At interdisciplinary conferences, these scholars listen politely enough to the views of one another and then retreat quickly to the very paradigms from which they began (see Sutton-Smith 2003, p. 262). In his view, play studies needs to transcend these limited frameworks by building models that incorporate the wonderful variety and ambiguity of play.

Sutton-Smith's own approach to these matters has been to emphasize the extent to which play researchers restrict themselves to certain settings or scenes of play—including schoolrooms, casinos, football fields, neighborhoods, and the minds of young children. Having situated themselves in this fashion, these scholars conduct their studies with a set of preconceived notions, reach the desired results, and then proclaim the truth of their findings for all forms of play. In that context, his *The Ambiguity of Play* is essentially an attempt to bind together these seven approaches, to discover what is common and different about them. For Sutton-Smith, that common thread is the extent to which all play activities cultivate the variability or flexibility of creatures, so that they may respond to ever-widening sets of challenges.

The current book attempts to participate in this project of theoretical synthesis in a different way. I argue that play studies has been dominated by the perspectives and concerns of certain disciplines within the social and behavioral sciences. These disciplines in my view are education, psychology, folklore, animal behavior studies, and anthropology. Taken together, these viewpoints have shaped the contemporary understanding of play. In what follows, I do not dispute the continuing importance of these fields but rather argue that these traditions need to be supplemented and integrated with other approaches.

For their part, educational researchers have emphasized the role of play in the lives of young children (see Sponseller, 1974; Smith, 1986; Klugman and Smilansky, 1990; Christie, 1991). In educational research, play activities are seen typically as opportunities to enrich regimens of school or home. Organized informally by small groups or under the guidance of a parent/teacher, play is understood to have numerous positive functions for human development. In that spirit, Lin and Reifel (1999, p. 151) list the following themes:

> Play is a remarkably important activity for children. Not only is it a means for expanding the self, but it is a major tool of self-preservation. Play is the province of the child. It is a "laboratory" where children can learn new skills and practice old ones in preparation for adult life in society. Play is also a social workshop, an area for trying out roles, both alone and with other children. Play is also an area for expression; it is concerned with the themes and emotions that are experienced in everyday life. By studying children's play, we can understand what they think and feel about the world around them. We also have a better understanding of all aspects of their development by studying play.

In this context, playful children are thought to acquire intellectual and social skills, stimulate their own creativity, and develop mastery of the object-world more quickly than their less playful peers. For such reasons, play has become a central element in the theory of active learning that now pervades educational practice from preschool through college.

Although education scholars have been perhaps the principal champions of Sutton-Smith's "play as progress" ideology, their viewpoints have been buttressed, for the most part, by studies from cognitive and developmental psychology (see Erikson, 1950; Vygotsky, 1962; Piaget, 1962; Bruner, Jolly, and Sylva, 1976; Rubin, 1980). Scholars in these fields foreground the extent to which play is an expression of the developing physical, mental, and emotional capabilities of the child. Assisting those patterns of development is a special kind of awareness, a recognition by players that they have entered an *autotelic* zone where distinctive rules and purposes pertain. With the matter so defined, participants seek optimal levels of stimulation (Berlyne, 1960), indulge their desires to "assimilate" the object-world (Piaget, 1962), pursue forbidden thoughts and behaviors (Freud, 1938), or become lost in a "flow" of momentary requirements (Csikszentmihalyi, 1990). So understood, playful activity becomes equivalent to a series of personal challenges and responses, connections and disconnections, successes and failures. By such processes, people experience the modalities of personal commitment and expand the range of their abilities.

As practiced by both educational researchers and psychologists then, play studies has tended to reflect an idealistic, somewhat romantic vision of the human being. Central to this vision is the belief that people—and especially young children—are naturally active and curious. If only we release them from the drudgery of routine social existence, they will fashion wonderful new worlds. Using their own sense of what is intrinsically satisfying as a guide, children will pull themselves upward. New challenges will be accepted, new skills developed. In this context, play is seen as a kind of reverberation between the emotional and the cognitive-moral aspects of experience. Learning advances quickly when it is associated with a distinctive range of emotions. In play studies, pleasure and related forms of excitement are thought to be more efficacious than boredom and pain. For such reasons, educational and psychological studies of play have focused less on schoolyard bullies and more on those imaginative, achieving children who will become—with only a little prodding from adults—their better selves.

The somewhat darker possibilities of children's play have been explored in folklore studies (see Opie and Opie, 1959; 1969; Sutton-Smith, Mechling, Johnson, and McMahon, 1995). Collecting and analyzing the songs, stories, jokes, rhymes, and games of past and present, folklorists expose the living heritage of children's culture. That culture, they assert, is no orderly, placid realm. Instead, the play world surges with creative, aggressive, and even sexual fascinations. At times, these songs and stories seem to reflect the efforts of adults to mystify and otherwise control children. But other expressions are clearly the work of children themselves, who use flamboyant imagery to mark the boundaries of the world. In such settings, players are frequently saboteurs, defilers of all that is ordinary and dear (Sutton-Smith, 1997, pp. 111–126).

This connection of play to individual development appears as well in studies of other types of mammals (see Fagen, 1981; Smith, 1982; Chick, 2001). In such accounts, animal play is presented as a special commitment of the young. Playfulness is associated not only with those species that possess a relatively large neocortex but also with those points in the life cycle when this portion of the brain is growing the fastest. Like humans, animal players seem to recognize a quality of pretense or make-believe in their activity and exhibit mannerisms consistent with human expressions of enjoyment. Why they play is a matter of some conjecture; however, the broadest interpretations suggest that play allows creatures to develop a range of skills fostering greater flexibility in the face of changing environmental conditions (Sutton-Smith, 2001). In other words, enhanced intellectual, physical, and social skills (including the ability to cooperate) promote the survival of both individuals and species.

As the reader will have noted, play studies tends to emphasize the positive rather than negative functions of play. In that sense, play is more the creator than the destroyer of worlds. Players build patterns—including strategies of emotional management, physical abilities, social skills, and broad cognitive frameworks—that may be useful to them later in life. Somewhat evangelically then, play scholars frequently tout the value of their subject matter as a stabilizing and integrating enterprise.

This emphasis on the functions of play is perpetuated in the anthropological tradition (see Lancy and Tindall, 1976; Mergen, 1986; Roopnarine, Johnson, and Hooper, 1994; Reifel, 1999). For its part, physical anthropology connects human biology and behavior to related mammalian forms. Play symbolizes our deep connection to other creatures at the same time that it illustrates distinctively human traits. In contrast, cultural anthropology explores variation in societal and subcultural expressions of play. More clearly than other disciplines, anthropology has been sensitive to play as a matter for adults rather than children and to the connections between play and other community activities like religious rituals, military exercises, courtship festivities, and sports. For such reasons, anthropological studies are explorations of the public as well as private meanings of play.

The Promise of Sociology for Play Studies

Despite the efforts of anthropologists and folklorists to broaden the examples and meanings of play, I think it is fair to say that play continues to be viewed through a rather narrow lens. That lens has allowed some aspects of play to be seen quite clearly while others appear only in vague or distant ways. Among the aspects emphasized has been the view of play as a relatively free or voluntaristic activity. Compared to other pursuits, play is usually thought to be a time when people "take over" their own affairs. Ideals of democratic governance, egalitarianism, friendly competition, and cooperation prevail. Rigidly proscriptive patterns from other institutional settings are commonly avoided, inverted, or mocked (see Handelman, 1998). In play, so it is argued, people can have the world to their liking.

Closely connected to this viewpoint is the premise that play features intrinsic satisfactions and the perception of "internal" (rather than "external") control of behavior. Again, in contrast to other activities, play gives people a chance to shape the world—and to do so according to their own terms and timing. In such ways, play is seen as the triumph of personal motivation over public constraint. Individual disposition and urgency are both instigators and sounding boards for a complicated chain of events.

Finally, the five disciplines in general have tended to see play from a constructivist or functionalist perspective. As noted above, players are seen as builders of natural and social relationships. What they build is thought to have consequences for the larger realms of order that are the contexts of their lives. Whether people are merely blowing off steam or escaping from the unpleasantness of life, play is thought to be an energizer and motivator of subsequent conduct. We not only build ourselves in play; we conceive and administer social arrangements that guide the lives of others.

If play studies can be seen as a party buoyed by the enthusiasm and idealism of its academic guests, then the sociologist may be seen as the person who arrives late and somehow manages to deflate the affair. In what follows, I focus on certain aspects of play that have not been prominently displayed in the individualistic orientation that dominates the discipline. These aspects, I argue, are fundamental themes of sociological analysis.

If play studies historically has emphasized the relative freedom and egalitarianism of players, then sociology directs us to patterns of social entanglement and hierarchy (see Gruneau, 1983; Henricks, 1991). The relatively intrinsic motives suggested by most students of play are countered by the sociologist's emphasis on external incentives and social functions. The individual or cultural focus of other disciplines is replaced by the more clearly organizational or group focus of the sociologist. Even the broad view of the player as person shifts toward a much narrower and more impersonal view of the participant as role performer (see Simmel, 1950; Goffman, 1961b; Aycock, 1998).

In general terms, sociology provides a set of qualifications on the nature of playful expression. At one level, this means that sociology questions the idea that individuals are freer in play than in other endeavors to pursue their own desires. Play, it will be argued, exhibits social structures only somewhat dissimilar from those found in other parts of life. These structures not only restrict people's personal freedom but also enable them to accomplish things they would be unable to do alone. The sociological contribution is the emphasis on the ways in which social structure acts as a framework for human endeavor. To play with others is to enter a realm of interconnection that is much more complicated than the play of individuals with the material world.

The issues having been defined in this fashion, this book will show the pertinence of sociology to play studies. To move forward in this way is not to claim that current orientations are somehow misguided or wrong but rather that other aspects of playful experience deserve attention. Also, it should be acknowledged quickly that sociological curiosity itself is not new to this field. Many scholars, including some prominent sociologists, have analyzed the social context of both youthful and adult play (see, e.g., Piaget, 1962; Erikson, 1950; Denzin, 1977; Fine, 1983); and many disciplines pride themselves on their sensitivity to social matters. Social psychology focuses on relationships between the personal and social; anthropology comments extensively on socio-cultural issues; and educational scholars are experts at describing the various social systems of playground and school. All this notwithstanding, I would argue that the sociological perspective itself rarely is presented in a systematic or specific way in the play studies literature. Even less prominent, I would claim, have been arguments shaped by sociology's great theorists and their respective traditions.

I advocate a return to these classic theorists in part because they frame sociological issues in very powerful and compelling ways. As is often said, contemporary scholars sometimes spend their entire careers only to come to places inhabited long ago by the classic thinkers. However, the greatness of these early writers also derives from the scope of their vision. That is, the classic thinkers were less constrained by the academic boundaries that we now recognize. Commenting on or otherwise organizing philosophical, historical, anthropological, and psychological matters was not at that point a sin. In that broad way then, these thinkers help us to understand play not as a solitary phenomenon but as an element within expressive life more generally. Even more profoundly, they make us confront the place of play within the patterning of human relationship.

Huizinga's Challenge to Play Studies

In any scholarly inquiry one must find a point of entry, a set of central questions to ask and answer. For the sociologist, those questions were asked most pointedly and profoundly by a Dutch historian, Johan Huizinga, during the late 1930s. Huizinga's (1955) *Homo Ludens: A Study of the Play-Element in Culture*, is by every standard a curious work. Written by a specialist in European cultural history and the social life of the Middle Ages, Huizinga's book is less an historical accounting than a gathering of information from all times and places to support an imaginative thesis. The thesis is that play—understood in a distinctive way—has been a central element in the development of societies. However, in Huizinga's view, the once prominent position of play has been eroded dramatically by the economic and political forces of the modern age.

Huizinga first defines play and then attempts to show how this activity was institutionalized in such aspects of early social life as language, games, law, war, philosophy, poetry, mythopoeisis, and art. In his view, the previous centuries of world history were marked by socially fixed occasions in which people competed with one another publicly. Such high-spirited and symbolically charged wrangling by prominent individuals was the way in which significant ideas were tried out, refuted, and reformed. In Huizinga's judgment, history is not only the accounting of technological progress or political and economic movements but also the analysis of cultural interchange and development. Thus, tennis courts, courts of law, debating and scientific societies, song duels, parliaments, potlatch festivals, and philosophical bantering find their places as crucibles of social change. For Huizinga play is not to be sought within some separate institution of society. Rather it is a distinctive form of relationship that stands at the center of public imagination and conduct.

Having defined his thesis so broadly, Huizinga was similarly ecumenical with his choice of supporting evidence. Ethnographic descriptions, studies in philology, histories of art, sociological accounts of the social structure of early societies, philosophical observations, and works of literature, are all cast into the fray. Moreover, Huizinga colors his arguments with a beautiful writing style that is as much art as social science. Time and again, the reader is stunned by the author's quality of insight and by the depth of his knowledge. For such reasons, many commentators (see Roszak, 1972; Ehrman, 1968; Levy, 1978; Sutton-Smith, 1997) have seen *Homo Ludens* as one of the most daringly conceived and erudite works in the history of the social sciences, a compelling depiction of the very course of civilization. However, others (see Geyl, 1963; Duncan, 1988; Gruneau, 1983; Nagel, 1998) have seen the book as sometimes vague and overblown, a selective commentary that ignores the grittier aspects of earlier centuries.

In my view, *Homo Ludens* remains, after more than sixty years, the greatest treatment of the socio-cultural implications of play. This status is due more to the nobility of its reach than to its grasp. Huizinga set forth in his opening pages a view of play that identifies many of the issues that modern scholars still struggle to understand. Likewise, his controversial thesis about the shifting status of play in human history is a profound commentary on the character of society itself. In the following, I will describe the challenge that his work raises for modern sociology.

Huizinga's Definition of Play

Surely the most well-known portion of *Homo Ludens* is the conception of play developed in the opening chapter. Like many other scholars, Huizinga wished to comprehend the nature of human capability, particularly as it is expressed in the development of social and cultural forms. Other writers, he notes in his foreword, have emphasized such themes as reasoning or toolmaking as distinctively human traits. However, Huizinga, who wrote his book in the shadow of the Nazi ascendancy in Europe, had come to doubt the virtues of naked reason. Similarly, the human ability to make and use tools is perhaps not distinctive; other animals transform the material world for their purposes as well. Alongside *homo sapiens* and *homo faber* then, Huizinga proposes a third theme. Humans have especially developed capacities to play, that is, to hold the world lightly and creatively. Our species, it seems, can step back from the grim necessities of life. In our minds, we can see new possibilities and together plot a common future.

In Huizinga's view, the capacity of human beings to play is primordial; that is, it precedes the development of society or culture. To support this view, he notes the role of play in the lives of various animal species. Indeed, he contends (1955, p. 1), with a certain overstatement, that animals "play just like men." Although he denies animals the level of rationality found in humans, he argues that their play is "minded." Said differently, play is an occasion when creatures transcend the immediate needs of life and impart instead a symbolic or relational significance to their actions. There is always something "at play," some shared object or pattern of connection that frames the behavior of the participants.

He points out that animal studies and psychology typically explain play in terms of its various "functions." Thus, individuals are said to play because they are driven to discharge excess energy, satisfy imitative instincts, train the young, exercise self-restraint, develop patterns of dominance, and so forth. For Huizinga, such consequences are more the results of play than reasons for its existence. In his view, play needs no set of ulterior motives. Rather play is driven by interior, phenomenological satisfactions. In "this intensity, this absorption, this power of maddening, lies the essence, the primordial quality of play" (p. 2).

In this sense, play is an aesthetic event, a time when experience is gathered and evaluated in terms of its emotional resonance. Play is marked typically by mirth, fun, and tension. For such reasons, play must not be understood as a demonstration of human rationality, a careful calculus of the effects of thought and action. However, as he (p. 3) famously puts it, "play only becomes possible, thinkable, and understandable when an influx of mind breaks down the absolute determinism of the cosmos." To that degree, play is about the expressive capacities of the mind, about the desire of creatures to make their mark upon the world and behold the effects of that activity.

Seen in this light, playfulness is a distinctive stance that humans take before the world. It is not only that we are able to play but also that we are able to know when we are playing. Furthermore, we are aware that there are differences between play and other modes of relating. For Huizinga (p. 4) play is a "special form of activity," a "well-defined quality of action which is different from ordinary life." Furthermore, play is not reducible to other forms of experience. However, it is curiously connected to such matters as laughter, comedy, folly, myth, ritual, and even beauty. Huizinga struggles with some of these distinctions throughout his book. Early in the text, though, he forsakes that task and instead produces his famous listing of the "chief characteristics" of play.

PLAY IS VOLUNTARY

For Huizinga, play is not part of the "natural process," the patterning of action and reaction that characterizes so much of existence. Instead, play is something added to or spread over life. In that sense, players are able to pause the customary chain of events; consciousness becomes reflexive. Although it does seem true that people and animals are "driven" to play, there is also a sense in which play opposes determinism. In play, we are able to choose courses of action and to adjust those courses based on the internal satisfactions we receive. Play, in its most essential form, is not a job or duty.

PLAY IS NOT ORDINARY OR REAL LIFE

In play, people are aware that they are doing something temporary and different. Even for children, play has a strong "only pretending" quality. To play is to cast a kind of spell over the moment, to suspend routine responsibilities and repercussions. However, players are also aware that this newly fashioned world may well be deemed trivial or transitory by customary standards. To play deeply is to commit oneself to a somewhat artificial, fictional version of the world. As Huizinga (p. 6) notes, sometimes this commitment takes the form of entrancement or rapture, and play becomes invested with the deepest levels of psychological seriousness.

This distinction between play and other patterns of interaction is also manifested in the "disinterestedness" of play. Here, Huizinga is thinking of the relative absence of material consequence. In his view, play is an interlude. It does not seek to satisfy our needs for food, shelter, sexual expression, and so on. Rather, it develops as a kind of personal and cultural adornment, a commentary on or reaffirmation of one's position in the world. For Huizinga (p. 9) play inhabits a "sphere superior to the strictly biological processes of nutrition, reproduction, and self-preservation." In play, we ascend to new levels that express the full dimensions of our humanity.

PLAY IS SECLUDED AND LIMITED

Our experience of the world is wrapped in space and time. To enter the playground is to adopt new understandings of these ideas. As Huizinga (p. 9) explains, play "contains its own course and meanings." In play, the demands—and clock time—of the outside world typically are set aside. Play is started with new notions of pace and pattern and continues until it reaches its own type of conclusion. However, Huizinga emphasizes, play displays a curious tension between the momentary and the eternal. Once played, the play event assumes a kind of historical status that can be referred to later. Furthermore, many types of play are structured by rules that allow the experience to be repeated, with nearly endless variation. Thus, to play a game is to reclaim suddenly experiences one has had before or even, more profoundly, to retrace the steps of anyone who has ever played the game.

Similarly, play is marked by new conventions regarding physical space. Boundary lines are established; objects within those boundaries take on new meanings. As Huizinga (p. 10) puts it, "The arena, the card table, the magic circle, the temple, the stage, the screen, the tennis court, the court of justice, etc., all are in form and function playgrounds, i.e., forbidden spots, isolated, hedged round, within which special rules obtain." To this degree, the playground resembles the "consecrated spot" so crucial to rituals.

PLAY CREATES ORDER, IS ORDER

Into a confused and complicated world, play brings a temporary sort of perfection. For Huizinga, play is especially order-making activity. That is, difficulties or challenges are (often artificially) created and then resolved. Play features an alternation between tension and completion, between opposition and union. For such reasons, the experience of play is commonly an aesthetic one, an encounter with rhythm and harmony.

Just as "successful" play must be tense, so it must have its rules. Rules are the framework that allows people to focus precisely, to repeat their activity, and to communicate with one another in joint play. About these rules, Huizinga (p. 10) states, there can be no dispute. For to claim the rules faulty or ridiculous is to be a "spoilsport," one who challenges the very legitimacy of the activity. Even the "cheat," someone who pretends to observe the rules, is less threatening. By contrast, spoilsports rob play of its quality of illusion. The entire affair becomes a sham.

PLAY SURROUNDS ITSELF WITH SECRECY

Part of the charm of play is the shared awareness that participants have separated themselves voluntarily from the normal course of events. To play together is to commit to one another, to affirm that these moments spent together (in what are often the silliest of endeavors) are valuable. Moreover, to play together is to make clear that others are not included. Those outsiders and their concerns are of no pertinence here. Thus, Huizinga's final characteristic of play is this quality of secrecy, the fact that some are "in the know" and others are not. To reinforce this distinction, players love to adorn themselves with elaborate costumes, curious equipment, and arcane expressions. By dressing up in this way players become other beings, people who have left behind their routine identities.

Huizinga's conception of play deserves its renown. Better than perhaps any other author, Huizinga describes the curious interplay between order and disorder that exists in play. Moreover, he illustrates well the scope of his subject. Play is not simply an activity of humans but of animals as well. Play is both mental and emotional, physical and symbolic. It can be a solitary enterprise but it is perhaps more interestingly an interactive endeavor. It touches adults as deeply as children.

More significant still is Huizinga's claim that play is not some isolated occasion but rather a crucial element of societal functioning. Playful activities may be structured into the conduct of public institutions or they may simply erupt, thereby stopping and transforming ordinary affairs. In that regard, play is often connected to ordinary life. Indeed, in its more stable forms, it frequently expresses itself as "a contest for something" of social value or, alternately, as a "representation of something" (p. 13). These two versions of play are the ones that Huizinga pursues in his treatment of the changing role of play in culture.

Play and Culture

Huizinga's controversial thesis is that play and culture were once connected in an intimate, almost living way. Indeed, early forms of play were sources of and contributors to cultural consciousness and creativity. However, if play once had an originative status with respect to culture, now that relationship has been reversed. Culture has captured and marginalized play and, in the process, stripped it of its possibilities.

Inherent in such a claim is the proposition that society itself has changed through the years. For Huizinga the historian, the task was also to indicate some of the changes in social structure that have occurred in the transition to the modern world. Arguably, play once occupied social spaces in traditional and archaic societies that either have been altered radically or no longer exist. Thus, to mourn the decline of play, as Huizinga does, is to mourn the decline of those societies. Indeed, it was during the writing of his great elegy to those earlier days, *The Waning of the Middle Ages*, that Huizinga (1954, p. 104) first became aware of the profound relationship between play and culture.

Although Huizinga does not systematically describe the transformation to the modern world, some of those changes can be pieced together in roughly the following way. Earlier societies were smaller and more local and anchored by patterns of oral communication. They were, to use modern sociological parlance, less "differentiated." That is, the different institutional spheres (economy, politics, education, religion, family, etc.) had not yet been separated—each with its distinctive organizations, personnel, and codes of conduct—as they are now. As a consequence, the relevant social bodies of the times (families, clans, tribes, village communities, etc.) were expected to handle most of the personal and social requirements of their members.

To the same degree, culture was not yet differentiated. Music, dance, philosophy, art, and religious belief and practice were not separate spheres. Knowledge was gathered in the person or group and often guarded in a jealous, secretive fashion. As Huizinga (chapter 6) emphasizes, in those pre–Socratic days, erudition was something of a medicine show filled with answerless puzzles, rhetorical displays, personal attacks, and evasive bombast. Under such circumstances, the goal of the mystagogue was more to defeat his rivals (and thereby augment his own status) than to promote general enlightenment.

Furthermore, the relationship of the person to the group was different from our current conceptions. Individualism as a concept was not well developed. Rather, people were members of social bodies that not only preceded them in time but also defined most aspects of their identity. And the leaders of those groups spoke for their members with a confidence perhaps lost to the modern world. Because of the tight connection between people and the groups that defined them, beliefs about honor, shame, and duty were felt profoundly.

Significantly, because writing had not yet trapped (and thereby rendered abstract) the world, social life had a vibrant, interactive quality that is missing in the contemporary era. Without the props and repositories of written culture, people were to a greater degree than now the vessels of culture. For such reasons, societal continuity depended on personal proclamations or other public enactments of belief and custom.

Although the common view of traditional societies is that of a largely changeless world anchored in myth and ritual, Huizinga tended to see past societies as much more contentious and dynamic. Although mythic forms were used to enforce a wider sense of social solidarity, there was, in his view, spectacular rivalry between subgroups and their respective champions. Thus, public ceremonies were occasions when groups could jockey for status, exchange prestige-laden goods, or otherwise show off.

To summarize, social life in earlier times was somewhat less articulated. The public and private dimensions of existence were not firmly separated; people were expected to express themselves publicly and to do so with the full measure of their being. Likewise, the intellectual, moral, and aesthetic aspects of culture were not yet parsed into distinct spheres, each with its own standards. Public expression involved all these elements at once; "common sense" was fashioned collectively through stinging verbal attacks, songs, stories, poems, sheer ranting, and physical display. In that sense, wisdom traditions were, at some level, collective theater. And, perhaps most profoundly, the contemplative dimension of life was not isolated from the world of action. To be sure, archaic societies were marked by deep mysteries and secrets; but there was a sense that these could not be figured out in a straightforward, logical way. Rather, knowledge had to be deduced or discovered by combinations of luck, ingenuity, personal courage, and trickery directed at the holders of the secrets. To live wisely and well, one had to court the favor of the gods.

In all these ways, Huizinga saw earlier civilizations as being somehow younger and less settled. For its part, the supernatural could be seen as especially quirky. Spirits and gods might have unclear, shifting relationships to one another, and their "personalities" could be as tempestuous and unpredictable as the weather. Thus, ordinary people were ever in the process of developing and repairing their relationships with spiritual forces. In that light, a key function of public events was the building of bridges between the supernatural realm and the world of ordinary affairs.

As Huizinga (1955, p. 31) emphasizes then, play was originally part of a broader "play-festival-rite complex," a mixture of institutionalized public events that served a range of purposes. In that light, the display-oriented or representative aspects of the event (the symbolic presentations and re-presentations typically associated with "ritual") mingled with the experience-oriented qualities thought to be essential to "play." Likewise, the serious purposes characteristic of ritual might coexist with the more energized, fanciful renderings typical of play. For such reasons, ritual and play are, at times, almost equivalents for Huizinga. As he (p. 18) puts it: "The ritual act has all the formal and essential characteristics of play which we enumerated above, particularly in so far as it transports the participants to another world. This identity of ritual and play was unreservedly recognized by Plato as a given fact." Said differently, ritual in earlier times was no simple enactment of abstract form. Rather it was an imaginative creation of order through the energy and inspiration of the participants. People "played out" symbolic events so that these might effect changes in cosmic order. In that sense, archaic play is understood by Huizinga to be a source of ritual; psychic commitments and enthusiasms preceded (and to some extent, controlled) cultural production. Furthermore, the play spirit ran roughshod over the boundaries of the serious. As he explains (p. 19), "In play, we may move below the level of the serious, as the child does; but we can also move above it—in the realm of the beautiful and the sacred." In these ways, play was a protest against the ordinary and the literal, an attempt to place human understanding and experience in a new key.

Such ideas about the effects of play on history are pushed forward in Huizinga's chapter on "play and contest as civilizing functions." In his view, the play of earlier societies was frequently articulated in two public forms: sacred performances and festal contests. If the former was especially important in reinforcing or otherwise "making real" collective ideals, the latter was the setting for dynamic interchanges that played out cultural possibilities in public ways. The histories of these contests—in such domains as law, poetry, philosophy, war, and so on—comprise the principal subject matter of the book.

It is not useful to review here the various examples and claims of those individual chapters (see instead Henricks, 2002). However, in general, Huizinga's argument is that play is a foundation for the contest.

Although he does not wish to equate play with contests that pursue material ends, he does acknowledge the playful aspects of competitions that pursue more symbolic or status-oriented outcomes. As he (p. 50) notes, competitions tend to be for something (such as a prize or rank), in something (such as a field of skill), and with something (such as the use of bodily strength or mental strategy). In such ways, play is connected closely to the valued skills and themes of societies.

Although his vision of the contest seems to parallel the "amateur" ideal in sport that was popular during his time, he does not incorporate that view in its entirety. For example, in contrast to the emphasis on gentlemanly control and fair play in the amateur ideal, Huizinga accepted cheating and trickery as legitimate elements in the contests (both mythic and real) of earlier times. Likewise, Huizinga admits gambling to be an interesting combination of play and seriousness. Moreover, the contests of traditional societies were often understood to be profound meetings between human activity and fate. The outcomes of the most carefully prepared and culturally central games might be interpreted as the will of the gods. To play in formally correct and competitively successful ways was to glimpse the future of the world.

Huizinga is emphatic about several key points. A first is that playful activities may address the most sublime and morally serious purposes. That is, although play may be a departure from ordinary life, this does not mean that it must be preoccupied only with trivial matters. Likewise, Huizinga disagrees with his mentor (and rival) Burckhardt about the place of the *agon* or social contest in history. Whereas Burckhardt has designated the sixth century B.C. in Greece as the key moment in the development of a culture of games, Huizinga argues that contests of this sort have been crucial in all types of societies over many centuries. Perhaps most critical is Huizinga's emphasis that play is not confined to contests of physical strength and skill. As noted above, *Homo Ludens* is a book about riddling games, potlatch festivals, trials by ordeal, philosophical dialectics, competitions in courtly manners, huffing barristers, competitive artisanship, and so forth. Indeed, it is this emphasis on the symbolic implications of play of many types that makes the book so remarkable.

In general, the existence of the "play-festival-rite" complex of earlier times made possible a host of social and cultural functions for play. As I have argued elsewhere (Henricks, 2002), play was a device that both dramatized existing social divisions and promoted the formation of new groupings centered on the playground. Furthermore, play permitted the negotiation of social identity in public ways. That is, winning or losing might reflect on social status more generally. More broadly, play was an integrative activity. All contestants (as well as judges and spectators) would be united under the common terms of the event.

Play events also commonly functioned as repositories of public memory. Great contests were remembered and became baselines against which more recent activity was judged. Likewise, playful contests were ways of identifying persisting cultural oppositions. Contestants frequently carried forward the values and beliefs of their sponsoring communities. The defeat of a warrior, artist, or philosopher could mean the humiliation of his ideas as well. Finally, contests were ways of demonstrating relevant cultural skills and commitments. To watch these matters played out was to contemplate the possibilities of living. For Huizinga, play in these settings was a kind of public dialectic in which people tried to advance their own personal, social, and cultural positions.

In these terms, Huizinga argues, the earlier centuries of European history were "played" in ways not known to us now. At times his commitment to this theme leads to enthusiastic overstatement. Thus (p. 179), "Medieval life was brimful of play, the joyous and unbuttoned play of the people." Shortly thereafter (p. 180), he portrays "the whole mental attitude of the Renaissance" as one of play. The seventeenth century, however angry and dour, is interpreted in his vision as a period of aristocratic delight. All this only prepares the way for the great and culminating century of play, the eighteenth, when the entire *zeitgeist* of the times is declared to have such qualities.

The great changeover occurred with the Industrial Revolution. The coming of the world of factories, capitalism, and cities—with their fundamentally materialistic sensibilities and bourgeois values—marked a different attitude toward life. Aesthetic feelings surrendered to economic desire; "work and production became the ideal, and then the idol, of the age" (p. 192). Society—at every point—was more strictly organized. Rule by principle replaced rule by personality. Gone now were those more ebullient days when princes gambled recklessly with the fate of their territories, when costume and artifice were sublime, when prominent people preened and posed and confounded others with their actions. In those bygone days, leisure was less an escape from work than a chartered opportunity for public expression. In privileged moments, life was held delicately, at a distance—and cultivated as a work of art. Now, in the industrial age, we have entered a period of "utilitarianism, prosaic efficiency, and the bourgeois ideal of social welfare" (pp. 191–192). "Portentous seriousness" pervades every aspect of life; people have become "earnest."

Few activities illustrate these changes better than sporting events. In archaic societies, physical contests might be swathed in myth. Players entered the fray at many different levels—as themselves, as representatives of their groups and communities, and as actors in events of (potentially) cosmic significance. Religious ritual, artistic expression, and sheer festivity surrounded the actual competitions. Sporting competitions were celebrations of the body in motion—exhibitions in grace, daring, and fortitude. People participated as children sometimes do now, to explore the boundaries of the physical world.

Now, in Huizinga's view, sports have become compartmentalized and rigid. Officialdom—with its leagues, schedules, training regimens, sponsoring organizations, and rulebooks—predominates. Sporting men and women aspire to what Huizinga terms at one point (p. 199) "sterile excellence"; quantitatively based records and record-keeping become key elements of the sports experience. Furthermore, like other modern activities, sport has become overrun by economic considerations; the success of sporting spectacles is judged by the criterion of profitability. For such reasons, the cult of the professional overwhelms amateurism. Indeed, those who play games for reasons of enjoyment or personal development now feel themselves inferior to the experts.

Huizinga argues that modern sport, despite its great cultural prominence, has no "culture-creating" capacity. Although based on play, sport has "stiffened into seriousness" (p. 199). Although showcased in vast stadiums and arenas and followed with fanatical interest through radio broadcasts and newspapers, sport seems curiously isolated from the deepest human concerns. In that sense, as Huizinga notes, it no longer qualifies as either play or seriousness. Instead, the sporting world has developed as an essentially profane diversion, guided by the technical and economic requirements of its sponsors.

Huizinga and His Critics

Few readers today will fail to note that Huizinga's writing seems guided by a set of values no longer fashionable in the modern world. As several commentators have emphasized (see Duncan, 1988; Lugones, 1987; Nagel, 1998), Huizinga was partial to the fundamentally ascriptive, group-centered societies of the past. In such a world, the fact of hierarchy itself (however those rankings might be apportioned to contending groups) was accepted as a natural or God-given state of affairs. At the uppermost reaches of that hierarchy were those families who derived their positions from the ownership of land. And the heads of those families were males.

During the Middle Ages, such titled men might claim their positions by military service to the king. At some point that warrior status shifted into mere gentility. Huizinga's theory of play is based, for the most part, on the exploits of these "leisure class" men.

Of course, Huizinga's sensibilities can be fitted within an elitist view of social order that reaches back to Plato and beyond. By such accounts, society needs its cadres of talented, privileged people. Such individuals must have the time, resources, and freedom to explore and otherwise comport themselves graciously within the world. They must have liberty in the older medieval sense of special privileges granted to some but not to others; however, they must also express liberality. That is, they must recognize publicly their social prominence and extend their blessings to those beholden to them. These leaders of society are also, for the most part, freed from the curse of work. Indeed, their responsibilities are to lead a culturally sophisticated life, maintain salubrious contacts with their peers, and more generally define the style of their age.

Although Huizinga sought examples for his theory from a very wide range of times and places, I think it is fair to say that he focused on the play life of highly placed individuals and groups. It is the agonistic competition of these well-placed peers—rather than cross-class rivalry or the competitions of less advantaged groups—that forms the subject matter of his book. The competitively structured arguments, teasing, chicanery, boasting, and material display of these prominent groups were the ways in which culture—as the symbolic framework for society—became articulated. The soundness of their public policies or the wider responsibilities of elites in general to those less fortunate is not examined. It is enough that culture can be fashioned as a work of art, that life at some level can be danced.

For his part, Huizinga acknowledged these aristocratic sympathies. Born in 1872 to a Dutch Mennonite family, Johan was a dreamy youth who enjoyed long walks through the countryside (see Colie, 1964). Although his family members were prominent medical doctors, he was deeply ambivalent about what he considered his rural, plebeian roots. By his own account, he fantasized about the gilded ages of the past. Moreover, his Mennonite roots nourished a somewhat disapproving attitude toward the world of everyday affairs. The grimy, bourgeois-dominated world of politics and economics seemed to him a stepping backwards from the beautiful models of the past.

During his university days, he was much influenced by a group of students who had become known as the Tachtigers (literally "men of the eighties"). That circle worked hard to introduce modern artists like Van

Gogh to the Dutch public and in general attempted to raise the level of literary and artistic sophistication within the universities. For his part, Huizinga was fascinated by what he understood to be a cultural approach to history, an exploration of critical ideas, artistic forms, social norms, and religious patterns that defined the spirit of an age. Conspicuously absent from that cultural mix were the tension-filled, material relations so crucial to the Marxists and utilitarians.

Huizinga's path through the university world was influenced by the old, patrimonial patterns as well. Not unlike many other academics of his time, social connections were critical to his receiving a university chair at Groningen, when he was thirty-two, and at Leiden ten years later. Ultimately, he became Rector at Leiden, where his duties included tutoring the young Princess Juliana. In such ways, he realized his dream of inhabiting the highest echelons of a tradition-ridden world.

Of course, none of this is to deny his tremendous talent, his ability to create portraits of every age that are as much art as history. But his seeming preference for the past did not go unnoticed by his contemporary critics (see Geyl, 1963). As Holland's most prominent academic, he should have been, they argued, more outspoken about the coming catastrophe in Europe. When he did speak, his arguments seemed to be wholesale indictments of the soulless materialism of his age rather than careful evaluations of realistic political options. At any rate, he did not survive the war. Arrested with other prominent Dutch academics in 1942, he was placed in a hostage camp, became ill, and died in February of 1945.

The Path Ahead

Homo Ludens is a remarkable book. More daringly than others, Huizinga demonstrated the importance of play for adults and revealed some of its implications for society as a whole. Like other classics, the book effectively conquers new territories for academic discourse and connects these discourses to what is fundamental about personal experience. This having been acknowledged, it would be hard to claim that Huizinga's work is entirely satisfactory in its conceptualization, its methods of inquiry, or its conclusions.

As well rendered as Huizinga's depiction of play may be, it perhaps suffers from an attempt to embrace too many aspects of expressive life and to explain too many things with one concept. Those with tidier dispositions will not care for the ways in which Huizinga posits the virtual identity of play with such matters as ritual, games, contests, or other forms of festive expression. Troubling also is the way in which he sees play both as order itself and as the creation of order, both formfulness and the dynamic interplay within and between these forms. Play theorists more generally have a penchant for emphasizing the paradoxical, elusive qualities of their subject matter. However, as Caillois (1961) argued, some recognition of the differences between the more rigidly organized and the more spontaneous, psychologically generated patterns of expression seems important. Moreover, Huizinga's idealist sensibilities prevented him from addressing either the material basis of play or its material consequences. In general, his descriptions of play are wonderful commentaries on the ways in which reality can be imagined in social settings through dialectical exchanges between rival actors; however, there is little to remind us of the actual thudding, sweating, sometimes breathless qualities of physical play. Finally, it should be noted that Huizinga himself was relatively disinterested in solitary play, which in his view does not contribute substantially to cultural maintenance or production.

Empirically oriented readers will not be satisfied with the way in which Huizinga presents his many examples of play. His arguments reveal the tremendous erudition of the author, but the supporting evidence is rarely presented in any concrete, detailed way. Nor are counter examples provided. Instead, the reader is carried along in a sort of cultural swoon, the mysteries of the centuries revealed in a couple hundred pages. Although Huizinga himself was very critical of Spengler's broad-brush treatments of the course of civilization, *Homo Ludens* generalizes too quickly as well. Indeed, so much of history is gathered up and presented here and there that the critical reader is hard pressed to refute or even comprehend fully what is presented.

His thesis—that play has been a generative activity in the course of civilization—remains unproven. Certainly, the play-festival-rite complex was a central part of orally based, traditional societies. His arguments have the ring of truth, yet little evidence is provided to show that societies are either made more stable—or helped to change—in these settings. Likewise, his examples of contentious play in European history are wonderful; yet he fails to show in any case how these dynamic exchanges actually produced changes in cultural policy or procedures. The sheer weight of examples perhaps convinces the reader that earlier centuries were more truly "played" and that aesthetic commitments were profoundly important elements in the social circles of the players themselves. It is less clear how these aesthetic commitments spread through society as a whole.

Nevertheless, *Homo Ludens* effectively challenges others to think deeply about the nature of play and about its connection to other patterns of activity. Such challenges are particularly pertinent to the discipline of sociology, which takes as its subject matter the patterning of human relationship and the role of personal agency in these matters. Huizinga's challenge to sociologists is a call to comprehend more fully the various ways in which human expression is organized in societies.

In what follows, I argue that such issues are not new to sociology. Indeed, they are fundamental to the work of those classic thinkers who established the dimensions of the discipline. Thus, an initial chapter examines the writings of Karl Marx and some of his descendants as attempts to understand both the material foundations of human expression and the various uses of social organization to misdirect or block that expression. In that regard, special attention is given to the contributions of the British school of cultural studies and to the writings of the Frankfurt School. The following chapter explores the perspectives of Emile Durkheim and his followers. The Durkheimian tradition, in which modern social anthropology has played a prominent role, not only describes the ways in which traditional societies organize expressive life but also articulates the relationship between ritual, play, and related forms of behavior.

The fourth chapter considers the contributions of Max Weber. Weber's famous commentaries on the "rationalization" process in Western societies are extended here to the more emotive aspects of life. In this context, Weber's ideas are contrasted with those of a later writer, Norbert Elias. An even sharper contrast to Weber's work is provided by the recent tradition known as postmodernism. The role of socio-cultural frameworks, as both constraints and enablements of expression, is explored further in a chapter on the writings of Georg Simmel. Among the early sociologists, Simmel had perhaps the deepest understanding of the aesthetic dimensions of social life. Our curious dependence on form and yet resistance to it are themes developed in his work. Simmel's understandings of the ways in which cultural forms articulate and preserve social distinction are extended through treatments of the work of two other thinkers, Thorstein Veblen and Pierre Bourdieu. A final substantive chapter is reserved for a more recent theorist, Erving Goffman, who was perhaps the principal inheritor of Simmel's subtlety and flair. As will be shown, Goffman's writing also brings together many of the themes of the other early thinkers into a broad portrait of the game-like features of social life in general. Goffman's attempt to unite the playful and ritualistic aspects of social order are considered through the work of Susan Birrell. Such themes are extended in a description of feminist authors who have explored the relationship of play and gender.

Certainly, the reader may wonder why concentrated attention was given to this set of authors and not to others. Furthermore, one may ask whether an approach that emphasizes contemporary paradigms of modern sociology, such as "exchange theory" or "symbolic interactionism," might address these issues more clearly. The sociologists featured above were chosen because, like Huizinga, they brilliantly frame the issues at hand. Moreover, although they draw sustenance from essentially the same conditions—the socio-cultural contexts of nineteenth- and twentieth-century societies in the West—they produce quite different accounts of the human predicament. Such differences are revealed most strikingly through their opposition.

To use a metaphor then, the status of the classic figures within the discipline of sociology may be likened to the towering trees of a forest. To be sure, there is much that is luxuriant and new growing wildly beneath that canopy. Yet, these modern movements exist in the shadows of what has come before. Although each chapter in the book "moves on," as it were, to more recent thinkers, it is to be understood that these subsequent writings are almost always extensions, modifications, or oppositions to earlier work. To explore this relationship between older and newer forms of thought is to participate in what Merton (1967, p. 35) once called the "dialogue" between the living and the dead.

It is customary, of course, for sociology books to genuflect to at least some of the classic thinkers. My intention here is not simply to defer to this work—or honor it—but to look for guidance in the structure of its ideas and arguments. Thus, examining the outlines and assumptions of a modern theoretical paradigm seems less useful than following the trail of a great writer's thought. The advantages of this latter approach are even more apparent when the topic is as elusive and subtle as play.

On the one hand, the following chapters are to be understood as attempts to use the insights of the classic sociologists to develop or refine Huizinga's conception of play. On the other hand, these chapters are attempts to reconsider the ideas of those same sociologists from the vantage point of Huizinga's concerns. In that light, it should be acknowledged that some of the authors focus more clearly than others on play itself. For example, Marx's writing explores creativity and alienation in labor processes, Durkheim was more interested in ritual than in play, and Weber was fascinated by the historical transformation of personal orientations and experience. However, Huizinga also shared these concerns, and the treatment of such themes by the classic sociologists effectively distinguishes play from related forms. To aid the comparison of the various authors, I try to show how each writer's thought may be applied to one type of behavior—sport—that is typically acknowledged to have playful aspects. Nevertheless, this book should not be interpreted as a theoretical analysis of modern sport; for that there are better sources (see Jarvie and Maguire, 1994; Hargreaves, 1994; Maguire and Young, 2002). Finally, for the sake of those less familiar with the sociological tradition—and because ideas only become meaningful in their wider contexts—the contributions of each classic thinker will be placed within the environment of the writer's life and within the broader animus of his work.

In a concluding chapter, I gather together these different ideas and approaches into a more general interpretation of the nature of play. As part of that process, play is compared to three other fundamental patterns of human expression—work, ritual, and communitas. Like play, these other forms are important activities in which people willingly declare their feelings and intentions toward the conditions of their lives. Ideally, such comments would be set within a wide-ranging theory about the organization and significance of human expression in societies. That goal can be addressed only in modest ways here.

As is sometimes noted, the ends of projects are usually found in their beginnings. Essentially, this book argues that sociological perspectives are valuable for the study of play, and will, at its conclusion, try to show the fruits of that approach. The contributions of other academic disciplines, however valuable, will be given less emphasis. Moreover, this book takes as its point of departure a set of theoretical viewpoints arising from the social conditions of modern, industrialized societies. Those concerns shape the arguments that follow. To be sure, I have tried to complement these approaches with contributions from later writers committed to understanding play in more recent historical periods, in other types of societies, or in contexts marked by differences in class, gender, ethnicity, and age. However, those deeper levels of understanding can be attained only by a wider community of social scientists.

2   *Karl Marx on Creativity and Alienation*

To understand a scholarly tradition one must sometimes step outside it, to thinkers who employ alternative ways of knowing, or even to those who oppose directly that tradition. Certainly, the inclusion of Karl Marx, the prophet of human labor, seems an odd choice for a book on play. For his part, Huizinga—who witnessed the ascendancy of Marxist thought and politics in Europe with an entirely unsympathetic eye—would have disapproved.

To be sure, the contrasts between Huizinga and Marx overwhelm the similarities. As Huizinga studied the nature, organization, and historical development of human play, so Marx considered such matters for the world of work. Huizinga's writing is part of an idealist, spiritual tradition that romanticizes previous centuries of European history. The style and substance of this tradition were anathema to Marx, even during the more soulful period of his career. Ever the materialist, Marx was the champion of the ordinary and practical, the man who proclaimed the "poverty of philosophy" (Marx, 1995) and trumpeted the virtues of economic study. From such a vantage point, it is hardly surprising that Marx should have placed technology and politics at the center of the world. Huizinga, it will be recalled, was criticized precisely for his neglect of these matters.

Both men were driven by a desire to understand the past as a kind of preparation for the future. However, Marx had the nineteenth-century person's optimism about the path ahead. Indeed, few thinkers have matched his quasi-religious certitude about the character and composition of future societies. The only sadness for Marx, it seems, is that so few people are willing to undertake the radical procedures needed to rush this world into being. Having experienced two World Wars, totalitarian regimes, and a worldwide depression, Huizinga had the twentieth-century person's doubts and anxieties. And by nature he was a pessimist. Like many conservative thinkers, Huizinga felt the great moments of history lay mainly in the past. Just how these better times can be reclaimed is never clearly developed in his writing. Perhaps we can look to our leaders for inspired acts of public creativity or, even more grandly, for a transformation in the style or *zeitgeist* of civilization itself. Marx, of course, is the champion of the working person. With a little help from the intellectuals, millions of disadvantaged people will lead us all out of the dingy industrial city into the light of day. With that ambition in mind, Marx's great contribution to modern thought is his wide-ranging intellectual system, which integrates so many aspects of capitalism with contemporary life. Such finely wrought systems commonly produce armies of disciples. At the other extreme, Huizinga worked as the solitary artist, creating his beautiful pictures of the past. Such canvases incite admiration for their ingenuity and craftsmanship and encourage reflection on the meaning of human possibility. Less frequently does intellectual work of this sort become developed by others.

All this having been acknowledged, the two thinkers are joined curiously by their common rejection of industrial, bourgeois society. Although their diagnoses of the regimented world of factory and office are quite different, both are haunted by a sense that a more colorful, spontaneous quality of life once existed and can somehow be restored. Both are fundamentally children of the Enlightenment, who believed that society can be criticized and re-shaped by reasoning that is sensitive to the broad range of human needs. Critically, both Marx and Huizinga approach these matters from a sociological rather than psychological viewpoint. Against the approaches of the utilitarians and liberals, both concluded that the needs of individual people are an appropriate starting point but not a basis for a theory of social order. Instead, each argued that one must study the great products of humanity—the wide range of social institutions, organizations, and practices—that not only reflect but also shape these human needs. Society may well be an artifice, but that creation rolls forward with the weight of centuries.

For this volume, the crucial link between Marx and Huizinga is their shared commitment to the creative possibilities of human beings. If we set aside the proletarian sensibilities of the one writer and the elit-ist sympathies of the other, we can see that both believed people can be engaged more critically and productively with their own lives. This restoration of "creative control" will be beneficial not only at the social and cultural level (where it finds expression in finely honed public institutions) but also in the quality of personal experience. Addressed to these purposes, Marx's account of human labor turns out to be not so different from Huizinga's depiction of play.

This chapter explores Marx's contributions to a sociological theory of personal control and creativity. Although many have claimed that Marx turned away from these matters to macro-level accounts of the history of capitalism and class-relations (see Gamble, 1999), other interpreters have emphasized that Marx held steady to his early humanistic concerns throughout his career (see, e.g., Fromm, 1999; Lefebvre, 1969; Marcuse, 1941). This chapter adopts the latter viewpoint. At any rate, the tension between individual freedom and historical necessity is the dynamic element of Marxism that has fascinated many different kinds of scholars for more than one hundred fifty years.

To be sure, Marx's work is focused ultimately on the development and consequences of economic organization. And other practices and ideas—carried forward by politics, religion, and other forms of public culture—typically are seen as derivatives or rationalizations of economic matters. For such reasons, we must turn to Marx's descendants for explanations of how expressive culture (in such areas as art, sport, and religion) can be misappropriated in capitalist societies. After a treatment of these more recent thinkers, some conclusions will be offered on the continuing significance of Marxian analysis for the study of play.

Marx's Intellectual Framework in Historical Context

Like other people, great social scientists ultimately are products of their times. After all, publicly circulated ideas, artifacts, and practices are frequently the subject matter of scholarly analysis. Sometimes this "cultural base" provides models to emulate or enhance; on other occasions, it serves as a goad for alternative or opposing viewpoints. Most frequently, creators pick their way through the vast assortment of prevailing ideas and practices—taking what seems to be useful, adding to the mixture in modest ways, and then organizing the whole affair in a manner thought to be new or intriguing. Those ideas prosper when they resonate deeply with the spirit of an age and when they find organized groups of supporters who have something to gain by their diffusion.

In that sense, Marx's writing is one of the great creations of the nineteenth century. As much as he fits our stereotype of the cranky and

isolated genius—working away all those years in the British Museum—
so also was he a gatherer and organizer of the intellectual and political
movements of his age. His theories of creativity and alienation are both
expressions of and reactions to such powerful social transformations
as the rise of industrialism, capitalism, and militarism; the ascendancy
of the bourgeoisie in public life; and the associated misery of the lower
classes.

Marx was born in 1818 in the small city of Trier, part of those borderlands that had been taken by Napoleon and then ceded back to Prussia
after his defeat. The second of eight children in a Jewish lawyer's family,
young Karl was strong-willed, unemotional, and intellectually voracious
(see Berlin, 1963). In such ways he contrasted with his more complacent
and socially skilled father, who supported the authoritarian regime and
had his family baptized as Lutherans. Karl's mother seems to have had
no prominent role in his life, nor does he appear to have had a strong
relationship with his siblings, apart from one sister.

Marx came to adulthood during a time when the towering academic
figure was still the philosopher Hegel, who died in 1831. Like other German intellectuals, the young Marx adopted major elements from Hegel;
and he remained an admiring critic throughout his lifetime (see Bottomore, 1964). Hegel's philosophy, which reaffirmed the legitimacy of the
Prussian monarchy, was in many ways a reaction to French thought. As
the leaders of the Enlightenment had championed the rights of individual citizens, doctrines of equality and democracy, and models of thought
derived from the natural sciences, so Hegel opposed these "universalistic" tendencies by emphasizing the historical particularity of societies. In Hegel's view, societies could not be reduced to the ambitions or
qualities of their individual members; rather they reflected a powerful,
world-transcending logic that was working itself out in a wide range of
social circumstances. In that sense, societies themselves may be seen
as great individuals, each with its distinctive purposes, eccentricities,
and character. Moreover, just as individuals embody culture in different
ways, so societies themselves embody distinctively that grander logic
or world-spirit that defines the course of civilization. In that light, every
society is engaged in a prolonged project of self-realization, an attempt to
discover and manifest the logic that stands behind its development. To
accomplish this end, philosophers must counterpose the actual institutional arrangements by which people live with that society's own best
set of intellectual principles. In Hegel's famous terms, the "real" and the
"rational" must be set against one another dialectically. Through processes of internal collision and synthesis, societies move forward. For

such reasons—and to the eminent satisfaction of the authorities—the Prussian state was held to be the moving edge of history.

From Hegel, the young Marx took his ideas about the ever-changing nature of societies, the importance of collision or dialectics, the legitimacy of institutional analysis, and the certitude that history is equivalent to progress. More important for our purposes was his adoption of the Hegelian viewpoint that history is ultimately a project of self-realization, an attempt to make the changing relations of the world conform to a deeper logic. To be separated from this logic, to live a life that denies its very foundations, is the essence of yet another Hegelian concept, alienation. Like his predecessor then, Marx spent his career attempting to discern the logic of history—to make explicit the nature of those patterns, to praise the various social elements that seem to embody the future, and to call into question occurrences that slow down or occlude that development.

Marx's original plans were to pursue a career in law at the University of Bonn. However, after only a year he transferred to the University of Berlin, where he studied history, philosophy, and languages in preparation for an academic career. He remained at Berlin to complete his doctorate, a study of rival Greek philosophies of nature, in 1841. During these years, Marx allied himself with the so-called Left Hegelians. Whereas conservative Hegelians accepted the doctrine that the Prussian state was the living realization of the rational, the Left Hegelians argued that only the rational was the real. Put differently, contemporary institutions could be criticized as poor representations of Hegel's deeper logic. The task of the intellectual was to hurry along the refinement of those institutions.

Marx's philosophical allegiances cost him his academic career, and he shifted to a career in political journalism. As editor of a publication in Cologne, he quickly attracted the censorship of the government, a state of affairs that led ultimately to his moving to Paris in 1843. In that freer setting, and again as editor of a radical publication, Marx discovered a new group of intellectuals and the set of themes that have become familiar elements of Marxism. From Saint-Simon and Fourier, Marx acquired a socialist version of history that emphasized the centrality of class struggle and the role of working people and intellectuals in that development. From Feuerbach came the revolutionary understanding that materialism rather than idealism is the driving force of history. From French thinkers like Voltaire and Rousseau came the belief that humans long ago had lived in better circumstances and that they were entitled to do so again. From the Scottish economists and Ricardo came understandings of those elements of capitalism such as free markets, exploitation, and the labor theory of value. Such writers were frequently subjected to excoriating criticism as Marx attempted to synthesize their views and distinguish his own work from what had come before.

The year 1848 was the banner year of proletarian revolt in Europe. To support those undertakings, Marx and his collaborator Friedrich Engels (whom he had met seven years before in Berlin) rushed the *Communist Manifesto* into print. A year later, he found himself banned from France. At age thirty-one he moved to London and recommitted himself to a life of independent scholarship and political organization. By that time, the major outlines of his intellectual life project had been drawn. He would fashion his monumental study of the nature of capitalism and assist the development of international socialism.

For more than thirty years, Marx pursued his studies in the Reading Room at the British Museum. Upon the museum's closing each day, he would return home for further hours of work. His family lived in poverty; four of his children died. He depended on the kindness of others, especially Engels, for financial support and for ten years (again with the help of Engels) wrote a weekly newspaper column for the *New York Daily Tribune* to secure a stable income. He lived among a relatively small circle of like-minded comrades in London and participated in the founding of the International Working Men's Association in 1864. Like Job, Marx suffered a great variety of difficult physical ailments that he bore without complaint. He lived to publish one volume of his masterwork *Capital.* The final two volumes were completed by Engels after Marx's death in 1883.

The popular image of Marx, at least in the West, is of a fiery-eyed, bristle-bearded man who was intolerant of opposition and vindictive in his revenge. We fancy him heartless because of the plight of his family. He was, according to the description of his friend Annenkov (quoted in Berlin, 1963, p. 88), the type of man who is "all energy, force of will, and unshakeable conviction. With a thick black mop of hair on his head, with hairy hands and a crookedly buttoned frock coat, he had the air of a man used to commanding the respect of others. His movements were clumsy but self-assured. His manners defied the accepted conventions of social intercourse and were haughty and almost contemptuous. His tone of voice was disagreeably harsh, and he spoke of men and things in the tone of one who would tolerate no contradiction."

Yet Marx the man was never equivalent to the ideologue that we envision. By the accounts of his wife and children (see Fromm, 1999, pp. 221–256), he was a loving husband and father. He enjoyed picnics in the park with his family and told them long, animated stories. Although never given to emotional exuberance or soaring rhetoric, he loved music and literature. Goethe's poetry was a favorite resource; and he re-read the works of Aeschylus and Shakespeare each year. He believed that such intellectual and aesthetic refinements could be spread to people of every type. Ever a hard man in his self-discipline and judgment of others, he brought some of the sensibilities of the eighteenth century into the more romantic, morally urgent century in which he lived. This is the Marx that informs the sections that follow.

Marx's View of Creativity

Marx's understanding of creativity is developed most fully in his *Economic and Philosophical Manuscripts* (Marx, 1999), a set of four short writings—some of them incomplete—composed between April and August of 1844. These essays comprise the core vision that has been developed by humanistic Marxists. It is notable, and perhaps not surprising in light of the resistance to Marxism in Western societies, that they were not translated into English until 1959.

As Lefebvre (1969, p. 8) has argued, perhaps the fundamental question for all Marxism is: What is the relation of human activity to its accomplishments? An initially descriptive project—exploring the variety of relationships between humans and their worlds—leads almost inevitably to a second, more evaluative set of concerns: Are some relationships better than others? And if so, how can these better modes of living be developed? Marx, at this age (he was twenty-six), addresses these matters in the manner of a philosopher. That is, he reflects on the meaning of human nature, on the complicated relationship to the world that develops as a result of distinctively human traits and abilities, and on the dangers that arise from new possibilities for living.

Huizinga (1955) it will be recalled, distinguished his own vision of the human (*homo ludens*) from those thinkers who had championed human rationality (*homo sapiens*) and human productivity (*homo faber*). This latter viewpoint, of humans as makers, is the theme developed by Marx. Consistently, in Marxian thought society is seen as something of a workshop (see Marx, 1964, p. 91). That is, the world is less an object to behold or contemplate than an artifice that has been created and then inhabited. This setting—with its machines, sawdust, and sweat—is the crucible of human experience.

Like other animals, humans exist in, and are constituted by, nature. We possess the same basic needs (to find shelter, feed ourselves, procreate, etc.) and live deeply in a world that is concrete and sensuous at every moment. But as Marx (1999, p. 183) explains, "man is not merely a natural being; he is a *human* natural being." In contrast to animals, humans have attained a degree of separation or freedom from their circumstances. Whereas "the animal is one with its life activity" (Marx, 1999, p. 101), human beings have a capacity to reflect upon and change the conditions of their existence. Animals produce only "what is strictly necessary for themselves or for their young" (p. 102); by comparison, people produce—and do so most effectively—when they are freed from direct physical need. Animals appropriate nature in response to the standards and needs of their species alone; humans can design responses to the needs of many species. Granted a distinctive vantage point within the vast machinery of nature, humans may even create "in accordance with the laws of beauty" (p. 102). In other words, people have a consciousness of the world, a self-consciousness, and a capacity for "will" that is quite different from the capabilities of animals.

This distinction between humans and animals finds its clearest expression in the idea of labor, that is, in the very act of creating and maintaining the material world. To a large extent, human beings are like bees or spiders, forever tending and expanding their habitats. However, as Fromm (1999, p. 41) puts it, humans differ by their ability to function as "architects." That is, they typically raise structures in their imaginations before they build. Plans are developed, modified, and abandoned—all without laying a brick. Furthermore, humans are able to pause or otherwise delay their responses to an incredibly wide range of desires and demands. For such reasons, human labor is different from the daily activities of animals.

Yet another distinction is the extent to which humans have invented tools and practices associated with their use. Human history may well be, as the Marxists would have it, a history of class relations; but it is just as profoundly a history of technology. Such tools and techniques empower people but are also problematic when they become established as objective characteristics of societies. Such problems notwithstanding, this mixing of material artifacts with the social practices that grow up around them becomes the basis of a human cultural world that is every bit as "real" as the organic world we share with the animals. Even more profoundly, this world intrudes upon consciousness itself. People are constituted not only as physical but also as socio-cultural beings. Thus, to such basic necessities as food and water is added a host of secondary or social "needs" that express the requirements of the societies in which we live.

As Rossiter (1960, pp. 63–92) argues, Marx's account of human nature is fundamentally a sociological rather than psychological description. That is, while humans are recognized to have certain physical needs, the outer dimensions of our psyches are transcribed by social practices. Human "interests" and yearnings are shaped directly by these circumstances. Furthermore, as societies move through their various stages of development, people's perceptions of these situations and of themselves shift as well. This vision of human mutability is deepened further when it is acknowledged that people create the world they live in and, to that degree, produce their own nature.

Clearly, Marx operated with a very wide conception of human productivity (see Lefebvre, 1969, pp. 25–58). Not only must people be concerned with those forms of labor that address their relationship to the material world and fulfill their basic economic needs (*poesis*), but they must also develop considerate, freedom-enhancing relationships with the social and political aspects of that world (*praxis*). In Marx's view, people are less by nature philosophers than they are tinkerers and artists engaged in the day-to-day manipulation of the world. The human project is not to escape or renounce concrete, sensuous productivity but rather to discover the conditions that express it most effectively.

Certainly, the popular conception of Marx is that of a writer who understood labor to be the material production of nineteenth-century industrial workers, and whose ideas led to the formation of state-dominated systems of economic activity. In actuality, Marx saw labor in a much looser, even pre-industrial, way; and he was profoundly ambivalent about the modern idea of work. In particular, he objected to—and considered "alienated"—labor that was only a "*means* for the satisfaction of a need, the need to maintain physical existence" (Marx, 1999, p. 101). Instead, the challenge to the free, enlightened person is to be productive in every aspect of his or her existence. By extension, too much concentration on the strictly economic part of life or too much emphasis on occupational specialization (both fundamental themes of Marx's century) was troubling. As he and Engels (1959, p. 254) somewhat romantically describe their vision in *The German Ideology*: "in communist society, where nobody has one exclusive sphere of activity but each can become accomplished in any branch he wishes, society regulates the general production and thus makes it possible for me to do one thing to-day and another to-morrow, to hunt in the morning, fish in the afternoon, rear cattle in the evening, criticize after dinner, just as I have a mind, without ever becoming hunter, fisherman, shepherd or critic." Within the terms of that pre-industrial sensibility then, Marx and Engels objected to the strict division that has developed between work and leisure. The human challenge is to be engaged actively and creatively throughout the day in a wide variety of ways.

In an argument that springs from Hegel, Marx claims that this project of self-realization is not merely a personal thing but is rather a vehicle that connects us with others. As he (1999, p. 101) puts it: "Productive life is, however, species-life. It is life creating life. In the type of life activity resides the whole character of a species, its species-character; and free, conscious activity is the species-character of human beings." In that sense, individuals engaged productively in the minutiae of their lives partake of the abstract or universal qualities of being human.

However, fulfilling oneself in an entirely private way is not enough. Working by day in the bustling economy and then retiring at night to one's home and garden is the purported failing of the bourgeoisie. Instead, Marx hearkens to the classical ideal in which private and public affairs are conjoined. In the Marxian vision of the good life, people participate together in communities on terms of relative equality. In that setting, they actively construct a world in which all of them live; so understood, identity becomes a matter of public definition. Emphatically then, Marx opposes the abstruse reckonings of the monk or philosopher as legitimate ways to know the world. Nor does he agree with Hegel that self-realization is fundamentally a process of intellectual or spiritual awareness. Instead, life is activity. To live fully is to creatively encounter one's circumstances and in so doing to experience acutely the human consequences of such transformation. What matters most then is not the freedom to think but the freedom to shape the public contours of the world.

Marx's dual commitment to sensuous experience and to sociology are displayed well in his treatment of the senses. As he argues, our five senses—our most private links to reality—are to some extent a public affair. Said directly (Marx, 1999, p. 134), "the *senses* of social man are *different* from those of non-social man." That is, our awareness or appreciation of the world is colored by the meanings that we attach to it. We perceive and respond to humanly created objects; our experience with these objects in turn shapes our sensibility. He (p. 134) continues: "It is only through the objectively deployed wealth of the human being that the wealth of subjective *human* sensibility (a musical ear, an eye which is sensitive to the beauty of form, in short, senses which are capable of human satisfaction and which confirm themselves as human faculties) is cultivated or created."

To this list of human capabilities then, he quickly adds a variety of other senses associated with "spiritual" and "practical" matters (loving, desiring, etc.). People live in a humanly colored world. A starving man may be reduced to the animal level in which food is merely nutrition; however, people in their full humanity appreciate food in much wider and more sophisticated ways. As he (p. 134) concludes, "the objectification of the human essence, both theoretically and practically, is necessary to *humanize* man's *senses,* and also to create the *human senses* corresponding to all the wealth of human and natural being."

By our actions, we assemble a world around us that both reflects our abilities and shapes them. For Marx, labor—in its ideal form—is that activity which expresses the special privilege of human beings to transform freely the conditions of their existence. Through the transformative action of labor, people discover the nature of the object-world and, in the process, their own qualities. While creativity may well occur in the airy spheres where intellectuals (like Marx himself) operate, the critical encounters occur in the concrete, tangible realms of the craftsman and artist. The objects we create—and the tools we use—not only reflect the human abilities we share with others but also provide the basis for our public lives together.

As one can see, Marx's account of labor brings together many different ideas—human nature, freedom, creativity, community, technology, psyche, and so on. Clearly, work in its deeper sense is no mere manipulation or production of objects. Indeed, the objects themselves are much less important than the experience of human relationship that derives from the activity. As Marx (quoted in Fromm, 1999, p. 38) puts it, a person is fully human only "if he affirms his individuality as a total man in each of his relations to the world, seeing, hearing, smelling, tasting, feeling, thinking, willing, loving—in short, if he affirms and expresses all organs of his individuality." In another passage (Marx, 1999, p. 135), this sense of connection or engagement reaches almost Taoist proportions: "It is only in a social context that subjectivism and objectivism, spiritualism and materialism, activity and passivity, cease to be antimonies and thus cease to exist as antimonies."

It may be claimed fairly that Marx in his later years turned more directly to economic and political matters. However, his youthful arguments about the connection between labor and human potential bear similarities to Huizinga's hopes for play. While the differences between play and labor will be discussed at the end of this chapter, we will continue with another theme shared by the two authors. That is, what causes this human potential to be blocked and what are the consequences of that blockage?

Marx's Theory of Alienation

For Marx, as for Huizinga, the world has gone astray. In the dreams of both writers, there was a time long ago when people lived in more creative and expressive ways. Social affairs were conducted in a manner that responded to the needs and interests of society's members; individuals were freer to shape their own destinies. For Huizinga, those better days existed only a couple centuries ago, before the reach of the Industrial Revolution. To support their account of primitive communism, Marx and Engels looked much farther, indeed beyond the boundaries of recorded history (see Engels, 1986).

Both men were troubled by the growing power of the bourgeoisie. The Industrial Age witnessed the ascendancy of once-humble capitalists and administrators, clerks and civil servants. Business interests were coloring public policy. The old agriculturally based society had its own set of tyrannies; but it seemed to be warmer and more personal than the city culture that replaced it. City life, with its capitalist support system, was moving forward under terms that were more formal, individualistic, and calculating than the culture of earlier times. For Huizinga, with his elitist sensibilities, the failing of the new order was largely a cultural problem. Civilization had stalled; and the great people of the modern era were being thwarted by all the mechanisms and controls. Although he was no admirer of agricultural societies, Marx saw the rise of capitalist industrialism instead as a social disaster. Indeed, its only redeeming feature was that it was preparing the way for another, more beneficent social form.

Not surprisingly, Marx's account of the alienated society is essentially the obverse of the creative, supportive order described in the section above (see Mandel and Novack, 1970). That is, images of unity, integration, freedom, sensuousness, equality, and human potential become replaced by their opposites. Instead of appropriating the object-world in ways that deepen self-understanding, people find themselves in conditions of misappropriation or even expropriation.

As mentioned above, Marx's idea of alienation derives from Hegel, and to some extent, Feuerbach. For Hegel (1977), the history of humanity was basically a process of self-realization, an attempt by individuals and societies to discover their most coherent and profound possibilities. Alienation is the condition of separation or otherness—not so different from the theological idea of sin—when people experience themselves at a distance from the great compelling logic that stands at the center of their being. For his part, Feuerbach transformed this issue from questions of spiritual-cognitive separation to separations from the concrete, physical settings of existence. In that latter context, the challenge for human beings is altered; people should not look to the heavens or to their inner selves for answers but rather should align their actions with the unfolding logic of material development.

For Marx, the fundamental problem of alienation is people's loss of control over the objects of their making. Labor, at least in the version presented by Marx, is primarily the rendering of the material world for human purposes. Through such rendering, the laborer appropriates the world; and by that act of possession and control, creates a kind of mirror for his or her qualities and abilities. In ideal settings, people maintain this transformative relationship with the natural (and now cultural) world. Just as they contribute to the human community through their labor so they must be allowed to use and enjoy the fruits of that activity. This connection between giving and receiving (i.e., how labor and its rewards should be apportioned in the good society) is computed somewhat differently in Marxism than in other social philosophies. For our purposes, it is enough to say that Marx believed physical labor to be the most valuable ingredient in humanly constructed objects. Laborers, like artists, should have proprietary rights over their creations.

This idealized relationship between maker and product has been disrupted throughout the course of history. For example, Marx had serious reservations about a process as old as civilization itself, that is, the division of labor (see Marx, 1964, pp. 92–93). Specialization entails a narrowing of human focus and effects a social order in which people need to barter with one another for their services. Such differentiation of function typically accompanies a growth of social hierarchy; people become separated into categories with differential access to the valued resources of their society. Marx was particularly interested in the emergence of wealth and property distinctions and connected these directly (see Marx, 1972, pp. 104–106) to alienation. Power, prestige, and knowledge differences were thought to follow in their wake. More generally, the bad society—again, practically all of human history—is marked by divisions over ownership and control.

Marx's theory details the various kinds of fragmentation and separation that occur under the conditions of alienation. Basically, alienation should be seen as a social malignancy that has profound personal repercussions. Throughout history people have constructed a series of social forms that have effectively blocked the Hegelian project of self-realization. At a very broad level, the fault may be traced to people themselves. Humans have created a magnificent world of objects and practices and then become dazzled by their own creations. As in the case of religious idolatry, the object itself becomes worshiped. People forget that they are the creators and sustainers of the socio-cultural world. Instead, they project their powers away by granting the object-world a life of its own. Like Hobbes' Leviathan, the vast machinery of society grows at the expense of its inhabitants. In the end, we become slaves to our own creations.

This theme—that people objectify society and, in turn, become objectified by it—is fundamental to humanistic Marxism. However, all Marxists would emphasize that some people have historically benefited more from the social apparatus than others. In nearly every society, and now under the conditions of capitalism, ownership and control have been the prerogatives of relatively small groups who, typically, do not "labor" in the proper use of that term. Remarkably, these powerful groups also experience an alienated sense of being.

Alienation occurs when the conditions of life and work cut people off from their proper economic, political, social, and psychological connections. People become estranged not only from their own plight but also from the circumstances of others. In the *Economic and Philosophical Manuscripts,* Marx develops the position that the bourgeoisie has become mystified by the prospect of acquisition. Living one's life to accumulate possessions is to lose one's life, or somewhat differently, to have that portion of one's self grow at the expense of all others. As he (1999, p. 131) emphasizes, the object-world "should not be taken only in the sense of *immediate,* exclusive *enjoyment,* or only in the sense of *possession* or having." The pursuit of purely private enjoyment is wrong because it cuts people off from the community that is one source of their being. Possession alone is a faulty enterprise because the owner reduces in importance "all his *human* relations to the world—seeing, hearing, smelling, tasting, touching, thinking, observing, feeling, desiring, acting, loving—in short all the organs of his individuality" (p. 131). Marx's goal then is to create the conditions for an integrated, public life in which all human faculties are in play. Economic specialization, however successful in those terms alone, is not enough.

Of course, those people inhabiting lower positions in the economic system encounter other aspects of alienation. Workers, in the modern sense of that term, commonly experience their labor as a narrow specialization whose pattern and pace are supervised by others. In that sense, workers have lost connection with the active, expressive portion of their being. This condition of powerlessness (and the resulting patterns of psychological awareness) is the theme that has been developed most fully in the alienation literature (see Murchland, 1971; Henricks, 1983). Because workers have been cut off from their rightful control, they have lost a meaningful connection with the products they make, with the rewards that derive from these, and with the community of working people. For our purposes, perhaps the deepest loss is the ability to learn from or grow psychologically from one's handiwork. Creativity flows outward into the object but the effects of that labor do not return to enrich the lives of the producer.

In general, the Marxian portrait of alienation is a description of arrested or disfigured creativity. People once produced with the fullness of their being; now that productivity is directed by others. Labor once united the various dimensions (physical, spiritual, social, psychological) of life; now it focuses on economic interests alone. Laborers themselves become workers, specialized and paid participants in a vast system of economic relationships. To this degree, they experience a split between the subjectifying and objectifying aspects of their being. Modern workers come to understand themselves as objects (or even "commodities" that are bought and sold) in a world of objects. Although objectification itself (the process of appraising one's traits and abilities in relation to the world) is a fundamental part of human awareness, the relatively passive status of modern laborers means that they do not control the terms by which they understand themselves. Under direst circumstances, subjectivity itself is dulled; people surrender to their own lethargy. Like leaves in a storm, they find themselves cast about by ideas and desires not of their own making.

As indicated above, Marx himself was especially concerned with the transformations of the natural world that occur in physical labor. That kind of creative mastery, particularly when done in the company of others, is the foundation of social order. For such reasons, Marx focused on the material, sensual side of existence and on the various social arrangements that have been devised historically to address this issue. That material/economic emphasis pushed into the background a host of other social and cultural processes, which he considered derivative or "epiphenomenal." To continue the Marxian treatment of creativity/alienation within the more broadly social and psychological aspects of life then, we must turn to later writers.

The Marxian Analysis of Culture

One of the characteristics of the modern world is the relative disconnection—or at least altered relationship—of culture from the social and personal settings that traditionally sustained it. Even Marx's nineteenth century was marked by a dramatic growth in the accessibility of various material forms and formats—newspapers, books, art, architecture, consumer goods—that stabilized and made "public" a range of visions about personal and social life. With the development of the electronic media during the twentieth century—such devices as radio, movies, and television—the study of mechanically produced culture as both cause and effect of human activity seemed even more legitimate. Although classical Marxism held hard to the position that cultural issues were essentially residues of socio-economic matters, writers like the Italian political theorist Antonio Gramsci argued that capitalism itself was shaped by the varying cultural contexts of the societies that harbored it, and that different ideologies would produce different effects on social development. Put differently, economism was being challenged by socio-cultural analyses utilizing the idea of hegemony (see Daly, 1999). I now turn briefly to a discussion of two traditions that have brought a Marxian concern for creativity and personal expression to the study of public culture in the contemporary era.

THE FRANKFURT SCHOOL

Endowed by the son of a wealthy grain merchant in 1923, the Institute for Social Research was a private study center located originally at the University of Frankfurt in Germany (see Jay, 1973; Held, 1980). Due to its socialist sympathies and to the fact that many of its famous members (including Theodor Adorno, Max Horkheimer, Herbert Marcuse, Walter Benjamin, and Leo Lowenthal) were Jewish, the Institute was forced to move twice—first to Geneva and then to New York City—during the Nazi ascendancy. The writers of the Frankfurt School remain influential today because of their efforts to apply many of Marx's economic concepts to the study of culture.

To be sure, the Frankfurt School carried forward the distinctively Western version of Marxism developed in this chapter. From this perspective, people in every society must receive not only material sustenance and social support but also opportunities for creative personal expression. Just as working people have been separated from their proper roles by capitalist economic organizations, so these processes are occurring as well within the realms of art and expressive culture. This essentially economic viewpoint is well represented in Horkheimer and Adorno's (1972) classic description of the "culture industry," written in 1944 in Los Angeles. By that account, cultural productions, such as dramatic performances or works of art, have been turned into commodities by businesses. Artistic or creative work has been wrenched from its originating contexts (seen largely in terms of Marx's workshop view of labor) to be "mechanically reproduced" in blander, conformity-inducing formats. Such softer, entertainment-oriented productions tend to coexist easily with the ambitions of the businesses (or governments) that sponsor the productions.

The Frankfurt School tended to view the recipients of these products as masses, as a relatively undifferentiated public "objectified" by an elite that controls the productive process. This shift—from the traditional Marxian emphasis on production to a new focus on consumption—was a substantial change; and it was buttressed by ideas about human personality that were being developed by Freud and his followers. This latter approach emphasized the extent to which people internalized the cultural mores of their society and, in the process, banished some of their own private desires to unconscious levels. Thus the Frankfurt thinkers argued that the masses were culturally alienated in a variety of ways. At a most basic level, they had become separated from the kinds of creative, public expression familiar to their ancestors. Rarely now did people make their own pleasures; instead they passively received the packaged amusements made available to them at commercial establishments or through the media.

However, such commercial fare was deemed unsuitable even on its own terms. Characterized by emphases on entertainment and escape, productions offered by the movies or advertising drew people away from more substantial matters (particularly questions of economic and social justice) or created a variety of phony allegiances (e.g., nationalistic pride) that replaced class-consciousness. Even more frequently, they celebrated the thoroughly private vision of life that Marx so adamantly opposed. Cultural expression developed as a series of grand distractions. Even more insidiously, the media commonly treated important issues in ways that trivialized or misdirected these concerns. Combining elements from both Marx and Freud, Marcuse (1964, pp. 56–83) discussed this issue as "repressive de-sublimation," the bringing forward of psychically important material in ways that are sexually explicit but inattentive to the full range of their sensuality. To express the matter in Freudian parlance, the "polymorphous perversity" that is every person's birthright was becoming "genitally organized."

Again, all this fits the broader Marxian vision of a populace that is honorable but easily distracted from its real needs. Individuals are stupefied by a bombardment of entertainment-oriented products. They fall victim to "false consciousness," the denial of their true (read, class-based) interests. They participate in "commodity fetishism" to the extent that they see life as an ongoing quest to obtain commercial products and experiences. Cultural consumption becomes a source of status and a center of being. The working class is no longer to be found at the picket lines but at the auto show.

BRITISH CULTURAL STUDIES

A guiding issue of critical theory was the "privatization" of experience under the conditions of a market economy. In this view, modern people spend too much time developing a quasi-unique style of personal and family consumption. Re-defining personal responsibility in this way (as a commitment to maintain the social status or lifestyle of one's family) has harmful effects on the social integration of communities and contributes to the individual alienation described earlier. People move away from public gathering spots to listening posts within their homes. This theme—the effect of mass culture on working class life—was a principal concern of a group of scholars who gathered at the Birmingham Centre for Contemporary Cultural Studies (CCCS) in the 1950s (see Brantlinger, 1990; During, 1993).

The cultural studies movement in Britain was to a large extent a response to the writings of the literary critic F. R. Leavis and his followers. The Leavisites believed that public culture in Britain was being destroyed by mass-produced consumer goods and entertainments. Stopping this decline required an infusion of "good" literature and art, which would restore moral sensibility. Government, through the auspices of the public education system, should accomplish this task.

Under the leadership of Richard Hoggart, the CCCS explored the nature of learning and literacy among working class people. Although Hoggart (with Raymond Williams, E. P. Thompson, Stuart Hall, and others) tended to be quite critical of media culture, the group also believed that Britain possessed a strong working-class tradition that was legitimate on its own terms. Working-class communities in England had their own pubs and working people's associations that were intimately connected with family practices and community life. In that sense, the CCCS rejected the idea of people as undifferentiated and passive masses. Likewise, the group disagreed with the Leavisites' view of culture as only the most refined practices and expressions of the upper classes. Instead, culture should be seen as a vast complex of lived practices (including music, family life, politics, recreation, and community relations) that characterizes and shapes a community. Just as people respond to the guidelines of their own local cultures in distinctive ways, so they interpret or "read" mass-produced consumer culture from their own vantage points.

The overall thrust of this approach was to highlight the active role of individuals and groups in producing and reacting to cultural forms. From the 1970s on, the CCCS increasingly incorporated the experiences of women, formerly colonized peoples, radical youth, and other historically marginalized groups to develop a view of culture as deeply historical and political. Just as every cultural form or expression (e.g., a billboard) carries a wealth of socio-historical references and insinuations, so individuals and groups read that sign in distinctive ways. Television shows, amusement parks, and public school classrooms are thereby always contested terrains. People more or less successfully resist the intentions of the producers and create their own realities in each setting.

As can be seen, British cultural studies began with a traditional Marxian commitment to understand the quality of working-class life in a capitalist society. However, it altered that approach by emphasizing people's ability to deflect or otherwise modify the messages of the commercial producers. Furthermore, the CCCS substituted smaller scale, ethnographic studies for the theory-dominated, macro-level approaches typical of Marxian analysis. In the British model, hegemony—again, the dominance of group-sponsored systems of ideas and practices—is a matter to be proved rather than claimed. While the power of the "culture industry" is not to be denied, other crucial social elements (communities, classes, ethnicities, age groups, genders, etc.) also contribute profoundly to a society's patterning of thought, moral valuation, and enjoyment.

A Marxian Analysis of Sport

As should be apparent, almost any human endeavor—love, religion, education, family life, art—is amenable to Marxian analysis. The various institutions of society tend to be integrated in some fashion; economic patterns reach into the other spheres of life. One institution that has been marked heavily by such economic patterns—and that, consequently, has received a full measure of Marxian analysis—is sport (see Beamish, 2002). In the following, I identify some themes of this scholarship. I use sport here to illustrate the Marxian approach not only because sport is commonly associated with play but also because sport makes central the concrete, sensual part of life emphasized in Marx's early writings. Typically, these Marxian elements are brought forward under a more general banner known in sociology as conflict theory (see Hoch, 1972; Brohm, 1978; Sage, 1990; Coakley, 1996b).

In general, sporting events are prominent features of societies that emphasize individualism, social mobility, and other competitively organized social institutions (see Henricks, 1991). While other styles of physical display (group dancing, mass exercise drills, public rituals) could receive equal or greater emphasis, modern societies have focused on the dramatic possibilities of sporting contests as a way to reaffirm selected cultural themes. At some level, a competitive exercise system has a natural affinity with a capitalist economic system.

Marxian analysis tends to focus on what is sometimes referred to as "big-time" sport. In this view, the sporting world is currently overrun by a commercial ethic (and related models for personal behavior) from the professional sports leagues. This professional model can be criticized on its own terms. That is, emphases on franchise profitability, player salaries, and television contracts have altered the public's understanding of its "community" teams. High-priced sporting paraphernalia, capitalizing on player and team "branding," is a central element in a huge secondary market of sports consumption. Communities routinely grant sports businesses a variety of tax-supported privileges, including publicly owned stadiums, road construction, and services of city personnel—all to prevent team owners from seeking better deals elsewhere. Some of these same taxpayers have little interest in sporting spectacles; others are too poor to attend the games. Making more in a season than most people do in a lifetime, sports celebrities have become the front men and women for huge conglomerates trading in fantasy, lifestyle, and the commodities that make real these ambitions.

More troubling is the intrusion of this model into the sporting activities of the universities, high schools, and youth leagues. Professionalization in this regard has tended to mean a specialized focus on sport (expressed through training regimens, travel expectations, coaching style, family commitment, etc.) that interferes with other important (if arguably less exciting) activities of young people. Just as athletic departments at large universities have acquired a semi-independent status, so this approach introduces an alternative set of values and commitments that compete with traditional academic expectations. Escalating salaries and benefits packages for coaches, frenzy for media exposure, corporate skyboxes, high ticket costs, low graduation rates for athletes, questionable "academic support" practices to sustain eligibility, corrupt recruiting activities, drug use, off-court violence, and so on, are familiar elements in a wide-ranging critique of big-time sport put forward by academics and disenchanted sports journalists. More specific themes are described below.

SPORT FEATURES AN ALIENATED FORM OF LABOR

In keeping with this portrait of big-time sports programs, the athletes themselves are sometimes compared to alienated laborers in the Marxian sense (see Edwards, 1984). Focusing on college athletes in the revenue-producing sports of men's basketball and football (and particularly on African-American athletes) it is argued that these students enter a system that profoundly controls their activity. After the heady experience of recruitment, they find themselves isolated geographically and socially from other students and subject to a rigorous daily schedule over which they have no control. Sometimes producing millions of dollars in revenue for the university, they are restricted to a set "maximum wage" (tuition and fees, room and board, etc.) and are prevented from seeking other available means of making money. Marginalized as students and frequently failing to graduate, these athletes are unable to transfer to other sports "employers" without a significant loss of time and series of special permissions. In general, athletes in the big-time programs are portrayed as creators who fail to receive the benefits of their creations. Attempts to legitimize the whole system—by citing cases of the few players moving on to the professional ranks or by emphasizing the public regard and alumni support that accrues to the university—are characterized as self-serving or otherwise unworthy.

SPORT IS AN ALIENATED FORM OF SELF-EXPERIENCE

A related matter is the extent to which sport (again, sport in its big-time version) mitigates against personal awareness and growth. At one level, concentrating on sport presents all the dangers consistent with any sort of specialization. Clearly, pursuing one course excessively prevents the taking of other paths. Again, Marx championed the person of wide-ranging appetites and abilities. The leisure specialist or sportsman—neither the conspicuously languorous dilettante made famous by Veblen (1953) nor those following the more modern "athletic" style—would have been approved. In particular, the athletic style has tended to emphasize an objectifying, ascetic attitude toward the body. Pain is frequently touted as the companion of gain, spirit is asked to conquer flesh. Furthermore, the experience of playing itself becomes secondary to the public display of skill and competitive success. Choosing such attitudes for oneself is one thing; adopting the performance-oriented viewpoints of nonplayers (owners, coaches, handlers, etc.) is another (see Rigauer, 1981). Like other forms of false consciousness, the so-called "sports creed" is thought to distract people from more ultimately beneficial approaches to physical experience.

SPORT IS A DISINTEGRATIVE FORCE IN COMMUNITY LIFE

Religion is seen in classical Marxism as a kind of opiate, a vehicle carrying people's thoughts away from the real (material) issues of their lives. Organized religion is said to focus attention on otherworldly matters, legitimize prevailing social hierarchies, and reconcile people to an ethic of obedience. Furthermore, religious rivalries are effective ways to divide communities when these same communities should be gathering themselves around common material concerns. Such charges can be levied against organized sport as well. That is, sports can be accused of bringing large numbers of people together for spectacularly pointless endeavors. Profounder questions—about the broader effects of the activity or the possibilities of redirecting this energy in more socially beneficial ways—are not encouraged.

Similarly, Marxist thinkers tend to downplay the importance of the community or educational divisions that constitute the typical rivalries of team sports. In brief, the wrong groups of people are set against one another in sports. Furthermore, athletes of every type participate in an institution that remains deeply divided along gender lines. Historically, sport has been a central setting for the development of a distinctive version of masculine identity and a bastion of sexist ideas. Looking at the sporting world in this broader way also reveals the extent to which class and ethnic differences have restricted sports participation and continue to do so. In essence, big-time sports is portrayed as an elaborate series of shows that stupefy or otherwise misdirect the public. The real beneficiaries of this "bread and circuses" approach are the property-owning groups, who watch the curiously misdirected rivalries of the groups situated below.

SPORT ALLIES ITSELF WITH OTHER FORMS OF OPPRESSION

To some extent sport glorifies—or at least reconciles people to—a worldview in which individual and group struggle is the normal state of affairs.

Life, it seems, must be populated with winners and losers, those who play the game effectively and those who do not. What is debatable about such arrangements is not the legitimacy of the interaction itself but rather the levels of commitment, preparation, and executive efficiency of the competitors. The triumph of the dominators is cause for mutual celebration; losers must content themselves with their more modest accomplishments and dream of future encounters.

Such ideas can be translated to the struggles of states in the emerging global economy (see Mandel, 1975; Brohm, 1978). As is shown clearly in the modern Olympic movement, nations vie with one another under terms that are equal only in the most superficial ways. Dominant countries apply their vast resources—economic, political, scientific, and technical—to the recruitment and training of their teams. Such countries pack the organizing bodies of the events with their own members and control the value frameworks that guide the competitions. They provide the bulk of the "qualifying" athletes and the "training centers" for many of the others. Most of the time (due to considerations of economic surplus, political security, transportation networks, and media facilities) they serve as "hosts" for the events as well. Styled as international gatherings, the Olympic Games are effectively occasions for the "world community" to witness the political and economic superiority of the great powers and, in the process, to reaffirm the status of the great and small.

MARX'S LEGACY

At a distance of one hundred fifty years, Marx's ideas are easy enough to criticize (see, e.g., Rossiter, 1960). Some predictions of the theory have been swept away by events of the twentieth century; other formulations were inadequate even in Marx's time. Marx's emphasis on economic issues as prime movers in history is a monumental contribution, but his dogged pursuit of this theme raises all the dangers of reductionism. To be sure, economic organization influences most aspects of life in modern societies; but relationships of power, prestige, and knowledge are crucial on their own terms. The interaction of these elements caused capitalism to evolve in directions Marx did not anticipate. The rise of the welfare state, income taxes, the development of the corporation, the thickening and diversification of the occupational structure, the growth of labor unions, and so on, were all factors that softened the harsh realities of the nineteenth century and, by some accounts, prevented Marx's revolution from occurring. More generally, Marx's analyses did not affect the history of capitalism in significant ways; and his certitude about the character of future societies seems, in retrospect, quaint.

Again, Marx's comments about the nature and significance of labor are profound. But his disregard for the occupations of the bourgeoisie seems misguided. His recollections about a stage of primitive or prehistoric communism are largely fables and his blueprint for political change seems insufficient. More problematic still is his conception of human personality. Real people are more complicated, and motivated by a wider range of forces, than is shown in the Marxian model.

All this notwithstanding, Marx's thought represents a powerful way of looking at the human condition. Some concluding thoughts about that legacy are offered below.

THE POWER OF TRANSFORMATION

Much of the appeal of Marx's work is due to its quality of hopefulness. The world, it seems, is always in a state of becoming; and humans can effect changes to assist that process. Even more fundamentally, Marxian thought is a statement about how people should address their circumstances. Both the material and socio-cultural worlds should be seen less as grim necessities than as opportunities for personal and public creativity. In a sense that must not be forgotten, people are the architects of their existence.

As mentioned above, Marx's early writings celebrate creative and expressive life in all its dimensions. By manipulating or rendering the object-world, people sharpen their skills and explore the possibilities of being human. The artifacts they produce reflect, like ornaments, these same attributes and capabilities. In the happiest circumstances, creators interact intimately with their creations. People make the world and in turn are made by it, empty themselves into it and find themselves filled again. By such lights, creativity is an attempt at personal and social self-realization, a step toward a more harmonious and engaged state of being.

Yet labor, in the Marxian sense, is not quite equivalent to Huizinga's descriptions of play. Fundamentally, labor is consequential. The making of the world is a real thing. The objects made have permanence and frequently influence, in large or small degrees, the remainder of people's lives. Furthermore, while Huizinga saw play as a kind of stepping back from the routine exigencies of life, Marx did not see labor in this way. Instead, he advocated a relatively seamless life. Public and private, work and leisure, contribution and reward, objectivity and subjectivity—somehow these customary antinomies should be resolved. People should not need protected spaces in which to operate freely; they should create a world that is free at every point.

THE VIRTUES OF MATERIALISM

It is sometimes said that Marx found Hegel standing on his head and set him aright. It may well be that Marx's work represents a kind of over-correction of Hegel's cultural-spiritual emphasis; however, Marx's commitment to the material part of life is helpful for the study of play. By focusing on people's relationship to the physical world and on the qualities they share with animals, Marx entered territory central to play studies. In the ways Marx emphasized, existence is indeed concrete and sensuous, and people attempt to apprehend the object-world with their five senses. Similarly, we possess the basic physical needs of animals and experience many of their limitations. Like the evolution of the brain itself, the more recent cultural portion of human nature has been built upon this core of physical-organic requirements.

However outdated by new knowledge in biology and the social sciences, Marx's work remains interesting because of his efforts to connect material relationships with intellectual-cultural development at the personal or social level. Again, labor for Marx was not a simple manipulation of the world to satisfy one's animal needs; rather it was a pathway for the fullest expression of human capability. To use Piaget's (1962) twentieth-century terminology, people are inevitably concrete-operational thinkers. While capable of occasional flights into airless abstraction, we typically interact with the physical world in forming our understandings. We manipulate and create and then adjust ourselves to these new creations. While hardly a complete theory of human knowledge or cultural development, Marx's emphasis on material exploration as a foundation for the house of consciousness remains a powerful tradition. Like children, we build so that we may appraise ourselves in our creations.

THE ADVANTAGES OF A
SOCIOLOGICAL APPROACH

Marx may be criticized for his incomplete understandings of human psychology, but he deserves credit for his attempt to build its complement, a broadly sociological approach to human nature and public life. Although he stressed the economic aspect above others, the overall spirit of his approach was to connect economic patterns of relationship with political and moral matters, in effect to create a portrait of the good society.

As described in the *Economic and Philosophic Manuscripts*, humans are social in their essence. They create a public life together and this context provides a framework for subsequent endeavors. Furthermore, people inhabit distinctive positions within the social order. These varying circumstances again determine how one sees the world. Marx is rightly famous for his attempts to connect material circumstance (in the full, socially enveloped sense of that term) with patterns of conception. Class position, arguably, is related to ideology. Formulations of government, education, religion, and so on, are connected to class-relations in some fashion.

For the study of expression then, this emphasis on social context is critical. As Marx reminded us, people do not shape the world on their own terms alone. We participate with others; we address the institutional realities that surround us. Private experience always has a powerful social dimension. Marx's standing as a sociologist derives from his imaginative ability to bring together these two realms.

EXPRESSION AS A SOCIAL PROBLEM

With an influence that has been unmatched by any other social scientist, Marx diagnosed the ailments of modern society and prescribed remedies for those complaints. While commentators disagree about the accuracy of his evaluation, the general themes pursued by Marx—the centrality of economic matters, the problematic nature of class-relations, and the prospects for a more humane and socially responsible future—continue to resonate within all fields of knowledge. Moreover, Marx's insistence that the potential of human beings can be either supported or blocked by social structure still guides humanistic thinkers. Alienation, that condition of disconnection or misdirection, is particularly important in this regard. People should not be made passive or marginalized or be turned into specialists by others. Nor should they hope to possess, and thereby stop, the world. Expression in every context is a human birthright and, ultimately, the basis of the good society.

3 Emile Durkheim on the Social Foundations of Expression

People diagnose the ailments of the world differently. For Marx, the crisis of industrial societies was the alienation of working people. Workers' rights must be protected by labor patterns that both satisfy the workers themselves and benefit the community at large. A quite different approach was taken by the French sociologist Emile Durkheim. For Durkheim, the crucial matters of the modern world were less the quality of economic relationships than the nature of people's moral and social connections. While Marx emphasized the ways in which individual needs served as touchstones in a radical critique of public order, Durkheim stressed the importance of society itself and the legitimacy of our obligations to it. On the basis of these commitments, it is odd perhaps that Marx should have become the best-known proponent of collectivist thought and Durkheim a self-styled champion of individualism.

As in the case of Marx, Durkheim's body of work seems at first glance to bear little relationship to Huizinga's concerns about play. Although Durkheim did share Huizinga's respect for society as a collective enterprise that should exhibit both civility and continuity, he did not share the latter's fascination with the disorderly qualities found in play. Huizinga, it will be recalled, emphasized the historical significance of the *agon* or interpersonal contest as an opportunity for social exploration. Durkheim, by contrast, was preoccupied with the possibilities for coordination and cooperation in societies. In a fashion still rare within the social sciences, Huizinga ruminated on the functions of joy as an element in the life of societies. Although Durkheim acknowledged this theme, he tended to focus more on the intellectual and ethical requirements of social experience. Indeed, one may ask how a writer so committed to the importance of societal integration, moral education, religion as a framework for belief and action, social responsibility, and self-discipline can be relevant to the matters at hand.

However, just as Marx's writing illuminates Huizinga's by forcing us to contemplate the relationship between work and play, so Durkheim's scholarship addresses matters that are ill-defined or dimly understood in *Homo Ludens*. Of special importance in this regard is the relationship between ritual and play, phenomena that sometimes appear as identities in Huizinga's writing. Furthermore, because Durkheim was perhaps the greatest commentator on morality in the history of sociology, we must turn to him to consider the relationship of social norms to human activity of every type. Through Durkheim, one learns about the relationship between social involvement and individual assertion and about the connections between the moral and aesthetic dimensions of life. Like Huizinga, he was a man who looked into the past to understand the future. His discoveries—about the meaning of obligation in societies—serve as a counterbalance to Huizinga's raptures about spontaneity and creative expression.

Durkheim's Intellectual Project

It is difficult to imagine a man less playful in his manner and commitments than Emile Durkheim (see Giddens, 1978; Lukes, 1985; Coser, 1977). Like Marx, Durkheim was a child of the Franco-Prussian borderlands, having been born in a village in the Lorraine in 1858. His career was marked by these small community origins and by the fact that his father was an orthodox rabbi. The Durkheim household was rooted firmly in the values of hard work, discipline, self-denial, and the importance of law. Although Durkheim considered rabbinical school, his scientific interests overwhelmed his religious feelings, and he determined instead to have an academic career. The traits he might have brought to the synagogue—moral seriousness, intellectual rigor, respect for community, steadfastness of purpose—were transferred to this new endeavor.

Like many other talented and ambitious French students, the eighteen-year-old Emile applied to the Ecole Normale Superiere in Paris. In a fashion that has heartened struggling sociology students everywhere, he twice failed the rigorously competitive entrance examinations. His ultimate admission led not only to brilliant success as a student but also to profound disillusion with the methods and curriculum of the school. Educational institutions in France were still much influenced by a humanities tradition that praised beautiful intellectual formulations. Durkheim disdained the flashy erudition of his times (see Pampel, 2000, pp. 43–48). Instead, he felt the academic world should be based on patient, systematic, and deep researches into the practical problems facing society. Like Marx, he steadfastly opposed empty eloquence; but unlike his German predecessor, he put his faith in science.

Durkheim's professional career is a testimony to his systematic and rigorous nature. The five years after graduation in 1882 were spent teaching philosophy in provincial high schools and studying social and political thought in Germany. His writings based on these matters helped him attain a position at the University of Bordeaux as a lecturer in social science and education in 1887. During the next fifteen years, he produced some of the most famous works in the social sciences. His doctoral dissertation (Durkheim, 1964a), published as the *Division of Labor in Society* in 1893, was a study of the differences in social integration between older and newer types of societies. This was followed in 1895 by *The Rules of Sociological Method* (Durkheim, 1964b), in which he argued for the use of scientific procedures in the study of social phenomena. A specific test of these methods was produced two years later in his classic *Suicide* (Durkheim, 1951). In that work, he used statistical data to demonstrate that "social facts" follow their own predictable patterns and influence even the most profound and difficult personal decisions. Of special importance during this period was his founding of *L'Année Sociologique*, a prominent journal in which he and his fellow proponents of scientific approaches strengthened their position within the European social sciences (see Clark, 1973).

In 1902, Durkheim moved to the top of the French academic world with his acceptance of a position at the Sorbonne. Because there was still strong resistance to the idea of sociology as a legitimate academic enterprise, his chair was in education and he focused his energies on studies in the history and practice of education in France. An expression of that period is his *Moral Education* (Durkheim, 1961), published by his students from lecture notes after his death. More important for our purposes is his 1912 classic *The Elementary Forms of the Religious Life*, a study of the origins and significance of religion in societies (Durkheim, 1965). In 1913, his chair was retitled to include the discipline of sociology, the first position of its type in France. During the ensuing World War, his only son was killed in the fighting. Durkheim never recovered from his grief. He died, from complications of a stroke, in 1917.

Like many other scholars of his time, Durkheim was troubled profoundly by the vicissitudes in French politics following 1789. The rapid swings between anarchy and despotism raised in Durkheim many of the concerns that had motivated Alexis de Tocqueville's (1945) classic study of democracy in the 1820s. That is, how can a society guarantee fundamental rights to all its citizens and, at the same time, promote civility, continuity, and order? Durkheim's famous responses to this question were in large part reactions to the prevailing ideologies of his time. Like Marx, he opposed the tradition of the utilitarians (and especially Herbert Spencer), who had argued that the good society is for the most part a result of the unfettered expression of economic self-interest by its millions of individual members. As Durkheim (1964a, pp. 200–229) argued compellingly, the "social contract" only exists because its participants share a wider set of commitments about their past and future relationships. In other words, some level of public trust must precede those hard negotiations so prized by the utilitarians. Furthermore, Durkheim opposed the "organicist" tradition represented by the so-called founder of sociology, Auguste Comte, and his disciples. Society may well be a reality of profound importance, but this does not mean that it is the only social reality that should be respected. One consequence of the French Revolution had been the supercession of smaller institutions like church, family, and community by the mighty state. For his part, Durkheim (1972, pp. 189–202) argued that society and government could never be made identical; rather the commitments of these two elements and of individuals themselves must be held in a kind of artful balance.

His avoidance of either extreme has made Durkheim's views difficult to classify. Some scholars (see, e.g., Coser, 1960; Nisbet, 1965) have tended to characterize Durkheim as a conservative. That is, his emphases on the primacy of society, on orderliness and public cooperation, on the necessity of authority, on moral education, and the need for social restraints on personal expression set him against some of the major themes of the Enlightenment and certain traditions of liberalism. However, others (see, e.g., Giddens, 1972; Richter, 1960) have emphasized the degree to which Durkheim was a defender of democracy and public welfare. He supported rights for citizens as a whole, envisioned an appropriate role for government in these terms, and advocated pluralism rather than uniformitarianism in public affairs. Moreover, he was a true child of the Enlightenment by virtue of his respect for science and rationality as vehicles in the creation of the good society.

Durkheim's distinctive perspective on modern society arguably stemmed from his early marginality. To a large extent, he brought many of the personal characteristics and moral concerns of the small community person (a sensibility that meshed with his foundations in Jewish cultural traditions) into the racy academic world centered in Paris. With a quality of vision denied to others, he was able to bind together the characteristics of these different settings into a wider portrait of society—one that tried to balance the national need for progress and economic coordination with the personal requirements for community and emotional intimacy.

In such ways, Durkheim's intellectual project is a refinement of the German Ferdinand Toennies's (1963) well-known distinction between *gemeinschaft* and *gesellschaft*. Toennies had witnessed in his own lifetime the widening contrast between the old village communities, still influenced by feudal traditions, and the more individualistic, worldly culture of the cities. *Gemeinschaft* was, by this account, traditional, informal, religious, personal, and sentimental. Community members commonly knew one another from birth to death. They worked side by side in the fields, played in public spaces together, and worshiped as one. *Gesellschaft* represented the greater world of citizens and publics. Economic matters and private calculation took center stage. Life became more impersonal, contractual, specialized, secular, and hard-boiled. As an integrative thinker, Durkheim could not countenance the simple replacement of one world by the other. Modern society, in the terms described by Toennies, would become an unworkable monstrosity. Some, though not all, of the qualities of the traditional community must be institutionalized into contemporary public life.

It is not the purpose of this chapter to develop Durkheim's response to these issues at length. However, a summary of his argument in the *Division of Labor* is that people in older, more traditional societies were held together somewhat differently than in the new nation-states. Because people in older societies performed many of the same economic tasks (in the process of caring for their own lands and households), they needed social devices to reassert their broader connections. Among these devices were periodic community rituals that reaffirmed their shared values, traditions, and lineage. This "mechanical" type of solidarity was different from that of the modern world in which people depended on each other "organically." That is, modern people tended to be economic specialists who contracted with others for the fulfillment of their needs. Much of Durkheim's intellectual career was a working out of the proper balance between these different forms of solidarity in the modern context. That is, to what extent did contemporary people still need the sense of belonging and periodic commitment to shared ideals that had enriched life in earlier times?

The Discovery of the Society

Among those "classic" sociologists who defined the discipline at the turn of the twentieth century, Durkheim is perhaps remembered best as the defender of the social, the man who most effectively pushed forward the position that social phenomena are realities of their own type that cannot be reduced to patterns of individual decision-making. He is also acknowledged as the great champion of scientifically based research strategies. Although different than the phenomena of the material world, social realities can be studied in ways that approximate the systematic rigor, objectivity, and propositional thinking associated with physical science. Less well remembered is his battle against the powerful Enlightenment tradition that people in their natural (i.e., pre-social) state have inherent qualities of ability and judgment. These indigenous capacities, it was commonly argued, should be the foundation of societies that represent and support their expression. To that degree, society itself was pictured as little more than an artifact, a product that results from (and safeguards) patterns of personal choice.

Like Comte and Saint-Simon before him, Durkheim was enough of a rationalist to recognize certain merits in this argument and to believe that a better society might be engineered at the national level. However, he shared with more conservative thinkers the sense that society was also an entity (with its own qualities and patterns) that preceded the experience of individuals. He also recognized that many aspects of people's decision-making are not clearly calculated but rather depend on an essentially nonrational acceptance of cognitive and moral frameworks from the communities in which they live. As Nisbet (1965, pp. 14–15) has argued, this recognition of the fundamentally nonrational character of human experience was as radical in its own way as the claims being put forward by Durkheim's contemporary Freud. However, while Freud emphasized nonrationality as an intra-personal conflict resulting largely from psycho-organic desires, Durkheim stressed instead our inevitable dependence on preexisting social forms. Indeed, many (see, e.g., Parsons, 1974) have discussed Durkheim's view of the person as essentially a form of "sociological Kantianism," that is, as a claim that our fundamental orientations toward the world (including our understandings of such basic categories as space, time, cause, hierarchy, etc.) derive from the structure of society.

It was not for Durkheim to regret or celebrate our dependence on the social; such matters are simply part of our nature. This dependence is developed most clearly in his book *Suicide*. Despite the variety of personal reasons leading to suicide, its rates in different countries and among different categories of people tend to follow predictable patterns. Hence, he concluded, such rates must be indicators of the quality and character of the persisting connections between people and the social bodies to which they belong. A major thrust in his book is the development of a typology of "egoistic" and "anomic" suicide, patterns in which people find themselves too little connected (intellectually or socially) with their environments. Thus, Protestants, men, city dwellers, single people, and so on, kill themselves with more regularity than those with different statuses.

Such a viewpoint has profound implications. If freedom is to be understood as sheer possibility of choice and movement, then perhaps freedom in that sense is dangerous. Too much choice—or too much change—can move people beyond their realms of comfort and stability. Durkheim argued that humans were different from other animals in that humans have few natural or biological limits set upon their appetites. For people, these limits must come from society. Like de Tocqueville then, Durkheim was a severe critic of "individuation," that largely unregulated condition of purely personal movement and decision-making (see Giddens, 1972). For humans to thrive, they must have socially defined channels of expression and recognized limits for action. A society in which sheer prerogative operates is a society characterized by anarchy. Social reality is needed to settle people down and shape their impulses.

Furthermore, society should not be seen merely as a necessary constraint. To be sure, social codes and patterns of enforcement keep people from various forms of deviance (including suicide). But society is more significantly a framework within which individuals can realize their ambitions (see Durkheim, 1964a, pp. 386–388; Richter, 1960). In this sense, freedom should be understood not only as a negative phenomenon (i.e., as an ability to escape the interference of others) but also as a positive one. Society creates the conditions of freedom. One cannot travel to a distant city or become skilled as a craftsperson or experience the pleasures of a hotel without the support of others. In such ways, social structure is a pattern of "enablement." All manner of human relationships, including the utilitarians' famous contracts, are possible only because of preexisting networks based on trust and cooperation.

Much of this puts Durkheim squarely within the traditionalist camp. Human beings must recognize their indebtedness to such social bodies as church, family, and community. Duty and responsibility are not just grim necessities but vehicles that shape and stabilize the person. Much of our behavior—and understanding—is influenced by social patterns beyond our control and ken. Society is an elaborately configured and profoundly important level of reality that we would do well to respect. However, Durkheim cannot be categorized so easily. Other portions of *Suicide* are about the conditions represented by "altruistic" or "fatalistic" suicide, about the dangers of over attachment to the social body. Nor does he defend a tyrannical social order. What he elsewhere (Durkheim, 1964a, pp. 374–387) terms the "forced division of labor" (covering all manner of servitude and false compliance) is held to be clearly wrong for our modern world.

Again, as an integrative thinker, Durkheim wished to combine the modern society's emphasis on personal choice and freedom of movement with the old world's sensitivity to responsibility and order. In that regard, he articulated the philosophical position of "individualism," a social system in which personal expression is both chartered and regulated in terms of its public consequences (See Durkheim, 1961, pp. 64–79; 1972, pp. 147–150; see also Neyer, 1960). Furthermore, he (Durkheim, 1964a, pp. 27–28) advocated the reestablishment of intermediate institutions (including occupational associations) that could broker some of the colder relationships between individual and state.

Durkheim's arguments about the importance of intermediate institutions, chartered liberties, and respect for social order at a society-wide level spoke clearly to a centralized but politically fragile society like France. His appeal within the more individualistic, largely Protestant countries to the North and within the United States was less pronounced. Indeed, in the United States, Durkheim's writings—including his ideas about the "functions" or social consequences of patterns of culture and behavior—were popularized only during the 1930s by the British social anthropologist A. R. Radcliffe-Brown (1972) and by the American social theorist Talcott Parsons (1968). During the 1950s, the theoretical position of structural-functionalism in sociology became fully developed; and Durkheim was installed as a revered ancestor within this tradition. Although some analysts have disagreed about the legitimacy of these claims of paternity (see, e.g., Pierce, 1960), Durkheim's search for the social consequences of human interaction remains one of the great contributions in the social sciences.

The Sacred and the Profane

To summarize to this point, Durkheim's intellectual project can be seen as an attempt to reverse contemporary understandings of the individual-society relationship. Society, in his view, is less a product of human ingenuity and enterprise than a creator and inspirer of such endeavors. This theme is developed most daringly in his 1912 work, *The Elementary Forms of the Religious Life*. The book's avowed purpose is to discover the origins of religious experience and practice by exploring these matters in one of the purportedly simplest societies in the world, the clan-based communities of the Australian aborigines. For our purposes however, the *Elementary Forms* will be seen as a more general argument about the relationship between social organization and human experience.

It should be noted that Durkheim's book represents a clear departure from the hostile treatment accorded religion by the French *philosophes* and their academic descendants (see Nisbet, 1966, pp. 221–231). In this tradition, religion was felt to be an unfortunate stage of human development, a collection of childish stories and regimens that block intelligent people from their true potential. Certainly, Marx was a standard-bearer for this argument. While not religious himself, Durkheim recognized that religion was profoundly important as an intellectual and social matter. The examination of religious beliefs and practices for Durkheim was a way to comprehend better the functioning of societies.

As Durkheim (1972, pp. 219–222) notes, theories about the origin and significance of religion tend to be of two types: those that see religion as a response to the need of individuals to comprehend and feel comfortable in the world and those that stress the role of religion in human sociability. *The Elementary Forms* not only emphasizes this latter viewpoint but also attempts to explain how religious experience itself derives from social matters. Durkheim argues that religion is essentially the recognition that there is a realm (of superior dignity and power) that stands beyond the comings and goings of the routine world. This realm, which he termed the sacred, was originally coextensive with the boundaries of society itself. People throughout history have acknowledged their dependence upon the oftentimes centuries-old collectivities to which they belong. Their postulation of a sacred realm (and sacred spaces and objects within the actual world) is fundamentally an act of humility in the face of these larger groups. In traditional societies, people typically cannot survive alone. It is through community membership that humans not only come to fullness as persons but also gain the set of ideas and practices that allow them to process their world. Thus, religious forms tend to reflect social forms. Aborigines possess religious beliefs and rituals consistent with their clan-based social divisions; ideas about gods, souls, and so on, are the products of later, more complex social orders.

Much of this is an elaboration of Fustel de Coulanges' (1980) descriptions of the sacred hearths found at the center of the Greek city-states.

Relying on the new ethnographic literature that had developed in the half century since the initial publication of Fustel's *The Ancient City* in 1864, Durkheim's contribution was to systematize and expand these considerations into a more general portrait of the social functions of religion. Significantly, his ideas about religion parallel his general response to utilitarian philosophy. That is, he argues that the hurly-burly world of economics and daily life (so prized by Marx and the utilitarians) is the inferior or "profane" realm. Transcending and informing this world is a superior set of social bonds, conceptualized as the sacred. Critically, the sacred is not a response to the solitary longings or confusion of individuals (as the utilitarians might claim); rather it is a social product. Indeed, true religion for Durkheim (1965, pp. 57–63) does not exist without a "church," an organized community of believers. Furthermore, it is not some intellectual scheme that can be entertained and dismissed at will. Again, true religion requires a system of well-guarded practices, obligatory customs of collective participation that shadow the activities of the mundane world.

In such ways, religion formalizes the social heritage of a people. For most of history, humans have looked about themselves for support—not only to the communities, clans, and families that surround them currently but also to those vanished generations that people feel closer to in sacred moments. Such matters, in Durkheim's view, are not issues to be approached instrumentally. Religion is an occasion for obligation, commitment, and respect. Even in moments of religious festivity or magical manipulation, there is tacit acknowledgment that the sacred is the superior realm and should be approached with some care.

Consistently, Durkheim's view about religion parallels his more general understanding of the relationship between institutionalized culture (culture as it is shared and enacted in social life) and human functioning. Remarkably, he compares the sacred-profane division found in society to the division between soul and body in the human personality. As he (Durkheim, 1960) explains, human beings have a "dual nature." Part of this nature derives from our kinship with other animals. We are physical creatures attempting to survive in a constantly changing world. Our existence is concrete and sensuous at every moment. And like animals, we must operate out of the physical structure of our organism. To this degree, our own bodies trap us into an experience of the world that is essentially isolated and individualized. We perceive and experience the world, but we have no way of knowing whether our sensations are equivalent to those of our neighbors.

However, this profane, sensory side of our nature is complemented by another (in his view, superior) side. Humans are able to develop and inhabit a world of conception. What thinkers historically have termed the soul—some transcendental, nonphysical aspect of the human essence—is in reality a recognition that there is a more abstract, intellectualized reality in which people participate. In a striking argument, Durkheim claims that this "sacred" conceptual realm is not a private but a public thing. That is, our ability to frame the world in our minds and to communicate with one another is dependent on a collective, largely impersonal edifice of ideas and language transcending time and space. Critically, it is this realm of conception that unites us as members of a human community moving together from past to future. In so doing, it breaks down the isolation that would otherwise be the central aspect of the human condition. The idea of the soul is merely the religious thinker's attempt to denote the connection of each person to this abstract community. By such lights, people are not condemned to live and die alone.

As Durkheim and his nephew Marcel Mauss argued in another context (Durkheim and Mauss, 1963), people's cognitive capabilities—that is, their abilities to classify and process the phenomena of the world—are indebted heavily to the societies in which they live. As French citizens, Americans, or Trobriand Islanders, we comprehend our own identities and our relationship to others through a distinctive cultural lens. Furthermore, such societies provide us with our moral sensibilities. Indeed, Durkheim is prominent among those who claim that moral matters are by definition different from individual ones. That is, true morality cannot be understood as a self-regarding maneuver, some fashioning of personal commitments to keep our own lives in order or gain the respect of others. It is not a cloak that we take on and off as situations demand. Rather, morality is an acceptance of the obligatory nature of social participation. To be moral is to acknowledge that the community must not be treated casually or instrumentally but rather is an object whose enhanced welfare is the appropriate end of action. To that extent, morality is the secularized development of themes that find their earliest (and most intense) expression in religion.

Durkheim's general view of mental life is represented well by his famous, if troublesome, description of the "collective conscience," that deep pool of public understandings and commandments that shape the lives of societies (see Durkheim, 1964a, pp. 79–82). In French *conscience* carries three rather different meanings: consciousness, conscience, and the concepts of which people are aware. As Bohannon (1960) has explained, these various meanings helped Durkheim construct the notion of a transpersonal symbolic realm holding sway over private thought and valuation. The idea of this symbolic realm contributed to the anthropological idea of culture. Durkheim's attempts to connect this realm with the boundaries and characteristics of various social bodies (such as local communities or society itself) led to an array of predictable criticisms by more individualistic thinkers (see Hinkle, 1960). Included among the charges were Durkheim's supposed mystification of social reality, congeniality with notions of a "group mind," and disregard for social differences and discord. However telling the criticisms, it is noteworthy that Durkheim's later writings (such as the *Elementary Forms*) tend to focus on "collective representations," specific socially shared ideas and norms, rather than "collective conscience" itself. However, he never renounced his ideas about societal representations being much more than the aggregation of individual ideas and values. In his view, collective frameworks guide and enrich the puny thinking that individuals can manage on their own.

Durkheim's ardent sociologism must be seen in the context of his times. In his view, the world was being overrun by an ethic of private interest. His response—to claim the historical and philosophical primacy of the community over the individual and to trumpet the virtues of abstract public thought over personal sensation—carries with it a certain missionary zeal. Furthermore, his dramatic separation of the sacred and profane spheres of life demands closer scrutiny. Indeed, the connections between the realms of conception and expression, permanence and transition, collectivity and person, and so on, are the matters to which we must now turn.

Ritual (and Play)

Although Durkheim was interested in collective representations as intellectual and moral abstractions (as philosophical matters), his principal commitment was to the sociological significance of these issues. In particular, that meant thinking about the social frameworks in which religious ideas are enacted and the relationship of these frameworks to other social processes. For such reasons, the latter portions of *The Elementary Forms* turn to the functions of ritual in societies.

It will be recalled that Huizinga too was interested in religious ritual and, more confusingly, in its relationship to play. As discussed in the first chapter, ritual seemed to Huizinga (1955, pp. 14–27) to have many of the same formal properties as play. That is, ritual is separated in space and time from routine affairs; it features distinctive costuming, manners, and ends of action; it is surrounded by strictly enforced rules. Like play, ritual produces no material product; instead its purpose is to "sort out" or otherwise define human relationships. Most strikingly, ritual encourages the same kinds of rapt attention so critical to play. Such similarities are most apparent in traditional societies. There, ritual and play seem to exist as closely entangled aspects of every public event.

Huizinga, of course, was more devoted to play than to its sober twin. After all, Huizinga was fascinated by a medieval world that largely accepted social division and hierarchy, emphasized the use of holidays to step away from routine, and acknowledged gaiety as a legitimate purpose for human interaction. And in other ways he embraced the sensibilities of essentially agricultural, tradition-bound societies. However, just as Huizinga relished the experiences of feudal aristocrats and peasants, so Durkheim was committed to understanding the dilemmas of the urban artisans and shopkeepers of his own time. Although he shared many of Huizinga's concerns about rampant individuation, instrumentalism, and the tyranny of nation-states, Durkheim was much more the modern thinker. In Durkheim's view, scholars should not romanticize the past but should instead examine the patterns of past societies as a way of thinking about new social forms (see Bellah, 1965). Consistent with this intellectual project—and with his own temperament and social background—Durkheim was drawn to the more socially stable, morally serious form of expression.

In brief, Durkheim's argument is that religious rituals in early societies were social practices that both clarified and reinforced the superiority of society over its members. This primacy of society was, as indicated above, expressed in the idea of the sacred. The function of individual rites (or the whole complex of ritual practices, which he termed the "cult") was to preserve the distinctive status of the sacred and to make people express publicly their commitment to it. In his view, religions tend to feature two different (though related) kinds of ritual practices—the negative cult and the positive cult.

Negative rituals are defined as symbolic practices that maintain the strict separation of the sacred and profane realms (see Durkheim, 1965, pp. 337–365). For the most part, these rites consist of a set of prohibitions, things that people must not possess or do. Some of these negative rituals address relations within the sacred space itself (e.g., words, gestures, and materials forbidden to ritual participants); however, Durkheim's principal interest is in the use of these rituals as gatekeeping devices.

As he (1965, pp. 52–54) explains, the sacred must be separated scrupulously from its profane rival. This is accomplished by special qualifications for ritual participants, holy places, special days and times reserved for religious expression, exotic costuming and paraphernalia, and so on. Such elements are exclusive to the sacred sphere; for example, a religious costume may not be worn in other settings. It is crucial that the sacred and profane not spill over their proper boundaries. Thus, much of the cult delineates sacred things that must not be touched, foods not to be eaten, or words not to be said outside their defining domain. Likewise, certain categories of people are forbidden to listen to (or even know the existence of) sacred songs and stories; and, if certain holy sights come before them, they are to avert their eyes. In the same way, participants may have special names used only within the ritual enclosure and not known to others.

Of course, profane people must be allowed to enter the sacred sphere at the proper time. Hence, many of the negative rituals focus on procedures people use to ready themselves for this transition. The self must be ridded of its impure, contagious qualities. As Durkheim (1965, p. 348) notes, some of this preparation may involve affirming actions such as "unctions, lustrations, and benedictions"; however, the "same results may be attained by means of vigils or retreats and silence, that is to say, by ritual abstinences, which are nothing more than certain interdictions put into practice." Neophytes routinely engage in acts of mortification, which may include denials of sleep, clothing, bathing privileges, personal possessions, permission to speak, and even the uses of their name.

It should be noted that play activities also frequently inhabit spaces and times set apart from ordinary affairs. However, play seldom requires such extraordinary procedures of preparation and denial unless it is formalized as a public event with heavily charged external meanings. The contrasting tendency of rituals to invoke just such regimens is explored by Durkheim in his discussion of asceticism. In his (1965, p. 350) view, asceticism is "nothing more than a hypertrophy of the negative cult." That is, asceticism is a philosophy that extends the elements of mortification rites into other aspects of life. As he (p. 351) continues: "We hold to the profane world by all the fibres of our being; our senses attach us to it; our life depends upon it. It is not merely the natural theatre of our activity; it penetrates us on every side; it is part of ourselves. So we cannot detach ourselves from it without doing violence to our nature and without painfully wounding our instincts. In other words, the negative cult cannot develop without causing suffering. Pain is one of its necessary conditions."

In this sense, asceticism reflects the triumph of abstract, conceptual commitment over the vagaries of flesh. It is a journey of personal purification, a project of remorselessly hunting down and conquering pain. The purpose of such activity is not to destroy the body but rather to strengthen it for the challenges of a higher moral calling.

Once the sacred spaces have been prepared and the ritual actors readied for their involvement, a host of other meanings prevails. After all, merely cleansing people of their profane qualities is not enough; the real work of rituals is the movement of participants through a range of public experiences. The broad purpose of this endeavor is to help everyone involved become more aware of the meaning of community itself and of their own places within that order. Such matters Durkheim (1965, pp. 361–461) discusses as aspects of the "positive cult."

There are, in his view, four different functions of positive rituals. Sometimes these functions are combined in the same ritual; alternately, rituals may focus on one meaning or another. In this latter spirit, he establishes a typology of *sacrificial, imitative, piacular,* and *representative* rites. For their part, sacrificial rites attempt to connect participants directly with the sacred realm by acts of transubstantiation—that is, by the public sharing (and frequently, eating) of some sanctified substance. Imitative rites, by contrast, try to enforce ideas of the sacred by setting forth exotic or inspiring models for actors to follow. Ritual participants dramatically reenact these models and in so doing "become" the totemic animals or mythic figures they portray. As Durkheim (1965, p. 408) explains, these different forms of communion teach people about the power of the sacred (and indeed, about the more general meaning of causation). By participating in the sacred, people feel their powers as individual beings grow tremendously. They are carried about by an energy (and sometimes clarity of vision) that has mysteriously entered their lives.

While the other forms of the positive cult tend to exhibit affirming or even joyful emotion, piacular rituals emphasize sorrow or fear. In this latter form, participants use their contact with the sacred as an occasion to wash away or atone for their failings. A specific example of this is mourning rituals, which reunite the community in common grief. Although mourning also tends to feature a range of negative rites (things that must not be said or done to those at the center of the event), the positive aspects (consisting of a wide range of gifts and gestures) help to rebuild the social order. Pointedly, these rituals are not an occasion for asceticism; instead sorrow is encouraged to flow as a public rather than private emotion. More profoundly, sorrow can be understood as a darker shade or prelude to joy. Publicly shared sorrow is a statement of community resolve that is followed, in certain mourning customs, by equally resolute acts of celebration and gaiety.

A final type, the representative (or commemorative) rite, connects people with the heritage of their community. Sometimes, this enactment of past events seems to have very specific purposes, for example, to ensure the reproduction of the totemic species. Other rites seem only to be processes of communal remembering, times for restating in mythic form the key moments from the past. However, as Durkheim (1965, pp. 424–425) emphasizes, these latter events frequently lose portions of their mythic significance over time and become predominantly aesthetic or even recreational activities. Like modern day Mardi Gras parades, the rites "go so far as to have the outward appearance of a recreation: the assistants may be seen laughing or amusing themselves openly."

In this regard, Durkheim (p. 425) points out the religious origins of many secular activities, including games and "the principal forms of art." His thesis is that the growing independence of games is merely one manifestation of a secularization process that has worked its way through society as a whole. As he (p. 425) puts it: "As the bonds by which the events and personages represented are attached to the history of the tribe relax, these take on a proportionately more unreal appearance, while the corresponding ceremonies change in nature. Thus men enter into the domain of pure fancy, and pass from the commemorative rite to the ordinary corrobori, a simple public merry-making, which has nothing religious about it and in which all may take part indifferently." This separation, he argues, is not at all surprising. After all, religion is fundamentally an attempt to describe what are essentially social feelings; but it often does this in ancient, fantastical ways that seem to have little (or only mysterious) connection to society as it is. Although religious events, by their public and collective nature, frequently bring out people's strongest imaginative and emotional capabilities, the specific forms themselves may not exhaust or thoroughly contain the emotions thus aroused. Durkheim believed that there are surpluses of creativity and energy that spill over in peripheral—and frequently secular—ways. A specific instance of this is the development of visual art. Early art, in his view, was not some decorative element added onto religious experience. Rather art was a natural extension of ritualized emotions. Ritual always contains a powerful aesthetic component that may draw people back to—or away from—the sacred context itself.

The most powerful example of this occurs in the state of ritual excitement Durkheim (p. 427) terms "collective effervescence." On certain ceremonial occasions, the energies of the participants seemingly overflow their banks. The mythic framework softens; worshipers give themselves over to "action, motion, gesticulation." While much of this energy serves

simply to reinforce the importance of the community, it may also contribute to a new sense of possibility for those involved. He even argues in
another context (1972, pp. 228–229) that it "is, in fact at such moments
of collective ferment that are born the great ideals upon which civilizations rest."

Durkheim's claim is a quite provocative one, which parallels in certain ways Huizinga's ideas about cultural change. Each author focuses
on the gathering of people in formalized, public settings. Somehow, the
spirit of play or human activity itself bursts control; the necessities of
the moment overwhelm traditional structures. The world is seen in a
new, "ecstatic" way. Of course, for Huizinga, the experience of rivalry
itself is a key ingredient in the creative process. For Durkheim, it is the
experience of collective unity that emboldens people and makes history
possible.

Durkheim's ideas about surplus energy as an element of play are not
new (see Ellis, 1973, pp. 23–48). His critical contribution to this theory
is instead his argument about the social foundations of exuberance. For
Durkheim, collective cooperation is an energizer and inspirer of people.
At such times, people encounter ideas that seem deeper and more powerful. To stand among or march with a thousand others is to feel braver and
more resolute. Furthermore, it is the mysterious interaction of thought
and activity that encourages these results. Belief and morality become
urgent through their application; we act out our ideals so that we may
experience their power.

The connection between the rituals and looser, more secular forms
of festivity having been acknowledged, it is important to emphasize that
Durkheim was clear about the differences between the two patterns. As
he (1965, p. 427) states: "When a rite serves only to distract, it is no longer a rite." Rites point to serious moral realities that exert significant
influence over people's lives. In that sense, they force people to return
to their sustaining communities. By contrast, activities like art or play
may have as their purpose only the stimulation of individual thought
or experience. They present images "which we may call up aimlessly
for the mere satisfaction of seeing them appear and combine before our
eyes."

In much the same sense (p. 427), "a rite is something different from a
game." Although recreation is "one of the forms of the moral re-making
which is the principal object of the positive rite," it is only a contributing element and not the abiding rationale. By our enactment of shared
symbolic forms, we may experience keen pleasure; and that pleasure may
refresh and strengthen us as we move back to our normal lives. However,

ritual always has an important social end. In sheer merry-making, this serious element is only an "echo," a distant acquaintance with things understood profoundly by our ancestors.

Since Durkheim: Themes from Social Anthropology

Durkheim's legacy for the study of ritual—and of public events more generally—is his sensitivity to the consequences of such activities for the groups that sponsor them. To the extent that these events are regular or patterned, their very existence can be attributed to these effects. In this light, Alpert (1965) has summarized Durkheim's theory of ritual in terms of four major effects or functions: disciplinary and preparatory, cohesive, revitalizing, and euphoric. Critically, such effects are group rather than individual matters; indeed, the participants and sponsors of rituals may be entirely unaware of the real (i.e., social) reasons that these events continue year after year.

It should be noted again that Durkheim's theory was not entirely original; some of his ideas come from de Tocqueville and Fustel de Coulanges; others derive from Robertson-Smith and other early anthropologists. Nineteenth-century intellectual life was marked by images of physical and social evolution; and Durkheim likewise saw in "primitive" people the fundament of our social and personal being. Similarly, he was influenced by traditions that ascribed to ritual a religious origin. Early society, in Durkheim's view, was centered in conceptions of the sacred; much of the secular world is simply an excrescence of these primordial patterns. To that degree, his sharp distinction between sacred and profane is an attempt to articulate and reestablish the ascendancy of the former realm.

It is not surprising then that anthropology should have been the discipline to consolidate and extend Durkheim's theory (see Lewis, 1980; Doty, 1986; Norget, 2000). As specialists in the traditional societies that Durkheim addressed in *The Elementary Forms*, anthropologists have, for the most part, maintained a community-based view of society in which a widely shared culture orients and directs the inhabitants. Moreover, in comparison to their more "modern" equivalents, traditional societies tend to feature small, socially stable populations; broadly shared responsibilities for members; few external information sources; and oral, face-to-face communication. In such settings, the social and cultural levels of reality continue to be connected closely. Hence, Durkheim's view of symbolic events as contributing elements in tightly integrated communities has maintained a certain appeal.

As mentioned previously, Radcliffe-Brown (1972) is the anthropologist most responsible for extending this approach. Rituals, in his view, could be understood as social devices that stabilize or otherwise help maintain the structure of the social units within which they are found. In that sense, the patterning of one part of society is to be explained by the necessities of the whole. This "structural" version of functionalism is to be contrasted with the "individual" functionalism of his contemporary Malinowski (1948), who argued that rituals typically address the natural anxieties and objective personal difficulties of society's members. For Radcliffe-Brown, as for Durkheim, it is not people who need religious ritual as much as it is the gods (i.e., society itself) who must be adored.

As might be anticipated, modern social anthropology has modified, or otherwise moved beyond, these understandings. The word "ritual" is now used to cover a wide range of events, both sacred and secular, in social settings of every type. Normally, these events are formalized (relatively prescriptive in thought, word, and action), fitted to some rhythmic or cyclical pattern in social or personal life, and focused on symbolic meanings. However, some rituals seem to serve clearly instrumental ends (growing crops, ensuring fertility, etc.) while others focus on more purely conceptual or experiential themes. Furthermore, most activities (games, pageants, dances, festivals, weddings, etc.) can be said to have ritualistic elements (see MacAloon, 1984).

In the following, some modern interpretations of ritual will be summarized briefly. These will be organized in terms of 1) ritual as a meaning system, 2) ritual in its social context, and 3) ritual as personal expression.

RITUAL AS A MEANING SYSTEM

For his part, Durkheim had only a modest interest in the exceedingly complex patterns of thought and action exhibited in sacred rituals. However, the ethnographic tradition in anthropology has continued to provide detailed descriptions of individual rites as windows into the intellectual life of each society. One such attempt to understand the thinking processes of traditional societies has been the "structuralist" model of Levi-Strauss (1967). He and his followers have tended to see myth and ritual as essentially "languages," as finely wrought collective products featuring both grammatical structures and symbolic meanings. Rituals in this sense are forms of communication, public devices that guide the way people categorize or otherwise process phenomena. To the structuralist, these patterns also reveal a universal quality of human beings, their ability to perform complicated cognitive maneuvers.

A rather different approach to rituals is taken in the "cultural systems" model of Geertz (1973) and his colleagues. While structuralists tend to explore rituals as logical, quasi-algebraic codes controlling societal thought processes, Geertz emphasizes the ways in which rituals are patterned symbol systems, that is, interrelated sets of ideas. In that sense, rituals can be read as "texts," socio-cultural creations that have multitudes of meanings, both explicit and implicit. To participate in ritual is to inhabit an intellectual microcosm that is filled not only with formal, publicly sanctioned belief but also with cognitive ambiguity, contradiction, and tension. And just because of this ambiguity and range of possibility, actors themselves must play a more active role in the process of interpreting its meaning.

As different as these approaches may be, both are natural extensions of the Durkheimian tradition. As Durkheim and Mauss (1963) argued, human consciousness does seem to be structured by institutionalized cultural frameworks, including some of our most fundamental procedures for categorizing and ranking. And meaning itself can be understood as an intra-cultural pattern, as a set of largely interdependent symbols positioned within some broader system. To that degree, culture—as a reality of its own type—parallels but does not duplicate the interdependent relationships of the social world.

RITUAL IN ITS SOCIAL CONTEXT

As indicated above, structural functionalism tends to emphasize the position of rituals as pieces in a larger social puzzle. These pieces not only help stabilize the puzzle but also allow viewers to form a vision of the entire work. Such an approach, however, has been criticized as an overemphasis on the conservative, stability-enhancing aspects of such events. Perhaps rituals are not only "models of" society (idealizing and reenforcing current practices) but also "models for" society (setting those very ideals against the status quo). In other words, the relationship between carefully crafted symbolic events and social life seems to be much more complicated than the early functionalists acknowledged.

Again, Geertz's work may be used as an example. In his celebrated account of Balinese cockfighting, Geertz (1972) explains how symbolically charged public events may have countervailing or "anti-structural" qualities. Although Balinese culture in general tends to praise civility and order, ritualized cockfights feature a tumultuous atmosphere full of wild gestures and rabid gambling. What the events reveal then are some of the social and personal tensions of Balinese life. As texts, they can be read in many different ways (as commentaries on masculinity, status-relations, sexuality, etc.), and the readings of the anthropologist may be different from those of the Balinese. In short, rituals are not simply formalized enactments of ideas but rather social constructs that must be intellectually completed and otherwise brought to life by their participants.

Such tensions and complexities are explored even more fully in the work of Victor Turner (1967, 1969). Building on the insights of the Belgian sociologist Van Gennep (1960), Turner shows how rituals are not so much systems of ideas as processes that move people from one status to another. In this approach, rituals are described as having three stages: an initial separation of the participant from his or her customary social standing followed by a period of deprivation and trial followed again by a re-granting of privileges consistent with one's newly gained status. For Turner, the most interesting of these stages is the middle or "liminal" period. This time of ritualized statuslessness—when initiates are frequently sequestered together and subjected to terrible ordeals—is also an occasion of powerful social bonding. In that light, Turner has commented on the degree to which such special moments of social solidarity or "communitas" become occasions to rethink the meaning of human possibility. To that degree, his work extends Durkheim's descriptions of collective effervescence.

A quite different treatment of the social effects of ritual is provided by the cultural ecologists. Ethnographers like Rappaport (1968) and Harris (1974) have argued that rituals frequently help communities adapt to the material/environmental conditions of their lives. By preventing people from eating certain categories of plants and animals or by assigning men and women to different roles, rituals may support political or economic patterns that help maintain population stability. In cultural ecology then, symbolic matters are wedded tightly to material concerns. However, as in functionalism more generally, the significance of these profound connections may be entirely unknown to the participants themselves.

RITUAL AS PERSONAL EXPRESSION

Among the advances of modern anthropology is an expanded understanding of the individual's role in rituals. For his part, Durkheim tended to see ritual participants as social categories, as sets of people who gather themselves under the terms provided by the event. However, later scholars (see Comaroff and Comaroff, 1993) have emphasized what humans, both in their physical and psychological capacities, bring to these social encounters. For example, both Turner (1967) and Douglas (1960) have stressed the extent to which symbols are products of "nature" as well as culture. That is, the biological or even visceral qualities of people are transcribed into symbolic events. Thus, rituals are not only exercises in abstract or logical thinking but also depictions of blood and bile and excrement. Personal intimacy and functioning become connected to societal dynamics.

Other approaches emphasize the activity rather than passivity of participants. In such views (see, e.g., MacAloon, 1984; Goffman, 1967; Turner, 1982), rituals are to be understood as lively performances or acts of communication. That is, ritual participants attempt to express themselves and produce reactions in specific others. Like actors in a drama, they bring culture to life in their own distinctive ways. Each behavior is attuned not only to their fellow actors and audience but also to themselves. In that sense, every wedding or funeral is different.

In all these ways, it seems clear that rituals are not merely symbolic enactments but rather social events that are colored by the status-relations and personal proclivities of those involved. So understood, ritual is less frequently some somber, collective march to an appointed destination than a spirited form of public expression. As Durkheim emphasized, the gathering of people under a collective banner creates a wonderful energy. How symbolic events like ritual effectively trap and channel all that energy is another issue.

A Durkheimian View of Sport

Durkheim's work, and functionalism more generally, has had a powerful influence on studies of modern sport (see, e.g., Luschen, 1967; Frey and Eitzen, 1991; Wohl, 1970; Coakley, 1996a; Loy and Booth, 2002). In part because of the legacy of Puritanism and the related ambivalence of academic institutions to sporting activity, sports practitioners and educators have felt a need to justify their subject. For the sports proponent, sports are not merely an escape or distraction from the more serious aspects of life but instead a contributor to the well-being of organizations and communities. Activities once thought to be purely expressive have taken on a deeply instrumental cast.

Such claims for the public benefits of sport are now familiar. Sport is an activity that frequently gathers a community and makes it confront its identity through opposition to other communities. Consistent with that project, sports are frequently frosted with a distinctive set of values, with a "sports creed" that makes them schools of moral as well as physical education (see Curry and Jiobu, 1984, pp. 46–53). For the most part, such values reflect selected commitments of the broader community. Just as young people are socialized into these values by sports participation, so the applauding spectators reaffirm such values as thoroughly legitimate ways to address human affairs.

For the participants themselves, there are a number of presumed benefits. Sport is commonly seen as a developer of character, as a setting in which people learn to subordinate their swirling emotions to the needs of the team (see Levine, 1986; Edwards, 1973). In that sense, a range of Durkheimian virtues—self-discipline, respect for authority, hard work, responsibility to the group, and so on—are thought to prevail. Furthermore, sport is seen frequently as a training ground in leadership skills. Whether the Battle of Waterloo was truly won on the playing fields of Eton or not, sport gives people opportunities to try out strategies against competing others, martial the support of teammates, and experience the vicissitudes of success and failure. In such ways, it serves as a kind of public laboratory, a place where people learn how to be successful in society's terms. Critically, such skills are seen not only as personal benefits but also as social ones. That is, it is society itself that needs great cadres of leaders who have honed those abilities in youthful sport.

Sports are also thought to serve various functions in the control and management of deviance (see Coakley, 1996a). The considerable energies of youth can be turned to socially destructive purposes. Sports then are devices (frequently adult-controlled) that frame or otherwise direct these enthusiasms. Just as sports may keep people out of trouble by the simple spending of energy, so they demonstrate to them the negative consequences of anti-social or "immoral" behavior. Missing practice, being lazy, or thinking only of personal success are all occasions for punishment in the sporting world. Perpetrators are singled out for public humiliation (running laps, doing push-ups); alternately they are made to carry the social stigma of having caused the team—and its sponsoring community—to lose. In their full glory then, sports programs are frequently schools of asceticism. As Durkheim explained, the intent of this approach is not to break the body and spirit but to strengthen it for the higher (i.e., public) purposes at hand.

Following Durkheim further, one could argue that sports allegiance mitigates against the massiveness of society itself. What the Marxists see as a misdirection of human commitment (a looking away from the natural allegiance to social class), the functionalists see as a beneficial unification of potentially cross-cutting divisions. Differences of race, class, age, sex, educational level, and religion are frequently "integrated" within the definition of community provided by the team. Such sponsoring schools, communities, and businesses might have little opportunity to enact these broader identities were it not for the artificial rivalries created by sports.

In all these ways, sport is sometimes said to function as a sort of "civil religion," as a periodic gathering of society under a relatively secularized (and vaguely defined) sense of shared moral purpose (see Bellah, 1967). In that regard, sport joins opponents together and affords them a glimpse of their collective heritage. Rivaling religion in its respect for tradition, sport preserves its rules and equipment standards so that modern people may judge themselves against the quasi-mythic exploits of their ancestors. To sit amidst the emptiness of an old gymnasium or walk the fairways of a legendary golf course is to have some sense of all the young people who once burned so brightly and now are gone. Amidst all its physicality and commotion then, sport touches on conceptual and moral themes. Within the Durkheimian tradition, these contemplative matters are rather more important than the sweaty rivalries of the moment.

As indicated in the previous chapter, one can quickly turn to all the abuses and dysfunctional aspects of the sporting world as well. A somewhat less ideological approach to these issues has been taken by Coakley (1996b), who identifies various structural and functional differences between formally organized and informally organized sport. Focusing on the example of kids' sport, he explains that it is organizational style and not field of endeavor that determines social effects.

Formally organized sport tends to be controlled by nonplayers, who are typically adults. Teams have stable memberships and feature elaborate recruitment and socialization procedures. People practice more than they play; issues of commitment and character take center stage. Typically, team games are set within the parameters of highly organized leagues, which are themselves controlled by external sports authorities. There is much ado about rules and records, which again are maintained by nonplayers. Participation in this type of sport means entry into a world of adult commitments and sensibilities.

Not surprisingly, kids in these types of programs tend to learn game rules and athletic skills more quickly. Players on successful teams acquire a certain celebrity and are ushered about in other adult-controlled settings (see Coleman, 1961). Likewise, successful performers develop (or perhaps only refine) character traits that can be transferred to other settings that demand respect for authority and self-denial. In such ways, this top-down model parallels the development of religious ritual in traditional, hierarchical societies. Young people must be stripped of some of the less appealing qualities of youth to emerge as quasi-adults, who bear the cultural commitments if not the social responsibilities of the older generation.

Quite different is the world of youth-controlled play. Here, social organization is predominantly local and interaction-focused. Sides are drawn from the people who show up; leaders emerge through a process of personal assertion. Rewards are intrinsic rather than extrinsic; that is, the effects of performances are restricted primarily to the playground itself. Groups are highly unstable; personal freedom—including the freedom to quit—is pronounced. Norms are informal and emergent. In other words, the group as a whole develops rules in situation-specific ways and then collectively alters those rules to meet the changing requirements of a "good game." It is argued then that informal sport produces other kinds of effects. People learn how to operate in egalitarian settings and refine leadership skills on their own terms. They develop relationship skills without the direction, or the safety net, of adults.

To conclude, social order can be constructed in quite different ways. The top-down model—represented by adult-controlled sport—strains to enforce continuity and order. People must be fitted to the collective will. Society's leaders must help to make these processes orderly and smooth. Whatever else, the social enterprise itself must sail. Durkheim's curiosities about ritual are shaped largely in these terms. However, he also understood that social order may emerge out of more egalitarian, participant-based contexts. Gathered together in a common enterprise without the usual trappings of status and routine, people can find themselves moving in fresh, unscripted ways. This bottom-up view of public life comes much closer to Huizinga's conception of play. In this latter tradition, people not only interpret but also build their world.

4 Max Weber and the
Rationalization of Play

For the most part, play scholars have accepted the idea that play is disconnected from the usual constraints and consequences of society. Players, we are told, are freer than other social agents. Entering the playground at will, they pursue those matters that fascinate or excite them. Failing to sustain these satisfactions, they abandon their enterprise. These qualities of personal freedom and social separation are elements crucial not only to play's charm but also to its ability to cast up alternative visions of life.

The matter having been defined in this way, it seems strange indeed that we live in an age of instrumental, socially controlled play. To be sure, play in past centuries was frequently harnessed to a variety of practical purposes (see, e.g., Malcolmson, 1973; Gruneau, 1980). Authorities, both secular and sacred, courted the support of their followers by sponsoring festive events. Moreover, the dramatic uses of such events—to showcase the social, psychological, and physical qualities of the participants or to affirm the social prominence of the sponsors—were always apparent. Just because play mattered in this broader sense, access to events was restricted in terms of gender, class, ethnicity, and age. Talented performers were sometimes paid or otherwise induced. Gambling and fraud were intermittent companions. However we idealize it now, play in its shifting historical contexts has often been compromised (see Sutton-Smith and Kelly-Byrne, 1984a).

Nevertheless, there is something curious—and perhaps unprecedented—about the current employments of play. In our purportedly post-industrial age, play (and the broader matter of human enjoyment) has become a public preoccupation. As Wolfenstein and Leites (1950) once explained, amusement has become somewhat obligatory. In a world that no longer comprehends the various categories of work, play has become a language of public discourse, a yardstick for invidious comparison between individuals and groups, and a vehicle for personal improvement. Seen in this way, play seems less an escape from social complexity than a rush toward it.

Whatever the private inclinations of individuals to become players, they are strongly encouraged to do so by a variety of organizations devoted to the "business" of play. Conspicuous in this regard are the commercial playhouses—selling packaged pleasure-experiences and related commodities like equipment, training, and inspirational literature. Such enterprises as sports arenas, amusement parks, casinos, fitness centers, and karaoke bars craft and sell play. This commercialization of pleasure has been an important social trend since at least the eighteenth century (see Plumb, 1973).

Somewhat odder has been the increasingly self-conscious use of play by other types of organizations. Many churches have modified the formal portions of their services with more joyful, spontaneous kinds of participation (see Cox, 1969). Counseling services have recognized the creative possibilities of art, puppets, and pets (see Rubin, Fein, and Vandenberg, 1983; Erikson, 1977). Politicians now acknowledge the value of televised debates—less as opportunities to inform the electorate than as occasions for public bantering and display. Most notably, educational organizations are employing a host of playful activities to engage or otherwise stimulate students (see Rogers and Sawyers, 1995). Creativity, active learning, and practical manipulation of all types prevail. Play is used less to divert or amuse than to inform. The successful classroom is thought to be the active, buzzing classroom. "Smart toys" and "Edu-play" have found their niche.

As noted in the first chapter, Huizinga (1955) claimed that forms of interpersonal creativity and rivalry have been central to the development of a society's institutional practices and self-understandings. However, in his view, this playful quality has been eroded by the bureaucratic regimes of the modern world. At least since the nineteenth century, public life in Europe and the United States has become a rather somber affair. The festivities of contemporary society, when they do occur, are commonly "false" or "puerile" charades run by manipulative administrators (Huizinga, 1955, pp. 205–206). In contrast to the play of the Middle Ages and

Renaissance, the events of the modern age have lost their dynamism and color.

As we have seen, Huizinga's remarks about contemporary play, however well aimed, never took the form of careful argument. Indeed, the unreceptive reader may dismiss them as part of a bad-tempered broadside against the modern world (see Huizinga, 1936). However, the bureaucratization of play (particularly by large businesses) has become an important element in the modern experience of play. Indeed, such socially constructed play is arguably a centerpiece of public life. To understand these matters more deeply, we must turn to another great commentator on the modern world, the German sociologist Max Weber.

An Introduction to Max Weber

Weber was born in 1864, and his life was in many ways an intersection of the political and economic currents that marked the late nineteenth and early twentieth century period (see Gerth and Mills, 1958; Bendix, 1960; Kasler, 1989). Weber's paternal grandfather had made a fortune by manufacturing textiles in western Germany. While Weber's uncle continued the linen trade, his father moved the family in 1869 to Berlin, where he developed a successful career as a lawyer and politician in the Reichstag. Comfortably positioned in a suburban neighborhood that included many well-known politicians and academics, the family symbolized all that Karl Marx despised: paternalistic capitalism, bourgeois liberalism, and a belief in Germany's imperial destiny. This broad theme—the changing character of capitalism and its implications for public life—would mark Weber's career.

Set against the moral complacency and political realism of his father's life was the world of Weber's mother. By the standards of the eighteenth century, the nineteenth was by turns humanitarian and morally severe. In an age of grand engineering projects, many believed that society itself could be made better, that the wretched conditions of many people's lives might be addressed and improved. Such beliefs, coupled with a certain abhorrence for the sensual indulgence of the previous period, were held by many bourgeois women. These concerns of Weber's mother—a wondering about religion, love of music and art, commitment to social justice, desire for public decency, and respect for the contemplative life—shaped the other dimensions of Weber's career.

As others have argued, Weber's own life story expresses the conflicts and contradictions of his century (see Mitzman, 1969). On the one hand, he was the bold, super-achieving male, a Prussian army officer with dueling scars on his face. He believed in a strong, expansionist Germany and pushed himself just as relentlessly to conquer the various fields of knowledge. A prolific and prodigiously talented scholar, he was appointed professor of political economy at Freiberg at the age of thirty and assumed the prestigious chair at Heidelberg only three years later. He was a famous adviser to politicians and had a commanding presence that could quiet a room with his entrance.

Alternately, Weber was a man who lived with his parents until that first appointment at Freiberg. He very much loved his mother and disapproved of the philistinism of his father and uncle. In 1897, when Max was thirty-two, his father died—not long after an intense argument in which the son defended his mother against his father. The following year, Max suffered an emotional breakdown that left him partially incapacitated for the rest of his life. Although he sometimes read and wrote in great bursts of energy, he didn't teach publicly again until the last year of his life.

Weber died at the age of fifty-six of pneumonia. He is considered by some (see Wrong, 1970, p. 1) to have been the last "universal genius" in the social sciences, the last person to have comprehended and contributed profoundly to all those branches of knowledge. Although he was trained as a lawyer and economic historian, Weber quickly broadened his interests to address the nature of political authority and administration, the distinctive character of capitalism, the strengths and limitations of modern science, religion in worldwide perspective, and ultimately, the foundations of social life itself.

Although Weber left behind no simplifying explanations of "society" or schools of disciples, his frameworks for thinking about social existence—the use of ideal-types to describe social phenomena; the distinction between traditional, rational-legal, and charismatic forms of authority; the recognition of values as key influences on economic development; the role of ethical neutrality in scientific research; the tension between formal and substantive rationality; the development of the concept of bureaucracy—are consulted still. Indeed, much of Weber's greatness stems from his willingness to accept the fact that social life cannot be universalized. Social structures and events are always embedded deeply in economic, political, and cultural circumstances that are themselves the moving edges of history. To appreciate the particular ways in which these circumstances combine, one must explore alternative patterns from other times and places.

Because he pushed himself to learn so much, Weber is often regarded as an intellectual hero who fought his own competing inclinations and who tried to reconcile the claims of science and citizenship, materialism and spirituality, past and present. Like his better-known contemporary Freud, Weber argued that people must face squarely the inevitable tensions and contradictions of the world. As Turner (2000, p. 1) claims, "Weber is widely regarded as the greatest figure in the history of social sciences" because he ranged over so many disciplines and because he was too honest to become ideological. For sociologists in particular (see Collins, 1986, p. 9), Weber is commonly held to be "the great master. He was intellectually the most comprehensive and historically the most learned of any of the leaders of the discipline. He asked the most profound questions and disciplined himself against providing easy answers."

A Guiding Theme: The Rationalization of the West

As wide-ranging as Weber's treatments of social life were (e.g., studies of ancient Judaism, medieval business organizations, Chinese literati, early Protestantism, capitalism, the Hindu caste system, contemporary German political parties), these diverse interests coalesced around a common theme. As many interpreters have noted (see, e.g., Loewith, 1970; Collins, 1986, pp. 61–75), Weber's work centers on the distinctive origins, character, and implications of modern Western culture. In a way that has never been equaled, Weber explained how each social institution in the West was fed by a great cultural transformation that he termed the rationalization process. In the realm of economics, this process unfolded as the development of capitalism; in politics, it expressed itself through parliamentarianism and rational-legal forms of political consent. In the case of administration, rationalization revealed itself as bureaucratization; in the fields of knowledge, it emerged as science and technology. Even morality and law became disconnected from their homespun origins and took shape as abstract, universalistic principles for conduct.

In this context, one may imagine Weber to have been a twentieth-century apologist for the Enlightenment, who celebrated the triumph of reason over tradition and superstition—and mentality itself over the vagaries of flesh. Certainly, in the view of the French *philosophes,* human rationality was the engine of progress and the avenger of social injustice. However, Weber held a darker, more pessimistic view. Reason, it seems, could be harnessed in various, sometimes contradictory, ways. The great social transformations described above might be rational enough in terms of organizational efficiency and yet irrational in terms of their consonance with fundamental human concerns. And, of course, rationality might develop differently in different institutional settings. In short, reasonableness in administrative matters could be different from reasonableness in science or electoral politics or religion.

Nevertheless, Weber's various treatments of rationalization tend to support a common thesis—that Western culture has been marked increasingly by an intellectually calculating attitude toward life (see Loewith, 1970). To this extent, Weber stands in a long line of thinkers (e.g., Voltaire, Montesquieu, Kant, and Hegel) who believed that European history features an unprecedented and profound shift in human thought and activity. Similarly, Weber's work is connected to that of other sociologists (e.g., Comte, Saint-Simon, Toennies, and Simmel) who argued that modern social life was becoming less personal, emotional, irrational, and spontaneous. The old world of the village communities—featuring long-standing intimate relationships and deeply held religious beliefs—was being replaced by something colder and more abstract. In this new world, large-scale "formal" organizations took center stage. People became "managed"—and in turn conducted their affairs in more specialized and emotionally distant ways.

In this manner, Weber's work represents a kind of culmination of the Enlightenment. Although he believed strongly that such changes as parliamentary government, bureaucracy, science, and capitalism represented significant advantages over what the world had known before, he agonized that these new frameworks were also degrading the quality of personal experience. The modern social organization—as an elaborate framework grounded in written codes—was, as he (1958b, p. 182) famously described it, an "iron cage."

Weber's Understanding of the Rational

To understand how rationality has captured creativity and pleasure in the modern world, one must look first at Weber's use of the term "rational." This project is made difficult by the fact that Weber himself was not always consistent in his writing about this concept. Indeed, Brubaker (1984) has discerned at least sixteen different meanings of "rational" in Weber's work, a list that includes: deliberate, systematic, calculable, impersonal, purely instrumental, exact, quantitative, rule-governed, predictable, sober, scrupulous, and logically intelligible. Despite this diversity, Weber's understandings may be explicated by describing three different levels at which rationality operates: 1) as a pattern of individual action and belief, 2) as a cultural principle, and 3) as a characteristic of social organizations.

RATIONALITY AS A PATTERN OF INDIVIDUAL
ACTION AND BELIEF

Perhaps the best starting point is Weber's (1964, pp. 115–118) distinction between "rational" and "nonrational" action. Nonrational behaviors were expressions arising from deeply held feelings (what he termed the *affectual* type) or from long-standing customs (the *traditional* type). Both types existed on the "borderline" of meaningful action; that is, they appeared more as momentary reactions or expressions than as carefully examined plans. Weber believed that nonrational forms of action were more commonplace—or at least more socially accepted—in earlier times. By contrast, the modern period encouraged a more self-conscious, deliberate quality of response in which individuals calculated the relative effectiveness of different strategies in meeting their goals. In most social settings, rational behaviors became favored over nonrational forms.

However, Weber realized that rational orientations themselves could take different forms. In that light, he articulated a distinction between *zweckrationalitat* (instrumental rationality) and *wertrationalitat* (value rationality). Instrumental rationality is a purely calculative kind of thought or behavior in which individuals assess the likely effects of different kinds of actions as means to reaching their goals. In this process, not only the means but also the goals may be juggled to find a pattern of best practices. Weber saw this type of action as quite different from value rationality, in which behavior is guided by a conscious belief in the "absolute value" of some ethical, aesthetic, or religious pattern. In other words, value-rational behavior features the self-conscious subordination of the individual to some principle or code (e.g., committing one's life to military service) so that meeting these principles is the "end" or measure of action. By contrast, instrumental rationality features ends that are held much more provisionally—as favored outcomes that are merely choices among possible alternatives.

This distinction between the two forms of rationality was crucial to Weber's understanding of modern life because he realized that people calculate or focus their energies in quite different ways. Those who hold no principles as sacred will operate differently from those who do. However, to behave in purely instrumental ways is to miss out on those possibilities for emotional and spiritual completion that derive from a firm commitment to worthy values. To that degree, the instrumental path leads to a restless life. However, even committed individuals may find themselves with internal value conflicts that complicate their choices. This confusion is exacerbated by the fact that certain institutional spheres (e.g., economics and politics) are often guided by principles of instrumental rationality, while others (such as religion, education, or art) tend to follow the opposite form. In other words, even as people aspire to be rational or reflective, they must always confront divergent goals that rest (typically) on nonrational foundations. To that degree, rationality finds its limits.

RATIONALITY AS A CULTURAL PRINCIPLE

People in all ages have calculated the relative effectiveness of various procedures for achieving their desires. In that sense, magical practices may be seen as efficacious or "rational" from the vantage point of the people who believe in them. Quite different, however, is the idea that certain actions are demonstrably more rational in some objective sense. For Weber, the development of science and its applications in technology represented a tremendous advance in human history. Seen as purely technical matters, certain practices could now be judged superior to others. And by extension, human behavior itself could be fitted to a growing body of scientific evidence about the workings of the world.

This type of knowledge ranged across groups and societies and led to the development of universal ideas and standards regarding the human condition. To that extent, such knowledge undermined not only the belief in human subjectivity itself but also the idea that decision-making should be grounded in the "particularistic" characteristics of the people involved. As a cultural principle then, rationality became a weapon that could be used against practices based on tradition (the blind following of what has been) and charisma (a faith in the judgments of inspired individuals).

RATIONALITY AS A CHARACTERISTIC OF SOCIAL ORGANIZATIONS

A third, and still different, issue is the way in which rationality is put into practice by groups and organizations. Indeed, one of the most prominent qualities of the modern age is the gradual subordination of groups to formal organizations. That is, social bodies composed of specific individuals (such as families and friends) have had many of their functions taken over by more abstract collectivities possessing definite structures and goals (such as businesses, voluntary associations, and schools). The culmination of this way of organizing people, for Weber, was the bureaucracy.

Weber's model of bureaucracy, which was based on the German civil service of his time, emphasized six traits (see Weber, 1958a, pp. 196–244).

According to this model, bureaucracy is a pyramid of administrative control that features: clear-cut lines of authority, written rules, impersonal relationships, selection of personnel by occupational merit, loyalty engendered through promotion and tenure, and distinct "offices" controlled by the organization. This pattern—which opposes such time-honored organizational practices as bribery, personal favoritism, the selling or inheritance of offices, and other informal types of influence—embodies the idea that groups should be governed by rules and not by the inspirations and prejudices of their members. To the extent that this model is implemented, personal discretion surrenders to the policy manual.

Although Weber applauded this movement toward fairness and impersonality in social relations, he also saw its failings. He described this tension in organizational decision-making as a distinction between "formal" and "substantive" rationality. As Brubaker (1984; pp. 35–43) explains, this distinction extends the previous opposition between instrumental and value rationality to issues of organizational culture. Formal rationality becomes essentially means-oriented action, practices that serve organizational demands for efficiency and technical excellence. To this end, organization leaders make decisions based on "what works" in this restricted sense; they may even choose policies simply to perpetuate the organization itself. Substantive rationality, on the other hand, concerns the degree to which actions serve the basic values of the organization or its surrounding community. As indicated above, Weber was keenly aware that bureaucracies might not serve some very basic needs of individuals and groups. Indeed, the future for such a technically advanced but spiritually eviscerated world was uncertain. He (1958b, p. 182) describes that dilemma in one of his best-known passages: "No one knows who will live in this cage in the future, or whether at the end of this tremendous development entirely new prophets will arise, or there will be a great rebirth of old ideas and models, or, if neither, mechanized petrifaction, embellished with a sort of convulsive self-importance. For of this last stage of cultural development, it might well truly be said: `Specialists without spirit, sensualists without heart, this nullity imagines that it has attained a level of civilization never before achieved.'"

With these distinctions in mind, the reader can more easily appreciate the depths of Weber's concern about the possibilities for satisfying personal experience in the modern world. To be sure, Weber, was no proponent of the unreflective or nonrational behaviors that were central to social life in the past. Yet, he realized that more rational behaviors carry with them their own liabilities. The incessant tinkering of people with every aspect of their lives led to the de-stabilization or de-mystification of human relationships. This sense for the artificiality of the world was exacerbated by value-conflicts between different institutions in society and between different societies. Furthermore, the growth of the predominant form of rationality (instrumental rationality) puts undue emphasis on the machinery of society rather than on fundamental human concerns. Indeed, subservience to this machinery and to the scientific knowledge that abetted its development, effectively "expropriated" individuals from their spiritual and emotional rights much as Marx's workers found themselves alienated in their factories. A cold, calculating framework had swept across the world. Technocracy reigned.

The Rationalization of the Expressive

Although Weber's analysis of the rationalization process seems almost encyclopedic in scope, there is at least one area that escaped the full measure of his scrutiny. As his wife Marianne Weber (1975; pp. 496–500) explained after his death, Weber's unrealized ambition was to write a "sociology embracing all the arts." As noted above, Weber understood well the distinctive way in which organizational culture had developed in the Western tradition. What he hungered to know still were the effects of these changes on the more intimate dimensions of life.

This issue was critical for Weber just because the supposedly nonrational areas of experience—such matters as religion, love, recreation, and art—are seen typically as refuges from the bureaucratic routines prevalent in the more "practical" portions of the world. That is, although the realms of politics, economy, and law might be heavy with regimentation and impersonality, the domains of the spirit should be something else. According to Freund (1969, pp. 25–32), Weber at one level believed that intellectualization and routinization stopped at the gates of the nonrational spheres of life; indeed, irrationality—as a personal response to rationalization—might even grow as a counterbalance to the predominant cultural trend. Certainly, Weber recognized that different "life spheres" could operate according to different principles. And, as Sica (2000, p. 57) has argued, he tended to condemn those adults who tried to escape from the complexities of practical life by flights into mystic religion or unreflective sensualism.

This viewpoint having been acknowledged, it seems clear that Weber also comprehended a different and more complicated theme: that in certain ways the rationalization process had already worked its way deeply into the realms of pleasure and faith. In other words, the predominant themes of the practical institutions—calculated order, written procedures, specialization, and so on—were becoming evident in the supposedly less rational institutions as well. To put it broadly, rationalization was a great net that had been thrown across the West. Art, music, religion, sexuality, and sport had been captured as well.

Weber died before developing the various individual histories (and cross-cultural comparisons) that would have satisfied his requirements for such a project. However, his classic works on world religions are to some extent attempts to show how people in different societies and historical epochs have tried to conceptualize fundamentally nonrational themes. Indeed, Weber's best-known book, *The Protestant Ethic and the Spirit of Capitalism* (1958b) is basically an exploration of the rationalizing of religious belief by certain forms of Protestantism in Northern Europe. In his account, this type of religious belief inspired careful, calculating activity in the world as a way of demonstrating to the believer (and to others) that he or she was among the saved. The resulting sense of vocation was one of the important sources of capitalist development and middle-class life in the North.

However, Weber was equally interested in the development of the great rival of religion for this-worldly satisfaction, the various forms of expressive culture including the arts (see Weber, 1964, pp. 223–245). Although his general comments on these matters are fragmentary, some themes can be constructed (see Martindale, 1958, pp. xxii; Kasler, 1989, p. 137). For example, Western painting in Weber's view (see 1958b, p. 15) was distinguished by a rational invention, linear perspective. Three-dimensionality in art was a geometrical device that could be learned and applied by any schoolchild. Earlier (and Eastern) styles of painting—in which the size of persons and objects in artistic representation was determined by their social or supernatural status—was replaced by a new formalism that placed the viewer in a mathematically plotted landscape. Similarly, Western architecture was the first to exploit the clear advantages of the arch as a principle of design. The scientific understanding of the arch and its supporting buttresses allowed architects to vault large quadratic spaces. Monumental buildings, like the great cathedrals, were the result. In yet another way, Western literature was marked heavily by a mechanical invention, the printing press. Although the press was created in China, its energetic development in the West as a device to reproduce writing brought forth a more standardized and widespread experience with wisdom traditions. People could now learn directly from cheaper, printed documents instead of through intermediaries like tutors and priests. Reading-directed contemplation for wider segments of the population, exemplified by Protestantism in religion, surged forward. Taken together, these changes illustrate the way in which technical invention frames human sensibility.

These changes also produced a shift in the social relationships of artists, audiences, and patrons. Aided by mathematical principles and technical inventions, art established itself increasingly as an independent, secular enterprise guided by formal techniques and understandings (see Weber, 1964, pp. 96–97). The sponsorship of princes and popes became secondary to bourgeois money and interests. Academic qualities, including those of an "art for art's sake" approach, increased.

The one place where Weber did develop his insights more fully is his book, *The Rational and Social Foundations of Music* (1958c). Published after his death by his wife and supporters, the manuscript addresses the purported uniqueness of Western music. At the heart of the argument is Weber's view that once again rationalization has profoundly marked a significant area of cultural expression. Western musical sensibility— embodied in such matters as the diatonic scale, rhythm, harmony, and even instruments—has been carefully standardized. Because of this, the performance of quite complicated music by large groups of players (especially, symphonic music) was made possible.

As might be anticipated, Weber studied musical expression in a number of different societies, past and present. Typically, ancient music was learned through listening; its performances showcased the religious or personal inspiration of the player. And for various technical reasons, these performances were largely solitary or small ensemble affairs.

Weber argued that the Western development of the twelve-tone scale (within the eight-note "octave") was a foundation for a more artificial, though ultimately more complex, experience of music. As he explains, tones were "fixed" (i.e., favored over the microtones or sliding tones used in non-Western music) and "moved" to satisfy almost mathematical assessments of harmony. By contrast, the Greek and Chinese scales (using five notes) and the Arabic scale (using seventeen) exhibited fewer harmonic possibilities. Since about 1500 in the West, the spaces between the notes in the scale were adjusted to permit specific harmonic sensations, for example, the so-called 4th (F in a C scale) and 5th (G in a C scale). This effect was even more pronounced when a third note was added.

The possibilities of a multi-note system (multivocality) were pursued further through the addition of different instruments. However, playing in concert required stricter coordination, especially a system of measuring time. Thus, the fixing of notes on a written staff (in measured time) arose during the twelfth century. Furthermore, the relatively standardized manufacture of (tunable) instruments—such as the violin, viola, cello, and brass instruments permitted conjoint playing. As the orchestra itself evolved, the roles of musician and composer became separated. Music became a composition, a written form which players interpreted.

As Collins (1986, p. 66) has noted, Western music—like other aspects of Western society—became "bureaucratized." Although irrational and improvisational elements remained important, music in general developed in the directions of quantification, impersonality, abstraction, regimentation, and "correctness." Requirements of social organization were set against—and to some extent triumphed over—the desires for spontaneity and for displays of virtuosity. As Martindale and his collaborators (1958, p. xxix) explain: "The protagonists of the aesthetic adventure of Western man are seen as driven to attain a maximum of logical order, rationality, on the one hand, and the intensified, lyric, free, creative expression, affectivity, on the other. This is the aesthetic counterpart of the drama of Western man in other areas of life."

It is my position then that Weber understood the extent to which rationality was both a framework and a trap for expressive life. As Levine (1981) explains, rationality serves as a block on personal freedom (by discouraging certain kinds of behavior) at the very time that it provides an avenue or enablement (allowing people to find new opportunities to express themselves). To use Weber's example, the formalization of Western music meant not only a host of new playing and listening possibilities but also an exclusion of other musical forms and styles. Rationalized music brought wider categories of people together on new terms; it created a music "public."

Implications of Weber's Work for the Study of Play

If Weber had lived to develop his portrait of expressive culture in the West, what would he have written? One can only surmise, but certain themes seem likely. His ideas about the intellectualization and systematization of music would have been pushed forward in such other spheres as the visual arts, architecture, and sexuality. He would have identified the persistent tension between the desire for spontaneity and improvisation (for being in moments that are fresh and creative) with the desire for continuity and control (consistent with the rationalization process). And of course, he would have contrasted the patterns of expressive life found in modern Europe with those from other times and places.

A somewhat different question concerns the pertinence of Weber's ideas for life today. After all, Weber died in 1920, before so many of the defining events of our times. He did not witness the increasingly power-ful uses of the aesthetic in European politics during the 1920s and 1930s. He did not anticipate or explore the close linkage between capitalism and expressive life that was developed by the critical theorists (such writers as Adorno, Horkheimer, Benjamin, and Marcuse) during this period and after World War II. Weber could not have foreseen the rapid development of the global political economy or the tremendous growth in information technology and consumer culture, themes developed by the postmod-ernist thinkers (Baudrillard, Derrida, Jameson et al.). And later writers (such as Gramsci, Foucault, and Bourdieu) went far beyond Weber—and Marx—in describing the uses and abuses of "cultural capital" by powerful groups. In short, Weber lived before the Jazz Age, the Great Depression, World War II, the atomic bomb, television, jet travel, the rise and fall of the Soviet empire, the liberation struggles of subjugated nations and groups, and the computer. Without the understandings based on these events and contexts, can the ideas of a turn-of-the-century German aca-demic be relevant now?

It will not surprise the reader that I think Weber's work remains per-tinent. I believe that expressive culture—and more specifically, play—has been developed in distinctive ways in the West. However, in an emerg-ing global society, Weber's notion of a Europe-centered West that may be contrasted with an Asiatic East needs revision. Instead, the pertinent question becomes: Is there a style of play that is characteristic of societ-ies that are adopting a constellation of institutional changes that include capitalist economies, strong middle classes, parliamentary government, relatively independent judicial systems, and science-based belief systems and technologies?

In what follows, I will apply some Weberian principles to the study of contemporary play (see also Cantelon and Ingham, 2002). In describing the special context for these ideas, I will use the term "modern" instead of "Western." However, this term must be understood as an ideal type in Weber's sense. That is, individual societies choose from the institu-tional practices described above in various ways and proceed to modernity along distinctive routes. Describing the above constellation of traits as "modern" is simply a heuristic decision based on certain changes that have occurred in a number of advanced industrial societies.

Furthermore, as Weber understood clearly, societies also provide pockets of opposition or anti-structure to counterbalance dominant cul-tural themes. Thus, one should expect to find play not only in its more formally organized, officially sanctioned versions but also in its more freewheeling, even rebellious forms. In that regard, Weber's ideas apply most clearly to those groups and organizations that have sponsored (and profited from) the rationalization of society's institutions. That is, the following principles seem especially pertinent to adult play within the business and professional classes and to the various activities that these adults control (play in schools, recreation leagues, music camps, etc.).

These limitations having been acknowledged, I would argue that modern play has been influenced profoundly by the rationalization process. In taking this position, I emphasize the extent to which rationalization exists as a cultural and social phenomenon. In other words, although play is profoundly a psychologically generated affair (i.e., a series of events driven by the energies and inspirations of players), it is also framed by societal patterns of understanding and artifact. These systems of ideas, organizations, and material implements channel thought and behavior. Thus modern play exists within an increasingly rationalized cultural context that nurtures imagining in distinctive ways.

Under such terms, I will propose a set of "implications" from Weber's work for the study of modern play. Of course, a simple listing of ideas is not equivalent to a substantiation of them. Such a project would require Weber's own cross-cultural and historical acumen. The following develops a brief rationale for each point and then use examples of these changes from the world of sport. In that process, some reference is made to the work of more recent thinkers who have developed these ideas.

MODERN PLAY TENDS TO HAVE AN ACTIVE, MANIPULATIVE QUALITY

At the heart of the rationalization process is a calculating, tinkering orientation of individuals toward the circumstances of their lives. Modern people are encouraged to be doubting, exploratory types; more and more dimensions of existence are held up for critical inspection. For Weber, rationalization (as a pattern of individual action) stands squarely against the old habits of social immersion and nonreflexive consciousness. With less taken for granted, people must discover who they are.

Play itself is commonly understood as an expression of this manipulative impulse. And festive events are typically an alternation between patterns of aggressive, creative activity and its opposite—a more receptive and adaptive mode. At such times, one gives and receives, manipulates and receives manipulation in turn. I have elsewhere (Henricks, 1999) described this opposition as a distinction between "ascending meaning" (expressed most purely in play) and "descending meaning" (expressed in communitas). While both play and communitas represent bounded events in which individuals explore the dimensions of life, they are otherwise different. Communitas describes the yielding, conformitive mode of relationship; people thrill to be part of that which is greater than themselves. By contrast, play emphasizes the transformative pattern of relationship; people discover the nature of existence through individual assertion and opposition.

I would contend that modern societies typically celebrate ascending meaning. Such cultural themes as freedom from control, achievement, rights, growth, and creativity are conceived as individual entitlements. The successful person—in business, politics, education, law, art—is understood to be the active, creative, changing person. Play becomes a crucible where these skills and aptitudes are developed. Less appreciated (as matters of public culture) are the qualities of boundedness, duty, security, stability, and conformity (see Bellah et al., 1985). Not surprisingly, modern societies proclaim the virtues of sport as a competitive version of physical exploration. Other forms of physical challenge like yoga or dance—which comprehend the virtues of yielding and cooperating as well as opposing—receive less cultural attention. Indeed, within the world of sport, such stereotypically "feminine" qualities as grace, flexibility, and balance receive less publicity than force, violence, and speed. Consistent with this emphasis is the development of sport as a showcase for this-worldly asceticism, a theme that Weber put at the heart of the rationalization process.

PLAY IN MODERN SOCIETIES TENDS TO FEATURE ORDER-MAKING BEHAVIOR

To the extent that play is active and manipulative, do players create or destroy? As Sutton-Smith and Kelly-Byrne (1984b) have noted, play is sometimes expressed as deviance and troublemaking. Players may be defilers and disrupters. Away from authority figures, they sometimes tease and bully and spray vulgarities on the wall. The pleasures of petty vandalism and social mischief having been acknowledged, the question remains whether such activities are seen more clearly as adventures in antinomianism and formlessness or rather as attempts by players to make their own marks upon the world and to create their own circles of control.

This opposition between formfulness and formlessness has been described by Handelman (1990). In this regard, he identifies two different styles of play. In traditional societies, play is sometimes comprehended as a mode of participative consciousness in which people move beyond order into a realm of transience and disorder. Indeed, the notion of a surging, disorderly cosmos guides and legitimizes the play. Those who experience this ebb and flow both play and are in play simultaneously. In the West, he argues, play is much more about the personal discovery of order; to that end one assembles and disassembles the world. Such play he (1992) has termed "bottom up," that is, the impetus of play comes from restless, disorderly selves.

While Handelman tends to emphasize the disorderly possibilities of play (see also Spariosu, 1989), the notion of orderliness in Western play is perhaps most well developed by Piaget (1962). The children Piaget studied were makers of ideas and rules. As amateur rationalists, they built frameworks for their collective experience and argued with those who would oppose them. In so doing, they assimilated "reality" into their personal plans and schemes.

To be sure, play exists in both orderly and disorderly ways. As a "modernist" himself, Weber was most attuned to the ways in which a certain type of orderliness—as a broad cultural principle—was tightening its grip on human behavior. Although the nonrational institutions of society (art, love, recreation, etc.) might provide alternative experiences to the routines of business, Weber was still committed to the principle of value-rationality rather than to sheer nonrationality or unreflective spontaneity. In other words, pleasure in his view should be guided by a self-conscious commitment to some principle or form. Some end or vision should guide the activity. To this degree, Weber's views of expressive life resemble the play theories of Huizinga or Schiller (see Henricks, 2001). Players (at their noblest) interpret sophisticated cultural forms or create their own works with this end in sight.

Sporting activities of course are significant examples of order-making. Players meet at the start of a game to agree on basic rules and boundaries. Opportunities for spontaneous self-expression are quite narrowly prescribed. At the end of the event, a hierarchy of winner and loser is established; and "good sports" are expected to acknowledge the worthiness of a competitor's play. Indeed, sporting events tend to have a self-congratulatory quality. Through self-discipline and a shared commitment to uniform rules, it is proclaimed, even the most heated rivalries can move to publicly acceptable conclusions.

MODERN PLAY TENDS TO BE ORGANIZED INSTRUMENTALLY

As noted above, play is defined typically as non-instrumental activity. By such lights, play is an opportunity to assess the world; it pursues no purposes beyond itself. Those who attach purposes to play activities are guilty of turning them into "work." However, in its contemporary setting, play is commonly connected to something else. Stranger still, play activities exhibit simultaneously a certain dependence on external patterns and yet separation from them. As many sociologists have indicated (see, e.g., Parsons, 1971), this pattern of institutional differentiation is a more general characteristic of modern societies. In other words, institutions like the family or economy develop distinctive cultural patterns, practices, and organizations; however, they also maintain systematic linkages with other institutions. A modern business or family may follow its own distinctive goals and norms at the same time that it contracts with organizations of other types (e.g., churches or schools) for the fulfillment of many of its needs. Families need medical care provided by external organizations; businesses need educated workers provided by high schools and colleges. In that sense, play activities and organizations both support and are supported by activities in other sectors of society.

As emphasized in the previous chapter, play provides services to organizations and individuals. Organizations need structured opportunities to establish informal social ties among their members and to facilitate tension-release. Play commonly allows people moments to engage in permissible deviance, assume alternate identities, affirm common values, and develop leadership skills. Perhaps most importantly, play provides a time to address organizational issues and concerns in creative but socially harmless forms. In all these ways, play provides a break from organizational routines and regimes. Similarly, play times give people a chance to assess their own characteristics and relationships. Such self-monitoring activity is important for individuals (and organizations) in a rapidly changing world.

On the other hand, play activities themselves need support from external organizations and individuals. At the most obvious level, play needs what Lieberman (1977) has called "playfulness," a set of creative, inquisitive orientations on the part of the players themselves. For play to be effective, people must want to participate and must have requisite play skills. In addition to this energy and inspiration, play typically requires shared knowledge. Communication depends on common cultural elements—ideas, ideals, and behavioral norms. This information, typically derived from settings external to the play event, not only frames the action but also provides themes for the players to explore. Play also requires material facilities from external organizations—playing equipment from manufacturers, play spaces from governments, businesses, families, and so on. It requires time (released from other social obligations) and often money (provided by individuals and organizations). In that sense, play rests on a bedrock of social opportunities and facilities that arise through the structure of society.

In modern societies play is put to work by every variety of organization. Play is used not only to integrate groups but also to accomplish goals quite specific to the organization itself. In schools, for example, play was formerly exemplified by recess or by the kinds of activities to which teachers objected. Now, students are placed in group whose projects foreground aesthetic themes, creativity of approach, and even the ability to entertain an audience. Teachers are being converted from dispensers of scholarly information and enforcers of discipline to personable guides who motivate and direct creativity. The educational theory behind such processes is that people learn better when they are emotionally committed to and otherwise in control of their own activities; learning should be fun.

Once again, sport provides examples of such themes. Playful sport serves functions for a wide range of organizations. Golf outings, company-sponsored teams, wilderness challenges, and betting pools are all devices to bond organization members. Competitions between schools, businesses, and churches are vehicles for corporate identity and pride. Likewise, sports experiences and abilities are ingredients in individual identity and personal relationships. "How one plays" becomes a public demonstration of character and social accomplishment.

PLAY IN MODERN SOCIETY TENDS TO OCCUR IN INSTITUTIONALIZED GAMES

In theory, play is distinguished from other forms of endeavor by its creativity and spontaneity. Compared to ordinary existence, play is exciting and inventive. Players are servants only to their imaginations. However, as Caillois (1961) emphasizes, play is changed by its manifestation in games. Games are cultural forms, rule-bound structures proceeding to definite ends. Furthermore, games typically take the form of contests, carefully regulated competitions resulting in winners and losers. By this process, play becomes a format for interpersonal comparison.

Weber's thesis is that human activity in modern societies has become more standardized through the application of rationally adjusted principles. Although their ends are nonrational or even pointlessly artificial, games are a good example of this tendency. Rules are established and adjusted to promote fairness of competition and optimum levels of enjoyment. Although the establishment of standardized rules limits the

inventiveness of the players, it nevertheless promotes the broader diffusion and greater sophistication of play. Likewise, the institutionalization of selected games (the process by which they become established
and accepted throughout society) further channels playful energy. People
choose to play Scrabble, checkers, and bridge rather than learn less well-
known games or invent ones of their own.

That these games should take the form of contests seems consistent
with the spirit of an economically competitive society. As Weber (1958b)
explained, capitalism and Protestantism are idea systems that promote
interpersonal competition. Electoral politics, adversarial systems of law,
races for scientific discovery, and the social class structure itself exhibit
similar qualities. In that light, institutionalized contests are ways for
people to affirm these values and to experience the vicissitudes of social
status.

As I have argued elsewhere (1991), sporting events emerged historically as identity ceremonies for achievement-based societies. That is,
societies that put forward ideas about the attainment of social status
through individual effort require public ceremonies dramatizing this doctrine. By showcasing the talents of selected categories of individuals and
by celebrating their competitive success, sports fulfilled (and continue
to fulfill) this function. Fairness and equality of competition became
ideological supports for a class system ridden with inequality.

MODERN PLAY TENDS TO HAVE AN AMORAL, TECHNICAL EMPHASIS

For Weber (1958a, pp. 295–301), one of the great transformations of modernity was the development of a "rational-legal" attitude toward organizations and authority figures. In earlier times, people more commonly followed their leaders either because they believed in the special personal
traits of these leaders (because of charisma) or because it was customary
that they obey in this way (because of tradition). By contrast, people in
the modern setting respect authority in a more neutral, provisional way.
Rules and leaders are seen as creations of the people themselves. For that
reason, they can be adjusted or eliminated. In that sense, rules and leaders are essentially conduits for communication. Although artificial in
nature, rules are respected because rules of some type seem necessary
and because people respect the process through which these rules are
created. Leaders are, for the most, merely position-holders who represent society's will.

It would not be surprising then that this more emotionally distanced, rational attitude should work its way into play. Modern forms of play do not descend from the gods or even the ancients; they are instead transient social conventions. Furthermore, the subject matter of modern play rarely concerns profound philosophical or moral matters. It will be recalled that Huizinga (1955, pp. 105–157) commented at length on the great puzzling games and cosmic riddles that preoccupied the ancient priests and philosophers. Modern play tends to have a narrower, less spiritual focus. Indeed, it seems that modern play has become a largely aesthetic event, an intellectualization of pleasure.

Just because the ends of modern play are typically frivolous or amoral, the emphasis for participants shifts to largely technical matters. How can I have the most fun? What strategies will help me be successful? With such concerns in mind, morality itself is repositioned as a fundamentally technocratic matter. That is, tests of virtue center around questions of how hard one perseveres (particularly in difficult circumstances) and whether one sacrifices oneself for the good of the team. Thus, character is revealed entirely by individual strategy and physical effort. The ultimate worth of the endeavor, since typically pointless or trivial, is not in view.

As before, modern sport exhibits these traits. The "sportsman" is one who observes the rules (however silly) simply because that was the agreement at the start of the game. This rational-legal commitment becomes even more neutral with the development of rule-making bodies and adjudicating officials. Under such conditions, rules become another aspect to be manipulated. Television time-outs in basketball, fist fights in hockey, and two-minute warnings in football, are all elements to be accounted for in coaching strategy. Rule-enforcement becomes the job of officials; players may adopt a "what the referee doesn't see doesn't count" ethos. Presumably, such short-range morality is transferable to other portions of life.

MODERN PLAY TENDS TO BE BUREAUCRATICALLY ORGANIZED

Few things are less playful in spirit than the modern bureaucracy. As Weber (1958a, pp. 196–244) describes it, bureaucracy is rigid in its principles and positions. Behavior is governed by written policy, relations are impersonal, chains of communication are narrow, quantification of procedures and outputs is paramount. In all these ways, individual spontaneity and discretion are minimized.

As discussed in chapter 2, the critical theorists believed that expressive culture was managed by a highly organized culture industry. This industry (whether controlled by a capitalist or socialist system) was hier-archical, regimented, impersonal, and governed by principles of mea-surement and efficiency. More recently, Ritzer (1994) has argued that these principles, epitomized by the organizational procedures of McDon-ald's restaurants, have moved into a great range of other organizations, both within the United States and internationally. Although Ritzer does not develop this theme explicitly, it seems clear that these principles have come to characterize the various commercial establishments that sell pleasure experiences. Thus, theme parks (epitomized by the Dis-ney chain), casinos, hotels and restaurants, cruises, and shopping malls have become carefully managed enterprises (see Schiller, 1989; Boorstin, 1962; Marling, 1997; Judd and Fainstein, 1999). Spaces are "themed" through careful attention to architectural detail and landscaping, music, attractions, and even items in the gift shop. Staff are closely supervised for appropriate dress and manner; ticket prices and other revenues are carefully projected. Even the capacity of people to wait patiently in line without distraction or reward is calculated. The commodity that is sold is not a series of amusement park rides or evening meals but rather a complete pleasure experience. This experience must be standardized (i.e., repeatable) so that patrons are able to anticipate a certain quality of experience and later be satisfied that this level was attained. As in the case of McDonald's, such standardization is commonly achieved through a franchise system.

Although the position of these pleasure-domes in the modern imagi-nation is incalculable, it seems clear that such packaged vacations and evenings-out are important ways in which people envision and then realize pleasure. Although each trip or event is "individualized" by the shifting interests and aptitudes of the patrons themselves, the setting for such personal exploration is carefully managed. Safety, cleanliness, and moderate levels of excitement prevail.

Organized sport fits these principles as well (see Cantelon and Ing-ham, 2002). Even at the level of youth sport, events are managed closely by officials (see Coakley, 1996b). Coaches typically dictate who plays where and when. Teams are placed within a league that has disciplin-ary powers. Rules—specifically rules regarding eligibility, team rights, and behavior codes—are written and maintained by the league. There are moments of spontaneity, but these are often confined to off-the-field horseplay; the overall atmosphere is one of control and discipline.

Such elements are magnified at the higher levels of play (see Sage, 1990). The arenas of big-time sport are carefully managed for season-ticket revenues and corporate sponsorships. Coaches and owners dominate. Players, to the extent that this term applies, are highly rewarded entertainers whose playing opportunities are closely supervised. Even fan behavior is coordinated. Guttmann (1978) has described these changes as long-term historical processes. He argues that modern sport has severed its long-standing connections to people and place and become instead a cultural artifice. In addition to the tightly managed regimes described above, sport has developed as a breeding ground for statistics and records. To that extent, sports are standard bearers for a myth of calculable human progress.

Reflections on the Iron Cage

Just as Marx's sociology is sensitive to the concerns of artisans and factory workers, much of Weber's work is preoccupied with the sensibilities and patterns of influence of the business and professional classes. In that light, Weber's analysis seems to beg the question: What will happen if personal and social experience surrenders to the principles of the self-important businessman, the civil servant, the accountant, the scout leader, the public school administrator, and the coach? Will creative expression be captured and managed in those officially "sanitized" ways described above?

The following section addresses this theme from two different directions. This first view is that of the sociologist Norbert Elias, who contends that the system of calculated control over personal behavior may be embedded in modern people even more deeply than Weber acknowledged. The second view is that of the postmodernists, who claim that the rational or logical dimension of modern culture and its organizations is very much overstated.

PLAY AND THE CIVILIZING PROCESS

Like Weber, the German sociologist Norbert Elias was driven to understand the directions of historical change in Europe; however, he took a different approach to these matters (see Mennell, 1992; Krieken, 1998). Although Elias shared Weber's interest in the changing role of the bourgeoisie, he was also interested in the influence of other classes, especially the old aristocracy, within the ever-changing amalgam that is the modern sensibility. He developed these ideas in an important book, *The Civilizing Process*, first published in Germany in the late 1930s (Elias, 2000). Among the contributions of that work is the idea that the rationalization process is broader (and somewhat differently focused) than Weber stated. However, as Elias (1986; 1996) explained in later works, this calculating impulse does not merely close off opportunities for emotional satisfaction but instigates and channels them as well.

Born in 1897, Elias was a relative outsider within the sociological establishment for most of his long career. However, as a young German academic in the 1920s and 1930s, he lived near the center of some of the most important intellectual and political movements of the modern age. After completing a first dissertation at Breslau in 1924, Elias moved to Heidelberg, where he was a student of Alfred Weber, Max's younger brother. There he also became good friends with the sociologist Karl Mannheim. In 1930, Elias moved to Frankfurt to become Mannheim's assistant at the university there. The Frankfurt sociology department was adjacent to the famed Institute for Social Research and Elias became acquainted with its community of thinkers. Like many other Jewish scholars, Elias emigrated to Paris and then London after the rise of the National Socialists in 1933. There he lived and worked for more than thirty years, becoming well known only after the English publication of *The Civilizing Process* in 1969. Since Elias's death in 1990, others—most notably his former colleagues at the University of Leicester and Dutch and German scholars—have carried forward his "figurational" approach to sociology (see, e.g., Mennell and Goudsblom, 1998; Van Krieken, 1998).

Weber is famous for his emphasis on the role of institutionalized values as directors and motivators of social (and personal) change. Like many other German academics of his time, Elias accepted the view that society must be understood historically and that these changing conditions are paralleled by changes in the world view or "ethic" of the inhabitants. Moreover, Elias shared Weber's position that idea systems and social forms typically are linked, even when the former is only a way of legitimizing patterns of economic and social inequality. However, like his mentor Mannheim, Elias tended to see ideas less as powerful instruments in their own right and more as products or expressions of the ever-precarious relationships between competing groups. Social relations are seen less as a structure or pattern than a patterning, a continuously shifting alignment of social units, who find themselves dependent upon one another in specified ways. Thus, Elias sometimes compared social life to a community dance or round, a comprehensible but not entirely predictable movement of the entire social body. To that degree, social activity is as much a series of reactions and adjustments as it is a consciously administered enterprise. Furthermore, the identities and behaviors of the individual participants are meaningless without an understanding of their placement within this wider social context.

Elias's book on the civilizing process is, at one level, an attempt to explain how and why a carefully calculated and refined style of social decorum developed in Europe. Basing his research on the collections of Renaissance etiquette books in the British Museum and drawing his inspiration from Huizinga's (1954) *The Waning of the Middle Ages*, Elias argued that social relationships in the medieval period were much more emotionally direct and volatile than in later centuries. In particular, the more visceral or bodily aspects of life—eating and drinking, personal hygiene, urination and defecation, sleeping, sexual relations, and so on—were approached in a less regulated and less self-conscious way. Gradually, new codes of public conduct about these matters came into being; eating with one's hands, spitting, or urinating in public were now thought to be shameful or disgusting.

Such changes were attributable not to the incursions of ministers and moralists but rather to new patterns of social dependence. Among these changes was the development of court life among the upper status groups. For a variety of reasons, isolated feudal lords found themselves drawn into a system of royal control. Coming to court meant seeking favors from the royal household and, in that process, displaying oneself publicly before rivalrous peers. Maneuvering in this complicated but confined environment required a new set of skills quite different from the military virtues of earlier times. Indeed, the modern view of the "Renaissance" person as someone accomplished in a great range of personal and social skills hearkens to those days. For Elias, the rationalization process—as the implementation of a carefully calculating approach to social life—was associated not only with the desires of bourgeois Protestants for economic and spiritual gain but also with the deadly social games of the court. In that light, those courtly behaviors so despised by Veblen (1953)—conspicuous consumption, studied languor, rhetorical and aesthetic flourish—must be understood as carefully crafted strategies designed to cement or advance social standing.

For years, this courtly style was opposed to the more rustic manners of lower status, "provincial" groups, and to the crass commercialism of the towns. However, the gradual thickening of society (through population growth, increasing complexity of the status system, economic interdependence, and other factors) encouraged the development of nation-states. In this wider framework, the bourgeoisie was recognized to play a vital role. Thus, an ethic of civility or gentility—as a style of individual self-control and courteous behavior toward wider categories of others—became established and spread. The pace and pattern of these changes was not even. Some countries, like England, embraced a broad definition of gentility and granted social and political rights to the bourgeoisie; other countries, like Elias's own Germany, lagged behind.

Elias's work is important here because it attempts to show how personal expression (and even the most enjoyable forms of physical behavior) are shaped by public codes that are themselves statements about social interdependence. In this project, he was very much influenced by Freud's (1962) view of the tension between psychic wishes and the efforts of "civilization" to repress or sublimate these desires. And, like Freud, Elias was drawn to the ways in which society's codes become internalized in the conscience of individuals. Thus social regulation is abetted by patterns of personal control. Moreover, as the "chains" of interdependence in society become longer and more complicated, so individuals gear their own behavior toward longer-term and more abstract social effects.

Although Elias shared Freud's fascination with both sexual and aggressive urges, he was especially concerned with the role of aggression, even violence, in our seemingly more pacified world. Of the latter danger, Elias knew a great deal. He had been a soldier in World War I; he had seen the fascination with violence in the Nazi movement; his parents died in Germany (his mother at Auschwitz) after he failed to convince them to remain with him in England. The latter stages of his career focused on his attempts to understand the connections between civilizing and de-civilizing processes. Was violent behavior merely an irregular, regressive response to the civilizing process? Was it a much more firmly established counter-tradition? Or was it contained—and even countenanced—by the coolly technocratic style of the wider movement?

For our purposes, these matters are addressed most clearly in a 1986 work coauthored by Elias and British sociologist Eric Dunning. Titled *The Quest for Excitement: Sport and Leisure in the Civilizing Process*, the book is essentially an argument that sporting activities in modern societies have developed as "an enjoyable and controlled de-controlling of emotions" (Elias and Dunning, 1986, p. 44). Many of the examples of this thesis come from England in the period between the seventeenth and nineteenth centuries, when arguably the modern version of sport was born. England was a particularly propitious setting for the development of sport just because it featured a wide range of contending status groups committed to a principle of national unity and to relatively broad participation in economic and political affairs. Thus "parliamentarization" in the political sphere was paralleled by a "sportization" of pastimes, that is, by the development of leisure activities within self-administered frameworks of associations and schools committed to fair and "gentlemanly" competition. Significantly, sporting activities became formats where persons of modestly different status could meet on terms of relative equality. Sporting language and lore became a kind of lingua franca for the socially connected; and the qualities of the "sportsman" became established as a broadly recognized public ideal.

As Elias and Dunning explain, sports like boxing, hunting, and football developed in ways that were more tightly regulated and significantly less violent than the contests of centuries past. With its written rules, gloves, rounds, officials, matching of competitors, association of sponsoring gentlemen, and so on, changes in boxing mimicked the more general pacification of society. Likewise, the violent and grueling hunts for the great beasts of the Middle Ages were replaced by softer, more thoroughly public forms, including those in which well-placed riders of both sexes competed to be first at the killing of a fox by hounds. Although hunting continued to require its kill, the target species was increasingly small or tame (birds or deer in parks) and killing at a distance (by bow and then gun) became preferred to more dangerous and intimate encounters. At any rate, these sports—and the proliferating forms of ball play—not only reflected the new balances between the various rural and urban social units but also articulated clearly the rules and standards by which such categories might relate to one another.

So understood, sport in its more "civilized" context presents socially approved pathways for participants to pursue together an anticipated range of pleasures that, for the most part, have been cleansed of their dangers. Societies that are centralized, democratic, competitive, individualistic, and pacified tend to produce sports that reflect those themes. Moreover, to the extent that sport matches relatively equal and socially assured competitors (under a framework of shared terms and goals) leisure becomes an exercise in social cooperation and comportment.

Spectator sports and their dramatic kindred display further opportunities for enjoyment. Indeed, in societies where ordinary existence has become fairly routinized, pacified, and sedentary, people may hunger for the exotic and dangerous. In that light, spectator sports, movies, rock concerts, and the like are devices to generate and then manage strong feelings in observers. In Elias and Dunning's (pp. 40–62) view, people do not attend such events to "release" emotional tension but rather to create it and explore its meanings. Having said this, the excitements raised must not be too strong (as might be occasioned by the spectacle of real rather than fictive death) or too modest (when the spectacle takes on the predictability and ordinariness or other portions of life). It should be emphasized that modern societies typically offer their inhabitants wide varieties of spectacles—with varying levels of excitement; and different categories of people have different appetites in this regard. However, in general, the danger and excitement levels of licit pleasures are situated at a strategic distance from the standards appropriate to broader social forms.

Recent trends in sports, including on-field violence and hooliganism by fans, seem to contradict these views. However, the civilizing process is less an historical judgment than a description of modes and manners appropriate to certain kinds of social formations. That is, when groups are not oriented to the broader frameworks uniting them—as is sometimes the case in international or inter-city play—or when groups feel actively excluded from those larger unities, they may behave in less than civil ways. As Dunning (1988) explains in another context, sometimes the loyalties of participants and spectators are only to their communities of origin, a condition that resembles the "ordered segmentation" or relatively isolated status of groups in the economically deprived areas of modern cities (see Suttles, 1968). Strong commitment to one's own group may be accompanied by callous disregard for outsiders.

It can be argued that a fundamentally "social" approach of this sort cannot fully explain so complex a matter as the public construction of excitement. Other factors like commercialization and professionalization; gambling; ethnicity, age, and gender issues; governmental and religious regulation; educational levels; advances in communication and transportation technology, and so forth also influence the possibilities for excitement. And, as Weber argued, value complexes drive history as much as they reflect it. However, Elias's attempt to show the connections between broad societal changes and patterns of individual orientation is an important contribution to historical sociology; and his return to essentially social themes is a useful correction to the somewhat more "cultural" emphasis of the Weberian tradition.

PLAY AND POSTMODERNISM

Is modern society, so full of instrumental rationality, the "iron cage" that Weber described? To a large extent, the foregoing arguments have presented a picture of the modern person as trapped in a kind of comfortable prison (see Foucault, 1979). Although the prisoners have consented to their surroundings—they recognize their confinement to be "legitimate" and even participate in the running of the establishment—there is a curious feeling of incompletion. The place is orderly and clean. Meals, health care, and visitation policies are adequate. Yet, experience has a rather scripted quality. Behavior is managed. Improbable, irrational, and passionate things are discouraged strongly. Residents know that some-thing is missing but they no longer have the vision (or the language) to talk about it. And the idea of a self-generated, caring community has somehow disappeared as well.

As Weber observed, it is natural that people in modern, bureaucratic settings should hunger for the intimate and the expressive. And funda-mentally nonrational commitments (such as love or religion) will con-tinue to hold their positions—if only as counterbalances—to the other forms of regimentation. Nevertheless it is striking that expressive forms of behavior in modern societies are not more rebellious or romantic. In societies of the past, exotic forms of expression—featuring status reversal, ecstatic (including drug-induced) psychological states, nonrational beliefs and puzzles, and so on—were built into the social fabric through public festivities. Now such activities are confined, for the most part, to small groups or are sold as commodities to private individuals. In other words, public culture—those beliefs and commitments promoted by prominent organizations and acknowledged by the social majority—seems relatively controlled and sanitized. Far from opposing this pattern, playful expres-sion tends to be organized as a series of pleasant individual escapades or interludes, officially permitted departures from public routine. In this way, even the "escape routes" for public expression have been anticipated and prepared by formal organizations.

Perhaps the sharpest alternative to this viewpoint comes from the intellectual movement known as postmodernism (see Bertens, 1995; Rosenau, 1992; Henricks, 2001). Consistent with its name, postmod-ernism claims that the era of wide-ranging administrative projects, rigid formalism, and universal belief-systems has ended. Such ideas, along with notions of an abstract and broadly human "self" and the orderly "progress" of societies, were the dreams of the Enlightenment and the centuries that followed. In the view of the postmodernists, a standardized and centrally administered world (subscribing to Eurocentric, masculine, and bourgeois principles) has not occurred, at least not in the fashion that the imperialists imagined. Instead, marginality, fragmentation, irra-tionality, and disorder are the watchwords of contemporary experience. Small communities of people huddle together and await their chances; anarchy abounds.

Just as society seems to be a centrifuge that throws people to its edges, so the prevailing cultural experience of most persons is not order but disorder. Although postmodernists acknowledge the persistence of large, bureaucratic organizations (giant businesses, nation-states, etc.) and the increasingly important role of culture in public life, they tend to see culture much more as a jungle of marginally related ideas and images than as a centralized system of interconnected principles. Although some postmodernists, following Jameson (1991), have connected this proliferation of quasi-meaningful information and artifacts to the rise of capitalist advertising, others (Baudrillard, 1983; Derrida, 1981) have stressed the extent to which information in general has become disconnected from its original settings. This process of "decontextualization" has meant that people are now subject to an electronically generated firestorm of marginally related words and images. To that degree, there is no unifying logic to public culture. What people experience instead is an ever-changing panoply of claims and gestures. No attempt is made at a public level to hold these claims (or organizational policies) to account. Indeed, as Derrida (1981) argues, even individual "arguments" do not possess logical meaning but exist only as exercises in "différance," endless trails of circular reasoning and willful ambiguity.

Perhaps even more profoundly, the historic linkage of culture to social and personal structures has come undone. For their part, modernist sociologists like Weber and Elias have stressed the intimate connections between these different kinds of patterns. Culture is seen as a powerful and heavily systematized framework that coordinates the life of societies and becomes internalized in the minds of its members. Indeed, it is commitment to these publicly shared ideas and values that gives social organizations their focus and human beings their energy. For their part, anthropologists have sometimes pictured culture as an integrated whole. Cultural beliefs, customs, and even artifacts are the very foundations of traditional societies; to change one important element is to cause the entire edifice to teeter.

In contrast, the more radical forms of postmodernism tend to see culture as a set of creations that have jumped out of the box of social structure and are now running about. In that sense, cultural expression is particular rather than universal, concrete rather than abstract, endlessly diverse rather than tightly integrated. To experience public culture is to channel surf through an endless display of theatrical appeals, gaudy objects, and buzzing noises—all demanding a moment's attention. Reality to that degree is "virtual," a series of artificial worlds disconnected from the concrete realities of life.

Within this context, postmodernists comprehend play as a pleasurable encounter with fragmentation and disorder (see Hans, 1981; Kuchler, 1994). Like patrons at a carnival, people wander through the world experiencing its sights and sounds. Individual manipulation of this environment takes the form of self-styled consumption or small acts of rebellion. Shopping, clubbing, and other types of connoisseurship become significant modes of personal expression. Creativity is reconfigured as a kind of collage making, an assembling of decontextualized images according to the maker's private inspirations. However, such activity is not an "escape" in the way previously described; it is simply the normal course of affairs. Moreover, in a posthumanist world, people's ability to actively manipulate the circumstances of their lives is less important than a broader point about the nature of reality itself. Radical postmodernists claim that the world—that swirling, shifting series of objects and events—is actually "at play" and that we are "in play." Amidst this semi-chaos, the best course of action is to do what parents do at amusements parks—hold tightly to your valued possessions, watch your children, and take what pleasures you can from the changing scenes.

Many of the postmodernist arguments were anticipated by Georg Simmel, the subject of the next chapter. Modern culture does seem increasingly artificial; marginality and disorder are important aspects of contemporary experience. We have become acquainted with the "pluralization" of life-worlds. However, culture (and society) can be discussed in many different ways at many different levels, and it would be foolish to disregard the monumental push of large bureaucratic organizations toward systematization and control or the more general powers of culture to frame human capacity. Perhaps it is enough to reiterate here the postmodern theme that contemporary culture is less an iron cage than a mirrored funhouse or labyrinth that even the keepers do not know. In the nooks and crannies, creative (even eccentric) life can be had. Nevertheless, such a portrait confines creativity and self-expression to private or small-scale settings and to the array of objects presented for one's inspection. From a broader viewpoint then, prison architecture and policies appear untouched. Guards continue to be paid. And the inhabitants accommodate themselves to the kinds of opportunities that this structure provides.

5 Georg Simmel and the Play-Forms of Social Life

For some sociologists, society resembles a great house or office building. A product of patient and ingenious design, the edifice looms over the street, both impressing passersby and regulating their entry. Within are many rooms, each with its own nomenclature, rules, and physical accommodations. People move about from one room to another, constantly adjusting their behavior to the different settings. Over time, many of these patterns of code and conduct acquire the feel of permanence. Like the stones and beams that support the building's physical structure, symbolic culture becomes a framework for every manner of activity; and these patterns become the basis for the security and identity of the inhabitants. Although each generation redecorates and expands in modest ways, the foundations of the building seem safe from all but the greatest of incursions. Wrapped in these assurances about past and future, social structure acquires its mighty weight.

The German philosopher and sociologist Georg Simmel understood this metaphor well enough. Yet he took another, more personal view of social order. For Simmel, social life is at its basis the comings and goings of people—the whispered conversation in the hall, the knowing glance, the love affair, the rivalry, the secret, the adventure. While other social scientists focused on structures of work and power that direct people along socially approved pathways, Simmel was more interested in the "social" in its purest forms. How is it that people sort out their relationships to one another? What factors influence their possibilities for doing so? And how does social involvement itself resonate with personal understanding and experience?

Within the context of such questions, Simmel was fascinated by the relationship between socio-cultural reality—as a kind of magnificent abstraction—and the inspired commitments of individuals in the moments of their lives. What he understood profoundly was that this tension-filled relationship between the abstract and concrete, timeless and momentary, impersonal and personal, is fundamental to the experience of being human. Probably better than any sociologist before or since, Simmel realized that humans encounter the world fundamentally through the construction and employment of symbolic forms. His ability to describe in striking ways the degree to which people create, inhabit, and oppose form makes him, arguably, the greatest of the sociological theorists of play.

In this chapter I first describe Simmel's general approach to human affairs within the context of his life and times. This is followed by an examination of expressive culture as developed in his essays on flirtation, the adventure, and sociability. Comments are offered on the value of Simmel's approach; and a concluding section discusses the work of other writers who have extended Simmel's concerns.

Simmel: The Man and His Work

It is sometimes observed that intellectual work is psychology writ large. At least if one expands the definition of personal circumstance to include the social settings in which writers are born and flourish, this maxim in Simmel's case seems true. As Levine (1971) has insisted, to understand Simmel's work one must first grasp his "marginality" within the academic world of his time. To say this is not to claim simply that he was an outsider or a failure. As will be indicated below, in some ways Simmel's academic career was spectacularly successful; in other ways he was blocked profoundly. This contradictory status of being both inside and outside the academy, of being "in" that world but not "of" it, influenced Simmel's more general portraits of social involvement. Like Marx, Simmel described human connections in terms of tension, distance, and alienation. Although people desire emotional completion, they seem destined for relationships that are irretrievably partial and impersonal.

Born in 1858 in Berlin, Simmel had a childhood reminiscent of that of Marx, born forty years before. The youngest of seven children, Simmel was part of a wealthy family whose fortune was based on the manufacture of chocolate (see Wolff, 1950, p. xviii). In this setting, he was exposed to a world of music, art, and drawing room conversation. Although his father died when Simmel was sixteen, his guardian was the owner of an internationally successful music publishing house. Under such auspices, Simmel was granted the funds to live in some style throughout his life and to pursue an academic career. However, like Marx, he seems to have been curiously remote from both his parents and his siblings (see Pampel, 2000, p. 129). Instead, he preferred the more abstract pleasures of art and philosophy, and the friendships that could be gained in this way.

At eighteen, Simmel entered the University of Berlin, beginning a relationship he would maintain for almost all his life. Settling on the study of history and philosophy, he was much influenced by his great predecessors Kant, Hegel, and Dilthey. The tradition of German idealism held that the world is seen through a series of perceptual screens expressed in such forms as language, law, art, and myth (see Collins and Makowsky, 1993, p. 167). Such structures help people process or otherwise make sense of the continually changing matters or "contents" of everyday life. Simmel's contribution, like Durkheim's, is ultimately a version of sociological Kantianism. However, Simmel was interested in a much wider range of social, cultural, and personal "forms" than Durkheim, and he always emphasized the dialectical, tension-ridden relationships between these patterns and levels. The forms of social and cultural life for Simmel are not merely objects of admiration or vehicles to help us think and feel; they may also oppose and frustrate our experience of the world.

Receiving his Ph.D. in 1881, Simmel was prepared to enter the professoriate. However, his much anticipated success was not to come (see Wolff, 1950). In 1885, he received an appointment at Berlin as a *privatdozent*, a lecturer dependent for his income on student fees. He remained in that position for fifteen years. In 1900, he advanced to the position of *aussenordenlicher professor* (extraordinary professor), but this was merely an honorary status with no change in income. He retained this status for another fourteen years.

Simmel's failure to advance in the German academic world, especially when compared with the success of his friend Max Weber, has been the subject of much speculation. By 1901, he had written seven books and more than seventy articles and had some measure of international renown (see Pampel, 2000, p. 140). Moreover, he was a dazzling lecturer, whose classes drew hundreds of students. Simmel and his wife Gertrude had a gracious home in Berlin that was the center for a collection of artists and intellectuals (see Frisby, 1984, p. 36). They counted among their friends such luminaries as Stefan George, Rilke, Bergson, and Troelstch.

Set against these successes, however, were two factors: the anti-Semitism of the German academy and Simmel's own intellectual style.

Again like Marx's, Simmel's parents had turned from Judaism in hopes of participating more fully in Bismarck's Germany. Simmel's father became a Catholic and his mother a Lutheran; and Simmel himself was baptized a Protestant. However, as Pampel (2000, p. 136) has noted, such converts were doubly suspicious in the climate of the times. Protestants might see them as opportunists; other Jews, as traitors. Like the sociologists described in the previous chapters, Simmel absolved himself early in life of any religious or ethnic commitment. Nevertheless, throughout his career the Protestant academic hierarchy saw him as an essentially Jewish scholar (see Pampel, 2000, p. 141).

More explicit objections focused on Simmel's intellectual style. Even sympathetic commentators have described Simmel as someone who approached scholarship as an art collector (Wolff, 1950, p. xx), as a philosophical squirrel jumping from branch to branch (Coser, 1965, p.3), and as a *flaneur*, the slightly curious onlooker who interrupts his afternoon stroll to watch the happenings of the world (see Frisby, 1981, pp. 68–101). What these depictions share is the view that Simmel approached his topics in a seemingly haphazard way—like someone who comes upon an object in the road and keeps turning it over with his foot to see its many facets. This style of "sociological impressionism," to use Frisby's (1984) term, was completely at odds with the prevailing traditions of German scholarship, which emphasized carefully plotted, deeply researched, and specialized inquiry. Furthermore, Simmel was very casual about his scholarly debts, rarely citing the work of others or developing their ideas at length. To his critics, he appeared to be a thinker who analyzed the world primarily for his own amusement. His choice of topics—essays on misers, romantic love, fashion, strangers, the nobility, creators like Goethe and Rodin, flirtation, and prostitution—seemed to support this judgment.

It is true that Simmel never arranged his topics—or his observations—in an organized or comprehensive way. However, in a different sense he was the most systematic of philosophers. What unites almost all of Simmel's writing is his manner of approach. Much like a mathematician who looks at figures of many sizes and colors and then organizes them as circles, rectangles, or triangles, Simmel sought to produce a geometry of social, cultural, and individual forms from the vast range of empirical examples. These distinctive forms were presented essentially as ideal types, that is as constellations of logically related traits that unify or otherwise impute coherence to the messy realities of everyday behavior. Simmel's gift was his ability to trace the implications of each distinctive type or form. Thus—to take one of his most famous examples—the three-person group is quite different from the two-person group (see Simmel, 1950, pp. 118–169). As ideal types, triads are more group-like, impersonal, formal, complicated, and full of new relationships and roles like coalitions, isolates, and spectators. People in the company of one other person tend to behave differently than those in the company of two. Consistently, Simmel was able to move his readers from the particular to the general and then back again—to show them how human possibility is framed in analytically coherent forms.

No introduction to Simmel and his work is complete without some reference to Berlin, the city that was a central source of his imagination and insight. Born and raised in one of the busiest sections of the city, Simmel was profoundly influenced by the city's flood of human traffic and discourse, the heterogeneity of activity, effulgent art and culture, economic and military adventurism, and the transitory and oddly impersonal quality of human contact. Like an amazing, self-replicating machine, the city developed in ever more articulated ways. In 1874, there were one million residents in Berlin; twenty years later, there were 1.7 million (Poggi, 1993, p. 35). For Simmel, the city was the great example of the accelerating possibilities of material and symbolic culture. However, he also sensed that this wonderful artifact was growing in ways that defied human control or even comprehension. As objectivity blossomed, subjectivity waned. The resulting quality of experience—distant yet specialized—was a theme developed in perhaps his most famous essay, "The Metropolis and Mental Life" (Simmel, 1971, pp. 324–339), itself a source for the noted studies of city life at the University of Chicago during the 1920s.

It is notable as well that Simmel did not live long after his departure from the city. In 1914, a few years after being rebuffed in his efforts to find a position at Heidelberg, he was offered a chair at Strausburg, again in those Franco-German borderlands that have figured so prominently in the lives of the other theorists. In this more provincial setting, Simmel was clearly out of his element. Simmel's initial enthusiasm for World War I was followed by disillusion and then, cancer of the liver. He spent his last years developing a general philosophy of life and died two months before Germany's surrender in 1918.

As Levine (1971) has argued, Simmel's body of work focuses primarily on the nature of culture, social life, and individual personality interpreted as forms of expression. Simmel sought to describe the origins, implications, and interrelationships of these forms. Again, his principal method was to seek similarity across diversity, to show how activities of the seemingly greatest variety might be organized as "types" following distinctive principles or logics.

CULTURE

Perhaps Simmel's towering achievement is his analysis of modern culture. Some of the elements of his argument are reminiscent of those of Marx and Weber; however, Simmel presents them in his own distinctive way. Like Marx, Simmel emphasizes the extent to which human cultural production is initially a practical matter connected to people's daily needs; however, these tools and technologies quickly acquire a status independent of their makers. In that sense, culture becomes "objectified." However, Simmel was much more interested than Marx in the full range of cultural products (language, art, religion, legal systems, moral codes, scientific ideas, etc.). These become linked to one another in a relatively self-contained world that confronts individuals and shapes their possibilities for expression. Furthermore, the elements of this cultural world are expanding at a rapid pace, not merely in number but also in variety (see Ritzer, 1983, pp. 170–172). At some point, these conditions of overwhelming size, independence, and diversity bewilder rather than support the individuals who would comprehend them. In that sense, Simmel's view of culture is much more pluralistic than Marx's; and parallels have been drawn between Simmel and later postmodernist thinkers (see Weinstein and Weinstein, 1993; Pescolido and Rubin, 2000). Most importantly, Simmel does not impute these problems to capitalism or class divisions. The expansion of culture is rather the condition of modernity itself.

Simmel shares with Weber the view that culture is becoming increasingly intellectualized or "rational" (see Adams and Sydie, 2001, pp. 197–198). Simmel's great commentary on this issue is his book on the "philosophy" of money (Simmel, 1978). Written in part as a response to Marx's Capital, the work argues that money in general represents a set of objects, ideas, and relationships that fundamentally alters the way human beings live. Specifically, money fosters a view of human interaction as an endless series of exchanges in which people calculate the costs and benefits of their participation. Indeed, life itself can be configured as a matter of gain and loss. Moreover, money allows people to escape the confines of locality and groups and to decorate their lives with the objects that they purchase and control; for such reasons, it fosters the growth of individualism. Both a medium of exchange and measure of value, money allows people to negotiate with distant others, postpone the acquisition and storage of goods, plan and develop large-scale enterprises, and quantify their relations to others. Indeed, the use of money to quantify precisely the rights and responsibilities of people within the terms of a relatively uniform system makes possible the fast-paced, specialized, wide-ranging, and mobile societies in which we live. However, it should also be acknowledged that money—and the skills associated with its accumulation—can quickly become ends in themselves. That is, as for the miser and spendthrift (see Simmel, 1971, pp. 179–186), life itself becomes understood as an exercise in getting and using money; and money values themselves (translated into ideas of "price") override other patterns of relationship. Even more generally, a fascination with cultural objects and principles replaces human connection. People surrender to abstraction.

SOCIAL INTERACTION

As noted at the beginning of this chapter, Simmel's portraits of social life tend to focus more on the interaction of individuals than on society (as an organism or machine composed of interrelated parts). In other words, the "social" for Simmel is less some chartered public framework than a series of patterns expressing (and coalescing) the interests and appetites of actors. "Society," to the extent that this term applies at all, is largely the recognition that the activities of individuals and groups may be summarized at some wide level of generality. This imputation of social totality (along with the idea that cultural contents are also shared at this wide level) becomes an important part of human social awareness and assists people's interaction with others. In such ways, Simmel builds upon Kant's argument that the supposed unity and structure of "nature" is, for the most part, a figment of the human desire to categorize or otherwise find order. In opposition to Durkheim—for whom society possesses the reality of an external, well-defended force—Simmel views society largely as a matter of personal consciousness. In that light, his descriptions of social life as process, shared symbols, the importance of everyday behavior, and the microscopic analysis of groups make him a spiritual ancestor of one of the most famous sociological traditions, symbolic interactionism.

Such ideas come together most clearly in Simmel's (1971, pp. 43–69) view of social life as "exchange." As they do in strictly economic activities, people in other aspects of their lives make decisions about social participation based on perceptions of potential costs and benefits. That is, social action of every type routinely produces changes in personal "condition" (Simmel, 1971, p. 45), including alterations in personal experience and social status. People participate with others when their projected involvement is anticipated to be "worth it"; social interaction itself is the result of two or more individuals deciding that this will be the case. If initially spontaneous and creative, exchanges typically develop into patterns in which ideas about "cost" or "value" become relatively standardized. A result of this process is that individuals adjust their own ideas about worth and worthiness to these forms. To this extent, social life itself may be seen as a process in which potentially severe and idiosyncratic kinds of conflict and competition drift toward more stable patterns of accommodation and compromise (Simmel, 1955). Moreover, our feelings about these patterns of exchange become the basis of the social bonds we share with others.

Such intellectual commitments might have led Simmel to see society in a thoroughly individualistic or utilitarian way. However, he was always much more interested in the "forms" of social life than he was in the specific motives of the actors themselves. Again, like a student of geometry or grammar, he was fascinated by the internal logic or organizing principles of social life. Thus city life, in its essence, is different from country life. Subordination to a person is quite different than subordination to an organization or, yet again, to a set of rules (see Simmel, 1950, pp. 181–306).

THE INDIVIDUAL

Not surprisingly, Simmel produced no extensive theory of personality or consciousness nor did he document at length the relationship of the individual to social and cultural forms. Rather, in keeping with his pluralistic spirit, he tended to focus on distinctive social "types" (like the miser or adventurer) or on the personal styles of creative artists and intellectuals (see Levine, 1971). However, like the theorists described above, Simmel had a deep interest in the effects of modern society on experience.

Simmel's treatment of the individual tends to emphasize the ways in which our involvement with others—and with culture—is always incomplete. To describe this quality of separation and fragmentation, he uses the metaphor of "distance" (see Levine, 1971, pp. xxxiv–xxxv). That is, people frequently find themselves to be held at arm's length in their dealings with others. They are expected to participate but they are also expected to respect established social divisions and roles. As in the case of Simmel's own experiences in the academic world, certain kinds of acceptance or involvement do not guarantee other kinds. His famous essay on this matter concerns the "stranger" (Simmel, 1971, pp. 143–149).

Unlike the traveler who is merely passing through, the stranger is an outsider who has come to stay within a community. Although strangers are quite recognizable members of the community, they are always felt to be different. Like foreign merchants or professionals, they are granted special, if limited, roles. That is, they may be seen as sources of new ideas and goods, as external critics of society, as arbiters of conflict, or even as confidantes. In such ways, Simmel anticipates now popular ideas about "marginality" or "status inconsistency." He (Simmel, 1950, pp. 345–378) developed this theme in an essay on the "secret society," which sees human experience as pervaded by a taste for differentiation and exclusion. To be in the group is to know that others are outside; to hold high rank is to sense the predicament of others placed below.

Just as our participation with others is typically specialized and fragmented, so our relationship to culture is tangential. As noted above, the expansion and diversification of objective culture in modern times has meant that individuals can no longer keep up. Although each of us builds his or her own "individual" or "subjective" culture from the offerings of society, it is clear that no one can incorporate or synthesize that vast array of elements. To that degree, individuality—as the self-styled fashioning of cultural elements—is a consequence of contemporary life. However, Simmel is also very concerned about the quality of such personal syntheses. In his view, the "tragedy" of modern culture is the extent to which objective culture has developed, according to its own logic, principles that have little to do with personal or psychological needs (see Simmel, 1997, pp. 55–107). Like Weber, Simmel is profoundly pessimistic about the possibilities of modern life. Objective culture is being fabricated at an exponential rate, while subjective culture—now little more than an adornment of styles and gestures—lags behind.

Reflections on the Expressive

Such viewpoints ultimately were consolidated as a broad philosophical distinction between "more-life" and "more-than-life" (see Weingartner, 1962, pp. 15–84). The first term in this pair embodies the idea that life is always reaching out beyond itself, changing and growing. While nonliving things tend to change mechanically, through a set of physical causes and effects, living things—and especially the human beings with whom Simmel is almost exclusively concerned—are characterized by a kind of internal awareness of their activity. In particular, human behavior is informed by past experiences. Because of the human capacity for memory and reflection, the past can be brought forward into the present as a set of problems or lessons. Furthermore, although humans are driven by physical needs or drives, they are able to become aware of these and act upon them with that knowledge. Simmel's general point is that human beings understand time—and indeed create it. Our adventures in the present are doubly informed, by our memories of past experiences and by our images of future possibilities. In that sense, the present does not lie at the front edge of experience but in its middle.

However, this process of growth and change is neither passive nor aimless. Rather, it is the nature of human beings to impart "form" to the world. Indeed, the substances or "contents" of life take shape in this way; experience is a process of mental and emotional imposition. However, Simmel also sees that there is a critical tension between life as a "forming" activity and those forms that have already taken shape (see Weingartner, 1962, p. 36). That is, in contrast to a purely subjective view of reality, Simmel argues that there are tremendous varieties of social and cultural forms, which having once been established, acquire a more or less objective status in the world. These stand against or confront the subjective flow of life. Simmel's emphasis on these objects and forms— what he calls "more-than-life"—establishes his view of experience as a dialectical process. Although people attempt to impart form to the world, they are equally dependent on and humbled by it.

Simmel's sociological and philosophical works are really commentaries on the human encounter with form. His greatness as a writer stems from his ability to identify the characteristics of different types of forms and to describe the complexity of our relationships to them. Form-making activity exists at the cultural, social, and personal levels. Forms may be expressed materially and symbolically. Form-making is not simply a matter of thinking or knowing but of acting and feeling as well. People internalize preexisting symbolic forms and use them to apprehend the world; however, they also synthesize these and apply their own patterns.

Although forms are normally patterns of activity or perspectives that we use to achieve our basic needs, that relationship can be reversed. In that regard, a key moment in human history is what Simmel called "the turning" (see Weingartner, 1962, pp. 49–55). This occurrence refers to the point at which humans are able to approach form "non-teleologically," that is, to escape the rule of their own existential necessities and desires. The artist, at some point, does not create in order live but lives in order to create; the philosopher lives in order to know, and so forth. In that sense, freedom entails the ability to participate in (more sublimated) realms of symbolic meaning. People are able to focus on external, "autocratic" forms; creative rendering of form—or alternately, service to it—becomes the issue. In the human condition the worlds of subject and object become divided. Although objectified forms make possible human endeavor of every type, they also restrict and oppose it. To that degree, the object world appears before us but always at a distance. Simultaneously, we stand within and without its boundaries. Metaphorically, forms are the symbolic dwellings we build and inhabit, but those accommodations feel oddly temporary and uncomfortable.

These qualities of experience will be explored by looking at three of Simmel's essays that address the playful and expressive aspects of life. The first is his essay on "flirtation" (Simmel, 1984, pp. 133–152), in which he considers the way in which erotic interests may be turned into a game or art form. In the second essay, on the "adventurer," (Simmel, 1971, pp. 187–198) he describes a type of individual who approaches the events of life—and sometimes life itself—as a form of play. Finally, the specifically social implications of interaction as a play-form are considered in Simmel's essay on "sociability" (Simmel, 1950, pp. 40–57).

FLIRTATION

Simmel's treatment of this topic begins as a commentary on Plato's view of erotic love as the desire to possess. For Plato, eros represents a kind of yearning, an intermediate state between having and not having. Simmel does not believe this conception to be an entirely adequate understanding of love; nevertheless, he develops the theme of longing and incompletion as the centerpiece of his essay.

The "flirt" is someone (for Simmel, female) who wishes to create erotic longing in others. However, this effort to please or entice is by no means equivalent to the wishes of a romantically serious woman to attract a lover. In the latter case, there is a desire to bring closure to the relationship, to complete the process of "having" for both people. "In the behavior of the flirt, the man feels the proximity and interpenetration of the ability and the inability to have something" (Simmel, 1984, p. 134). That is, the desire of the flirt is to keep her suitor in a state of suspended animation, in which he alternately (or simultaneously) experiences the prospects of both accommodation and denial. Put differently, the flirt desires only to manipulate the emotions of her suitors and to study their reactions to her enticements. To that degree, she has the satisfactions of romantic success without having to confront its normal consequences.

As noted above, Simmel's view of social life emphasizes the idea of interpersonal exchange. Socially valued objects are desirable not only on their own terms but because of their inherent scarcity or because of the artificial difficulties set up to prevent their attainment. By making her romantic favors seem both probable and improbable at the same time, the flirt both holds the attention of her suitor and inflates her own desirability. For Simmel, the most commonplace example of flirting is the side-long glance with the head half-turned, often as the woman is walking past. The motions of her body suggest that she is not interested, and yet the flashing glance encourages one to follow. By contrast, the "full, face-to-face glance, no matter how penetrating and compelling it may be, never has this distinctive quality of flirtation" (Simmel, 1984, p. 135).In a sense, flirtation is an exaggerated version of that more general pattern of social relationship found in all of Simmel's writing—to feel both close and far away, to find oneself invited in and then rejected at the same occasion.

This ability to keep admirers in a state of tension and ambiguity can be displayed in many ways. For example, Simmel discusses the use of "extraneous objects," such as dogs, flowers, and children, as props. The flirt may use these to display her capacities for affection and physical intimacy. However, these objects are not the focus of her activity. Rather, they are vehicles to create jealousy in her admirer, on whom she bestows the occasional glance. In the same way, a woman may appear to flirt with one man when the real object of her flirtation is another man who is thought to be watching. Other vehicles include ornaments like clothing, hairstyles, and jewelry. Such devices may seem to conceal certain portions of the body. In reality, they draw attention to them; the covered part is made artificially scarce and thereby desirable. Much superior to complete covering, however, is a certain tension as to whether something will be revealed or concealed. Like dresses with plunging necklines, artistic fig leaves are not attempts at modesty but acts of sexual provocation.

Among the most frequently employed devices of flirtation are words themselves. Although they lack the inherent ambiguity of glances and gestures, words can have multiple meanings and can be said in different tones and contexts. Even more confusing is the intention of the speaker. Does she really mean what she is saying or is she not "serious"? Are her comments directed to all her listeners, to herself, to another admirer, or to me? Should I be encouraged or discouraged by what I hear and see? In such ways, flirtation luxuriates in verbal ambiguity. Such confusion itself would provide little pleasure to anyone. However, the conversation turns on a topic in which the admirers are hotly interested, the romantic availability of the woman. For Simmel, flirtation centers on the role of woman as sexual chooser. In his (early twentieth-century) view, men are expected to pursue women; women in the end must make discriminating choices. Although women lead typically much more restricted lives, they are able to explore the pleasures of power and choice in this particular way. Again, in the view of his time, a bride is seen as someone who resists and then, ultimately, surrenders; a coquette is someone who does neither. To that degree, flirtation pauses and accentuates the first moments in the process of romantic choice.

If the flirt's suitors are serious and she is not, then the activity in question is quite unbalanced—play for her and torment for them. Flirtation as a social form comes into full flower when the man understands and plays his distinctive role. That role is to make declarations of romantic intent that are similarly ambiguous. If there is no genuine interest or feeling on either side, then the whole affair becomes an empty game with no enthusiasm or energy. But flirtation succeeds best when both players recognize the desirability of the other and appreciate these romantic gestures. In that sense, both partners should enjoy the fickle manner in which they are treated. The real pleasures are the satisfactions of the moment and the anticipation of sexual pleasure, which may or may not come. In such ways, flirtation emerges as a sojourn in the meanings of erotic possibility, a form of sublimation. As Simmel explains (p. 144), it is at this point that the "art of *pleasing*" becomes replaced by the "*art* of pleasing."

Such subtle distinctions encourage Simmel to think about the differences between art and play. Following Kant, he argues that art is "purposiveness without purpose" (p. 144). That is, artworks are carefully related sets of elements, explorations in pattern and meaning. Whatever significance these artifacts and performances have for the audience, they bear no immediate connection to action in the world. Like art, flirtation also has this quality of purposiveness without consequence. Participants are entranced by form. However, flirtation is differentiated from art by the relationship of each to reality. Art takes themes from reality and places them into a sheltered context where they can be considered in a focused way. Observers of art know that they have entered a specialized, separate world. Although flirtation also takes fundamental themes of life as its subject matter, it explores these themes in real-life settings. Indeed, flirtation draws its strength from the fact that the genuine motives and feelings of the actors are always unclear. In that sense, flirtation is an elaborate form of play-acting, performed without the benefits of a stage, audience, and script. More curiously still, the actors perform primarily for one another; and no one knows where the play will lead or how it will end.

THE ADVENTURER

Simmel's essay on flirtation is fundamentally a study of the ways in which people willfully make ambiguous their words and gestures. By contrast, his treatment of the "adventure" is a commentary on the meaning of eventfulness in people's lives (Simmel, 1971, pp. 187–198). Thus, the love affair—for Simmel, one of the great examples of the adventure—is profoundly different from the playful bantering of the flirt. To deserve their name, love affairs should express the deepest, most sincere commitments on the part of their participants. Nevertheless, they too are cut away from the routine activities and responsibilities of the world and, in that sense, are different from love itself.

Simmel begins his essay with an analysis of the "event," that stretch of activity-in-time that we formulate in our minds as a relatively coherent or unified whole. That segment of life may be considered on its own terms; that is, "it revolves about its own center, [and] contains as much breadth and depth, joy and suffering, as the immediate experiencing gives it" (Simmel, 1971, p. 187). However, just as we understand events to be more or less unified worlds following their own principles and timing, so we typically place those events into the overall pattern of the life course. This positioning of events within the stream of life is the theme that Simmel develops here.

To experience something as an adventure is to find oneself isolated from the normal activities of life. However, life in general is marked by patterns of discontinuity; one set of activities ends and another begins. Processes of bathing, dressing, and shopping, are hardly adventures. What distinguishes the adventure then is, first, the degree of separation. To illustrate this idea, Simmel compares adventures to dreams. The greatest adventures are so tangentially related to the other elements of life that we assign them a special place in our imagination and memory. In looking back, it may seem as if our adventures were the actions of someone else, or at least a version of ourselves who now seems alien to us.

Still, adventures are different from other profound, dream-like segments of life like illnesses, accidents, and disasters. These latter events are, for the most part, things that happen to us. But the adventure is an occasion when the person somewhat willfully seeks out or decides to remain within that isolated setting. As he (p. 189) puts, it, "We speak of an adventure when continuity with life is thus disregarded on principle." The adventure is an island, far away from the great continents on which we live our ordinary lives; yet part of us wishes to live on this island forever. In this context, Simmel describes the willfulness of the erotic adventurer Casanova, who typically convinced himself that his current paramour was the only woman he had ever loved or ever would. Because of this level of commitment to the moment, the spell of the adventure may not be broken easily. And even disasters and accidents may take on qualities of adventure for people who find themselves oddly entranced by their common fate.

Simmel also emphasizes that adventures are different from not only the trivial interruptions of life but also the chaotic occurrences that we can never comprehend or control. In his distinctive way, Simmel tells us that the remotest, most exotic events are sometimes the closest to us. That is, however curious the people, places, and activities of the adventure, such matters speak centrally to the psychological needs of the person. As in so much of Simmel's writing, this desire of people to comprehend themselves in the ever-changing environments of existence—to provide form to confusing reality—is the driving energy of the adventure. Adventures are thus like works of art. In each case, the maker takes some small segment from the stream of life and works it into a kind of self-sufficient totality. Both artworks and adventures explore, in their respective settings, fundamental issues. Of course—like flirts instead of artists—those who craft adventures are creators of real world events, dabblers in time.

These issues are brought together in Simmel's depiction of the "adventurer," the *ahistorical* individual who seeks out and relishes these experiences. Adventurers desire the isolated and the accidental (what Simmel calls the "extra-territorial"), but they are in other ways the most insular of people. That is, adventurers see exotic events largely as occasions to test character and expand identity. Moreover, adventurers are similar to gamblers in that they actively court randomness or fate. Like gamblers, adventurers believe that ultimately the uncertainties of the world will not conquer or destroy them. With that optimism, they throw themselves into the void. Even the philosopher is, in that way, an "adventurer of the spirit" (p. 194). Like other adventurers, philosophers set off into fundamentally unknown (and unknowable) terrain, buoyed by the generally unfounded optimism that they can bring order to it.

Critically then, the adventure is a "third something" (p. 192) that sits between chance and necessity. At the former pole lies the world of abrupt, seemingly unrelated matters; at the other end are those consistent, well-integrated sequences that seem knowable to us. Adventurers believe that they can make or find passageways through the unknown, can play with fire and be unburned. Such willingness to embrace uncertainty can extend to the whole of life. That is, life itself can be seen as a string of adventures, united only by the psychological constancy of the adventurer himself. Again, this quality of disconnection is not mourned but celebrated. For such reasons, Simmel feels that adventurism is more common to the young than to the old (p. 198). Older people, to his mind, are preoccupied with integrating and restricting their spheres of activity, or more generally in finding meaning in the whole of life. The young are more likely to be fascinated by life's variety and by their own abilities to confront the unknown.

Finally, Simmel suggests that life itself can be seen as an adventure. For this to be accomplished, one must be able to see life as an episode in a much longer, though by no means clearly knowable, chain of events. The true adventurer is buoyed by the belief that the spirit can pass through the murkiest of predicaments, that this particular fashioning of the world is merely an "exclave" (p. 196), which we will taste fully and abandon without remorse. To that degree, the adventurer approaches reality itself in a light-hearted and playful manner. Our few moments of life, however passionately lived, are but interludes in a much longer and more mysterious journey.

SOCIABILITY

The specifically social implications of play are developed most fully in Simmel's (1950, pp. 40–57) essay on "sociability," the autonomous or "play" form of human interaction. As Levine (1971, p. xxvii) has explained, Simmel's sociological descriptions tend to focus on four different kinds or levels of interaction; elementary patterns like exchange and competition, institutionalized structures, society itself, and autonomous play-forms. While human relationships typically develop as responses to the desires and interests of the people involved or to the specific requirements of some cultural domain, the play-forms of interaction are different. In the latter case, social form itself becomes the "content" or focus of the interaction.

In Simmel's view, the great examples of this phenomenon come from the world of play. In his (p. 42) words, "Actual forces, needs, [and] impulses of life produce the forms of our behavior that are suitable for play. These forms, however, become independent contents and stimuli within play itself or, rather, as play. There are, for instance, the hunt; the gain by ruse; the proving of physical and intellectual strength; competition; and the dependence on chance and on the favor of powers that cannot be influenced. All these forms are lifted out of the flux of life." In contrast to other types of activities, the specific actions and objects of autonomous events are chosen primarily because they allow the possibilities of the form to be experienced in the clearest or most satisfying way. In this sense again, play is similar to art. Each becomes constituted as a little world within which certain principles and understandings pertain. Moreover, this separation from material consequences "gives play both its gaiety and the symbolic significance by which it is distinguished from mere joke."

The subject of Simmel's essay is a particular type of play-form, which he terms "sociability." Historically, people have banded together as blood brothers, guild members, participants in religious sects, and so on, and in these settings have experienced powerful feelings of shared circumstance and commitment. The events that Simmel terms sociability are activities (now cut loose from these originating purposes and commitments) in which people gather to celebrate their common connections. Sociability is an exploration into the meaning of community and, more precisely, social form. Simmel's principal examples of sociability are the festive gatherings of his own circle—fancy dress balls, dinner parties, and evenings at the salon. However, his ideas extend to all fundamentally social gatherings—reunions, block parties, baby showers, wedding festivities, charity benefits, church suppers, and so on—where people reaffirm their connections to others.

Like other forms of play (or at least play in its most idealized versions), sociability entails no purposes beyond the event itself. Rather, its "aim is nothing but the success of the sociable moment and, at most, a memory of it" (Simmel, 1950, p. 45). That success is to be understood as a time of collective bonding accomplished through the good will of those involved. So understood, sociability requires that certain psychological traits be brought into play; such qualities include amiability, refinement, and cordiality. Even more critical is the employment of "tact," which for Simmel is the quality of judgment that keeps people focused on the proper purposes of the event.

In this light, Simmel makes the striking assertion that sociability must always be somewhat impersonal. Although the liveliness of such occasions depends on the proper mix of backgrounds, interests, and preoccupations of those attending, such matters must also be kept in check. In particular, differences in wealth, erudition, fame, and social position must be downplayed to support the sense of unanimity. Even more surprisingly, "the purely and deeply personal traits of one's life, character, mood, and fate must likewise be eliminated" (p. 46). Thus, one can be a bore by allowing one's personal preoccupations or interests to overwhelm others. Those who talk endlessly about public issues, ideas, and events commit another type of social error. That is, to focus on cultural content in this way is to miss the point of the gathering, which is to please others and reaffirm the value of all. Simmel frames these matters as two types of "sociability thresholds." To embrace either too much "objectivity" or too much "subjectivity" is to move outside the doorways of the experience. Again, the tactful person is the one who not only can steer the conversation in pleasant but lively ways but can also repair matters when others are being bored or otherwise made uncomfortable.

These elements of unreality and impersonality seem to limit the possibilities for personal expression. Yet Simmel argues that they also heighten these possibilities, albeit in a special way. His example is a lady who wears a low-cut dress to a ball. Although this outfit would be inappropriate in a more intimate circle of friends, the very impersonality and formality of the bigger setting makes such behavior (and related customs of flirting, dancing, etc.) acceptable. In that sense, the woman at the ball appears as a carefully stylized version of herself, much as if she were wearing a mask. More broadly, invitees to sociability circles know that they will be expected to adopt quite specialized (and closely interrelated) roles; people attending bridal showers, bachelor parties, reunions, and so on prepare themselves accordingly.

To describe the ideal relationship between these attendees, Simmel emphasizes the "democratic nature" of sociability. Again following Kant, he formulates (p. 47) a "principle of sociability" in which "each individual should offer the maximum of sociable values (of joy, relief, liveliness, etc.) that is compatible with the maximum of values he himself receives." When the participants in sociable occasions are too different or unequal, this quality of reciprocal exchange is made difficult. However, even when the participants are in reality quite similar in background, the sense of equality is only a fiction that is developed and sustained. As he (p. 48) puts it, "nobody can find satisfaction here if it has to be at the cost of diametrically opposed feelings which the other may have." Although other social situations emphasize good manners as a moral imperative, in sociability these are simply requirements of the form itself.

Again, sociability resembles art or play more generally. In such cases, people do "as if" reality were constituted in a certain fashion. In sociability, one does as if all were equal. This deception is not a "lie" in Simmel's view, but rather a commonly understood pretense. The real lie occurs when participants manipulate this situation to achieve their unannounced purposes, a state of affairs described fifty years later by Simmel's intellectual heir, Erving Goffman. Similarly, the stylized presentation of self at festive occasions is not a falsehood but simply a recognition by everyone that personal concerns must be refashioned to fit the occasion. As Simmel (p. 50) puts it, sociability is a "social game" in a double sense. Not only is the game played in society as "its external medium" but people also fundamentally "play society." Robbed of their normal powers, social customs (and cultural beliefs) are held lightly, twisted, and deflated. What matters most is that the group be made stronger by this process, that social affiliation itself can be shown to be more important than the public passions and proclivities of the world.

Simmel concludes his essay by demonstrating the special ways in which society is "played." He reprises his description of the coquette to emphasize the lightness or ambiguity of commitment that are general qualities of the event. In that broader sense, all of us play with one another's feelings. People should be courted and flattered but they must know that none of this is to be taken too seriously. Similarly, Simmel comments on the distinctive qualities of conversation in such settings. Here, people talk for the "sake of talking." However, conversation must not be mere chatter but rather a collective "artistic" form to which all contribute. Like flirtation, conversation may move forward in spirited ways and then suddenly change directions or be abandoned. Such sudden shifts are not exercises in rudeness but rather recognitions that it is the amusement of the people involved, not the conversational topic itself, which matters. Finally, Simmel remarks on the transient quality of interaction in sociability. People begin conversations with one another, part company, and begin the process again. Party-goers may excuse themselves from one group on the grounds that they are leaving, only to be found conversing animatedly with someone else thirty minutes later. As he (p. 54) explains, "The ways in which groups form and split up and in which conversations called forth by mere impulse and occasion, begin, deepen, loosen, and terminate at a social gathering give a miniature picture of the societal ideal that might be called the freedom to be tied down."

In sociability people experience—in a protected way—the dynamics of social involvement. In contrast to other play-forms, which cultivate the competitive and acquisitive appetites of their participants, sociability emphasizes the themes of joining and cooperation. Society, from this perspective, is an exercise in collective good will. Moreover, sociable interaction with others is to be seen not as a duty but as an act of volition and pleasure. The moral imperatives of real social existence are thus translated into aesthetic matters based on an immersion into artificial social form (Simmel, 1950, p. 54). For Simmel, such forms must not become too artificial or disconnected from the currents of real society, a phenomenon that occurred in the court life of eighteenth-century France. Rather, play-forms depend on the delicate interpenetration—and appropriate sense of distance—between those realms that are serious and fanciful, routine and spontaneous, moral and amoral.

Evaluating Simmel

Surely, among the sociologists considered in this work, Simmel is the one who most resembles Huizinga in spirit and intention. Like Huizinga, Simmel was fascinated by the elegancies of the elite. Both writers chose to focus on culture in its broadest sense rather than on the economic and political passions of their day. Both were critics of the modern world who were preoccupied with the relationship between culture and personal experience. Both emphasized the role of the aesthetic in the character of societies. Both brought an artistic sensibility—expressed in their style of argument and choice of topics—to their academic work. Finally, both emphasized the significance of play-forms in society and were deeply curious about the relationship of these to art, ritual, and the patterns of practical life.

Not surprisingly then, Simmel's work may be criticized in many of the same ways as Huizinga's. As noted above, Simmel's somewhat literary style of writing makes his arguments sometimes hard to decipher or refute. The reader is impressed by the sheer power of his insights and by his ability to look deeply into pertinent examples of human interaction. Still, many of his essays stand as exercises in the "principles supported by examples" tradition of sociological discourse. One learns much about the pervasive influence of shared symbols on human conduct, but these symbols are rarely worked into larger portraits of the overall workings of society. Indeed, Levine (1971, pp. xv) has argued that Simmel did little to spell out the relationships between the social and cultural forms that he described so beautifully.

Similarly, one learns little about the motivations of flesh-and-blood people involved in the social life of their times. Simmel's actors exist as types of people who find themselves in types of situations. Little is said about how people actually bring about or energize their encounters and events. Instead, social existence is largely a process of adjustment to prevailing collective forms. People synthesize these patterns as well as they can but there is always a failure to fit or adapt completely. To that degree, life is characterized by tension and marginality.

For such reasons, some critics (see Collins and Makowsky, 1993, p. 168) have concluded that Simmel's "payoff is aesthetic rather than sociological." That is, his real contribution is his understanding of the implications of certain types of social and cultural forms for human experience. Stated even more broadly, Simmel's work may be understood as a philosophical statement on the relationship between life and form. However, to say this is not to negate Simmel's great contribution, which was to think through the logical implications of different types of social, cultural, and personal patterns. Nor can one easily dispute Nisbet's (1966, p.19) judgment that Simmel was "in many ways the most imaginative and intuitive of all the great sociologists." Perhaps a more useful conclusion then is a statement of what I believe to be some of Simmel's most important contributions to the study of human play.

PLAY IS AN ENCOUNTER WITH FORM

Most commentaries on play have tended to describe the activity as a distinctive type of interaction with objects and people. Thus, we climb mountains, work crossword puzzles, dance with our partners, build castles out of blocks and knock them down, and so on. By encountering the world in this way we discover the boundaries of our lives. However, Simmel's great contribution is his insistence that play is, first of all, a recognition of and entry into "form." However much we wish to conceive of play as an escape from the restricting patterns of the world or even a wild leap into formlessness, Simmel reminds us that players willfully impose limits on their endeavors. That is, to play fully and well, one must accept a framework of understandings about the play sphere; a rock is first base, shirtless friends are the enemy team, three strikes and you're out. Even more critical is his recognition that the "game is on" at many levels. Again, to continue the baseball example, playful activity is more than a physical attempt to hit a ball with a stick and race around bases. It is equally an exploration in the meaning of social opposition and support. Batters sense the will of the opposing team to put them out, the energy of their teammates, the impartiality of the umpire, and so forth. Even more profoundly, play is an acquaintance with symbolic order. At every moment, we learn what it means to take on a specialized identity, to see objects in new ways, to understand success and failure in an altered context.

PLAY IS DIALECTICAL

If players were simply to acquiesce to these forms or march along them to their appointed destinations, the result would be something akin to ritual. However, Simmel's view of human experience (and of play) is more dualistic and tension-ridden than this. At one level, this means that play is an interaction of individual life with the objectified forms of the world. We appraise and manipulate these forms; we test their solidity by trying to evade their influence or by flaunting them openly. We judge these actions by the ways in which they resonate with our own experiences and with the responses of others. In that sense, play always has a tentative, oppositional quality. Our acceptance of the rules and regimens of the play sphere is undertaken in full awareness that we could behave differently. To play is to contemplate the world as an artifice; life operates in the subjunctive tense.

However, more clearly than other theorists, Simmel sees that play is no simple encounter between life—conceived as some untrammeled personal yearning to create or express—and form. Rather, individuals themselves are synthesizing, formful creatures who operate out of these frameworks. We enter the play sphere with our own characteristic patterns of curiosity, desire, anxiety, and commitment. Thus play exhibits the most fascinating interactions between the personal motives and ambitions of the player and the qualities of the object-world. Players drive the interaction forward but they do not do this just as they please.

PLAY IS CHARACTERIZED BY SEPARATION AND "DISTANCE"

Again, the prevailing view of play has been that this activity allows people to pull the world close to themselves, to experience it in more intimate and fulfilling ways than is normally the case. Those who play are said to be engaged or entranced; in the other portions of their lives, people purportedly feel their relationships to be more remote and complicated. By contrast, Simmel argues that play is always characterized by feelings of separation and distance; indeed, this quality is central to the success of the event.

Like Huizinga, Simmel emphasizes the ways in which space and time are reconfigured to help focus the attention of the players. Playgrounds are frequently marked off; players know that they have entered unusual terrain. This exotic quality, however, is problematic. On the one hand, isolation from ordinary experience means, among other things, fewer distractions and interruptions. Play can proceed on its own terms. However, too much separation can destroy play by sheer irrelevance. Like the jaded aristocrats of the *Ancien Regime,* people can discover their own exploits to be pointless and boring. When the gulf between play and real life is profound (as in the more exotic locales of the "adventure"), play activities must speak clearly to the psychological centers of being. Play cannot live in a vacuum; there must always be a connection to what is continuous or ordinary.

Said most generally then, play draws its energy from the tensions of real life. Something must be there to be played with. Relevant issues, beliefs, and skills must be imported to the play sphere. And much of the pleasure of play comes from this sense of dislocation and escape. Players are routinely the possessors of "stolen goods" from their societies, which they have taken to their hideaways to savor and explore. In such ways, players separate themselves from the usual claims of culture and, indeed, from the other portions of their own identities.

This separation of play from other activities or occupations is also a basis for the formation of social groups that are able to distinguish themselves from various categories of nonplayers. Being able to play at certain times and places, in the company of selected others, in certain activities, or with certain equipment—all are capabilities that potentially separate people from one another. In such ways, distinctive play activities display differences in social standing. To play is to make claims about one's own abilities and opportunities and to mark oneself off from all those others unable to join in the fun.

PLAY IS (SOMEWHAT) IMPERSONAL

As we have seen, Simmel tended to stress the ways in which human expression is wrapped in form. For that reason, his accounts of people often make them appear to be abstractions or types. Nevertheless, this understanding—that individuals adjust their behavior to the requirements or logic of symbolic form—is a profound alternative to traditional viewpoints of play. As noted above, play is seen typically as an occasion for spontaneous, even eccentric expression. In play, we can be ourselves. Simmel argues strongly that this is not the case, at least not in the more social settings of play. Human communication requires commitment to a common language, a modification of private impulse for the sake of the whole. Although some disclosure of personal concerns and feelings is crucial for play to gather its collective energy, too much of this is distracting or even destructive. Play is first of all a form; much must be held back so that the proper matters may come into the light.

Moreover, to play is to play a role. Even in private, people adopt stylized images for themselves and move forward in those terms. Collective fantasy requires even stronger commitment to these versions of the self. Players of every age know that they must ready themselves in these specialized terms. Playing fully then is not quite equivalent to working, or loving, or immersing oneself in the deepest solemnities of religious expression.

PLAY IS FOSTERED BY SOCIAL EQUALITY

Like Huizinga, Simmel was less interested in the private creativity of people than in the relationships they forge together. In that regard, he attempted to describe some of the optimal social conditions for play. Of special interest is his claim that play-forms are enabled by social equality. As noted above in the discussion of sociability, too much differentiation or inequality between potential participants makes interaction difficult. Such people may have too little in common to develop comfortable conversations, or worse, they may be unable to forget the patterns of deference that exist customarily between them. Moreover, the satisfactions that they give one another may not be equivalent. That is, one person's expression of enthusiasm or support may be highly valued by the group, another's not at all. Furthermore, even people who are relative peers must work hard to see that social distinctions do not distract from the collective spirit of the event. In sociability, each person must be held to be valuable. Manners and tact are key elements. Injured feelings are indicators of collective failure.

For such reasons, games are based typically on equality of opportunity among participants. Outside statuses are disregarded; games typically begin from conditions of absolute equality. But Simmel pursues these ideas in more complicated ways in his general theory of social life. Simmel's view of social life as "exchange" emphasizes the degree to which people make agreements about the patterns they will follow. Each party must sacrifice certain benefits so that others may be claimed. Even relations between rich and poor or between powerful and weak (see Simmel, 1950, pp. 268–306) are marked by some degree of mutual assent. However, to acknowledge reciprocity in this way is not to claim that each side always benefits equally or that both play equivalent roles. As described in his essay on flirtation, men and women frequently play quite different roles. And people can switch roles, moving from "offense" to "defense." In that light, play-forms are often alternations between giving and receiving, between pain and pleasure. Players find themselves rejected and then, just as suddenly, accepted. Success is made sweeter by opposition and failure. What is critical to the collective success of play-forms is the obligation that participants not only commit themselves openly to their respective roles but also honor the satisfactions that the other provides.

Simmel and Beyond: Studies of Social Distance

One of Simmel's principal contributions to the study of play is his under-standing of the ways in which forms may function as markers of personal or group identity. Social circles—and the cultural forms they practice—are simultaneously devices to include and exclude an array of willing participants. However, Simmel was interested in these matters primarily as a study of the emergence and maintenance of social form. He was much less interested in the economic and political causes of these processes or even in the Weberian theme that historical circumstances and events shape those "types" and make them irrevocably different from one another. Furthermore, Simmel's interest in individuals as abstract categories prevented him from exploring personal involvement and "form-fulness" in deeper and more productive ways. The following section comments further on the role of play in processes of social distinction, especially as this theme has been developed by Thorstein Veblen and Pierre Bourdieu.

Simmel's own thoughts on these matters are presented most clearly in his writings on fashion and adornment (see Simmel, 1997, pp. 187–218). Although clothing has historically been a cultural response to the material needs of its possessors, modern societies are marked by rapid changes in clothing styles for reasons that are largely social or honorific. Especially in settings where large numbers of relatively unfamiliar (and potentially rivalrous) individuals meet and interact, clothing styles are important symbols not only of group membership but also of personal status within groups. In particular among the upper classes in modern cities, fashion develops as a largely autonomous form characterized by artificiality and transience.

For those who would be fashionable, choices of clothing and other aspects of personal "style" (such as hair style, jewelry, use of language, posture, etc.) are parts of processes in which people simultaneously embrace and oppose group norms. On the one hand, people desire to be "fashionable," to be knowledgeable about current trends and to dem-onstrate that knowledge through their selection of objects and personal behavior. Notably, such forms are constantly moving targets. Just as con-tending groups seek to imitate the styles of the day, so fashion-setters must distinguish themselves from outsiders who have the economic and social resources to imitate their style. To be in fashion is to live precari-ously within the present. Nor can individuals easily escape the logic of the system. Those who defy these conventions are deemed simply "out of fashion"; others are located within the changing styles appropriate to their social class or adopt "classic" styles that are themselves indicators of taste and wealth.

Within the fashionable group itself, processes of greater subtlety pertain. The power of the "general style" is such that fashionable individuals do not wish to clash with that style but only to "stand out" from it (Simmel, 1997, p. 191). Truly fashionable people either incorporate the styles of the moment in ways that their poorer or less assured rivals cannot match or manipulate these styles in quite modest forms to show their own taste and flair. For the most part then, fashion is a fundamentally conservative enterprise, a way of showing distinction through the quality of one's conformity. For people like the upper-class women who figure so frequently as Simmel's examples, fashion is a chance to garner the respect of a social circle for oneself (and for one's family) when other, more substantial opportunities are blocked.

More curiously, fashion can be a cloak behind which the truly innovative person may hide. Using Goethe as his example (and perhaps thinking of himself as well), Simmel (p. 200) argues that the appearance of conventionality gives the artist an interior freedom that he or she would otherwise be unable to find. For Simmel, fashion and other types of adornment tend to be relatively transient, impersonal, removable—and ultimately superfluous—forms. They do not touch the center of one's being but are instead gestures to others. Even so, the well-adorned person typically expands his or her sphere of social worth. Expensive jewelry captures (and focuses) the attention of others; expensive tailoring substitutes for other, more substantial skills and accomplishments. Again, such superficial indicators are critically important in the transient, competitive, and semi-anonymous conditions so characteristic of modern life.

Simmel was quite clear that considerations of style extend far beyond clothing and adornment to choices in art and music, personal conduct, opinion, and leisure habits. One straightforward attempt to apply Simmel's insights—and to describe the shifting historical conditions behind changes in style—is my own *Disputed Pleasures: Sport and Society in Preindustrial England* (Henricks, 1991). That work attempts to show how the sporting choices of different status groups—like fashion choices—became separated from their original, practical contexts and then developed as some of the most highly regulated (and thoroughly artificial) patternings of human expression. Thus, sporting activities were as much commentaries on social and cultural form as they were forms of physical exploration.

Simmel's more general treatment of culture focuses on the extent to which symbolic forms somehow escape their originating contexts.

However practical their beginnings, patterns of human expression typically become "objectified" and sustained by their own internal logics. As these forms become more abstract and diversified, the "satisfactions" of participants become more refined and sublimated. Emotion becomes separated from (and ultimately subordinated to) intellectual processes; publicly objectified conceptual models transfigure subjectivity. So constructed, modern culture is both a glittering artifice that cannot be captured or contained as well as a phantasm haunting personal experience. Such is the tragedy of the modern world.

To examine English sporting history is to confront the separation of sports from their practical bases. Activities like hunting, hawking, and the various forms of fighting (such as the military tournament, swordplay, and hand-to-hand fighting) became increasingly disconnected from military and economic matters. Furthermore, these activities became differentiated from one another in the manner of games. That is, each was soon associated with its own set of rules, values, fields of play, material equipment, and honored traditions. This growing artificiality of sports (as play-forms) accelerated in the fourteenth century with the popularization of ball games. By the end of the sixteenth century, general claims for the practical benefits of sports—as training for militias or encouragements of physical health—were losing their rationale. For the upper classes at least, sports became almost entirely exercises in civility, class tradition, and personal display.

Much of this transformation seems attributable to processes of social differentiation or, to use Simmel's terms, to the attempts of groups to articulate their "social distance" from one another. Human beings (and social units of every type) characteristically maintain their identity through complementary processes. On the one hand, people wish to be connected to desirable groups or statuses; on the other, they separate themselves from discredited or threatening others. To maintain social distance is to mark oneself off, to keep identities clear and distinct. In this context, sports historically have been important mechanisms for the maintenance of social distance.

Elite groups in particular wish to make their activities distinctive from those of contending groups. What the study of the English context reveals is the extent to which well-placed groups used the social resources at their disposal—wealth, power, prestige, and knowledge—to safeguard their sports from the incursions of lower status groups. Unqualified people were kept way from many types of sporting activity by law, by considerations of "propriety" or social knowledge, by access to specialized grounds and equipment, and even by understandings of terminology and craft. When contending groups successfully invaded those domains, the elite developed their distinctive sports in ever more articulated ways or chose new, unspoiled endeavors.

By contrast, those "qualified" to participate were ushered into elaborate worlds in which sportsmanship became equated with conformity to strict patterns of social decorum and public belief. Considerations of sociability prevailed. In such settings, playing well meant playing in these terms; distinction was obtained through excellence "in form." Sporting life featured (and continues to feature) a profound tension between social exclusion and inclusion. Such tensions are heightened in the spectatorial forms of sport, when play becomes display.

For such reasons, *Disputed Pleasures* describes public sporting events as "identity ceremonies" in which participants are allowed to compete— and otherwise express themselves—in carefully defined settings. From this perspective, sporting history has very much been a socio-political matter, focusing on questions of who (i.e., what categories of people) gets to perform with—and against—whom in what ways before whom and for what reasons. Certain categories of people have had superior access to the sporting ground and in those settings have been celebrated for their physical and psychological accomplishments. Others have been consigned to the viewing areas or even banned entirely. For those allowed to play, identity is revealed through a process of cooperation and competition. To repeat Simmel's argument, we huddle with socially similar others and then try to distinguish ourselves from them in narrow (and often entirely artificial) ways.

VEBLEN AND THE LEISURE CLASS

Probably the most important general treatment of these matters is Thorstein Veblen's *The Theory of the Leisure Class* (1934), first published in 1899. Like Simmel, Veblen was fascinated by modern people's efforts to distinguish themselves from relatively similar others. However, in contrast to Simmel, Veblen was also determined to show how these processes of invidious comparison emerged historically and how they were related to economic patterns. Central to his argument was the widely accepted thesis of nineteenth-century anthropology (see Morgan, 2000) that societies are evolving through a series of stages (and sub-stages) from savagery to barbarism to civilization. However, progress along these lines is neither simple nor automatic. Indeed, many of the traits of the modern world can be seen as holdovers or refinements of the barbarism of earlier times. In Veblen's mind, the quest for social distinction—and the compulsion to display its attainment—was one of these traits, evidence that contemporary society lingers in a state of advanced barbarism.

Barbarism itself was associated with societies that possessed systems of private property, a division of labor, social hierarchy, and expanding populations. Life was seen as restless and "predatory," centering originally on hunting and warfare but moving on to other forms of seizure and control. Barbarians began to travel more and had wider ranges of social contacts, many of these with relative strangers. Under such circumstances, systems of status display developed. Although the vast majority of the population continued to labor and produce for society as a whole, certain categories of people (especially property-owning groups) became free of these obligations. Thus was born a "leisure class." This social elite focused its energies on what Fernandez (2003, p. 179) terms the "holy trinity" of Veblen's thought: coercion, exploitation, and seizure. The operational mode of the upper-status groups in such systems was the honoring of the military heritage of their ancestors, expanding their holdings, and menacing and controlling those who threaten them. "Conspicuous" leisure and consumption were behaviors and expenditures designed to impress rivals. The relative magnificence of such displays was thought to be an indicator of the levels of surplus wealth and power possessed by the sponsoring grandee himself. Consistently, the size and character of family domiciles, furnishings, staffs of liveried servants, food, travel, entertainments, hunting grounds and lodges, dogs and horses, and so forth, were matters of profound social importance. For under such competitive and unsettled conditions, public regard was everything.

Of course, Veblen's real interest was not the past but rather the conditions of contemporary life. What he saw during the second half of the nineteenth century in Europe and America was the rapid growth of a class of fabulously wealthy business people who resembled in many ways the grandees of earlier times. Like Marx, he was troubled by the relationship of these new "captains of industry" to the productive process. From the vantage point of his rural background and Norwegian ancestry, Veblen understood the good society to be one that honors hard work, creativity, efficiency, and thrift. Indeed, there is, he felt, an "instinct of workmanship" that people widely recognize. To move beyond barbarism, society must honor those who produce in the most efficient and publicly useful ways. Engineers and their machines should guide us in the path ahead.

Unfortunately, modern societies were ruled by a class of rapacious entrepreneurs who cared less about public utility than about their own profits and social standing. Price-fixing, intimidation of competitors, restrictions on over-production that would reduce profits, and other forms of collusion were the order of the day. True competition and efficient production were blocked. In his view, these practices of the economic elite were largely remnants of a barbarism that had shifted onto new "pecuniary" targets.

The Theory of the Leisure Class is fascinating as an account of the devices used by the higher classes to display status, part of a broader system that touched most facets of modern life. The leisure class had shifted its interests away from economic productivity toward four central lines of activity: government, war, religion, and sport (Veblen, 1934, p. 2). Each of these institutions (as well as education, for which he reserved a special invective) was organized in a fashion that protected the interests of the business classes, courted their favor, and otherwise bloated their prestige. As in previous centuries, the world seemed to be divided between those who worked in productive ways and those who did not, and the latter group was intent on maintaining the distinctiveness of their leisure status. Thus, to return to Simmel's example, the fashion of higher-class men was to wear clothing that publicized their distance from manual labor—highly polished shoes, long coats, lustrous cylindrical hats, and even walking sticks. When carried by able-bodied men, the latter "serves the purpose of an advertisement that the bearer's hands are employed otherwise than in useful effort" at the same time that it functions when needed "as a weapon" (p. 363). Even more exaggerated was the costuming of the bourgeois woman. Like captive birds, such women advertised their family status by elaborately plumed hats, high-heeled shoes, long skirts, painstakingly bound hair, and of course, corsets. With their (idealized) pale skin, small hands, slender figures, and fragile constitutions, such women displayed the qualities of essentially interior creatures who appeared not to work. Such refinements were extended within the class of domestic servants, to whom Veblen frequently compared the upper-class women themselves. If a family could afford a huge staff of uniformed servants—who did not work productively but merely waited on family members and maintained their household at extraordinarily high (and thoroughly artificial) levels—then that family must be very wealthy indeed.

At its upper levels, society is driven by largely wasteful patterns of dressing up, parading about, and spending. Moreover, the gentleman or lady of leisure is expected to partake of a whole range of "quasi-scholarly and quasi-artistic accomplishments" (p. 45). Such "immaterial goods," he continues, include a knowledge of "the dead languages and the occult sciences; of correct spelling; of syntax and prosody; of the various forms of domestic music and other household art; of the latest proprieties of dress, furniture, and equipage; of games, sports, and fancy-bred animals, such as dogs and horses." Participation in such forms acquires an almost sacramental character. Moreover, although these accomplishments are the epitome of useless endeavor, they are also difficult to obtain. As he explains, "good breeding" requires years of instruction, application, and expense.

As noted above, the sporting enthusiasms of the middle and upper classes were especially troubling. To play is to spend one's time in economically nonproductive ways. Veblen was not such a Puritan that he despised any activity of this sort; however, he did object to the distinctive cast of modern sport and leisure. He felt that modern sport preserves in a rather atavistic way themes from the barbarian era. Sport itself is not playful exercise or experience, but an activity that centers on predation, competition, and the desire for trophies and other forms of symbolic "booty." Sport is fundamentally about domination and the regard that follows its accomplishment. To such ends, sportsmen cultivate "ferocity and cunning" (p. 262). One does not hunt to "enjoy nature"—as there are other ways of seeking this enjoyment; one hunts to kill. Likewise, athletic sports and games are not merely opportunities to commune with others but chances to prance and rant and swagger (p. 256). In such a view, sports are essentially emulative activities, practices in public prowess. Put differently, sports are forms of regression that seek to return their participants not only to earlier stages in the development of societies but also to earlier stages in the life of the person. In that light, an addiction to sport marks "an arrested development of the man's moral nature" (p. 256).

For Veblen, it mattered little that sports can be surrounded with a variety of other social purposes beyond emulation or that they can entail the most diligent kinds of discipline and calculation. Such goals are only attempts to distract participants from the otherwise overwhelming boredom and unpleasantness of this type of physical exertion by turning the whole affair into a charming fiction—of pseudo-restrictions and purposes. As he (p. 256) famously put the matter: "Sports satisfy these requirements of substantial futility together with a colourable make-believe of purpose." One plays in order to show others that he has the personal capacity—and the time—to do so and to reanimate his personal commitment to an economic system based on pointless competition and reward.

BOURDIEU ON SOCIAL DISTINCTION

In our own era, perhaps the most important commentator on the social foundations of aesthetic style is the French sociologist Pierre Bourdieu.

His understanding of these matters is displayed most clearly in his *Distinction: A Social Critique of the Judgement of Taste* (Bourdieu, 1984). Based on a set of surveys of French citizens during the 1960s, *Distinction* is an attempt to describe the taste-cultures of various occupational categories (what Bourdieu calls "class fractions") and to comprehend these patterns and preferences within a broader vision of social structure. Like Veblen, Bourdieu (who died in 2002) was committed to understanding a wide range of aesthetic choices and behaviors—practices that include reading habits; tastes in radio, television, and cinema; food and drink; decoration and clothing; sport; music and art; and public manners—and to demonstrating the political, economic, and educational sources of those patterns. However, in a style reminiscent of Simmel's subtle arguments, Bourdieu's commentaries are as much analyses of social distance and false choice as they are straightforward accounts of what people prefer.

In my view, Bourdieu is the modern representative of many of the intellectual commitments of Simmel and Veblen. However, *Distinction* is not grounded explicitly in the work of those theorists but is instead an empirical work, in which survey data is the basis for the theoretical flourishes of its author. To the extent that so creative a writer can genuflect to other sociologists, Bourdieu's principal acknowledgments are to Marx, Weber, and Durkheim.

Summarizing the intellectual framework of any writer—and especially a thinker as elusive as Bourdieu—in a few paragraphs is a risky and ultimately unsatisfactory enterprise. However, understanding *Distinction* requires some act of theoretical (if not social and cultural) location. As the subtitle suggests, the book is first of all a response to Kant's (1968) view of aesthetic judgment as something that is natural or inherent in humans (see Allsion, 2001). Like most of the classic thinkers presented in this book, Bourdieu presents what is essentially a type of sociological Kantianism, an attempt to show how human orientations, judgments, and value frameworks are influenced by the social and cultural conditions in which people live. In that light, the "aesthetic gaze" is not a pure form of human relationship with art or culture but instead a product of the viewer's distinctive position in the class system. Furthermore, Bourdieu's work may be seen as an attempt to stand between—and even overcome—the division between two of the great French thinkers of his day, Claude Levi-Strauss and Jean-Paul Sartre.

Following Durkheim and his anthropological descendants, Levi-Strauss (1967) emphasized the way in which the deeper logics expressed in language, myth, and normative code effectively frame thought and behavior. Culture is seen fundamentally as a symbolic order that allows people to notice, classify, and interrelate the phenomena of the world. Within these preestablished frameworks, our individual thinking finds its place. In contrast, Sartre's (1956) existentialism foregrounds the powers and responsibilities of subjectivity. Culture—and meaning itself—is ultimately an artifice created and sustained by interested actors. To deny the status of individuals as creators of that cultural world is an act of capitulation or "bad faith," sacrilege to the self. For his part, Bourdieu rejects both the view of Levi-Strauss that aesthetic choices are basically accommodations to logically interrelated ideas and objects of culture as well as Sartre's position that such choices express the interests and concerns of existentially situated persons. Instead, people's preferences are wrapped in patterns of personal and social commitment, which are themselves worked into the broader arrangements of society. Entangled in these circumstances, we typically reproduce our behaviors in ways that make sense to us and, by those decisions, effectively move society ahead. In such ways, *Distinction* describes the sequestering of people inside specialized social habitats. With our visions so narrowed, we routinely fail to understand the political and cultural choices of differently situated others and angrily condemn them for their ignorance and impropriety.

Bourdieu is well known for his extension of Marx's thought into the realm of contemporary culture or, more precisely, for his combination of Marx's economic focus with Weber's interest in status and lifestyle. In particular, Bourdieu (1993) extends Marx's concept of economic capital to other institutional arenas. Thus, "cultural capital" refers to the possession and use of publicly valued forms of knowledge, "social capital" to advantageous placement within important social networks, and "symbolic capital" to placement within societal models for individual honor or prestige. Other applications include "body capital" (one's location in an idealized system of appearance, age, and health) and "political capital" (standing in the realms of power). In each case, the possession of capital refers to an advantageous stance within those diverse systems that produce and distribute the valued resources of society. Clearly then, human capability is not limited to economic resourcefulness but applies to a much wider range of social possessions and placements that allow individuals and groups to define themselves and pursue their relationships with others.

Like Weber, Bourdieu understood that the resources listed above are somewhat different in character and implication. That is, people may have different sorts of social utility (beauty, artistic ability, skill at sports, etc.) and certain forms of capital may have to be spent or "converted" to get others. Moreover, contending groups frequently tout the value of the distinctive forms of capital they possess. Thus, business people at a social gathering may turn the conversation to discussions of homes and vacations; professors, to intellectual or artistic matters. However, society is not divided simply into little social circles, each with its own standards for what is appropriate and important. Like Marx, Bourdieu understood that politically and economically powerful groups have tried throughout history to control—or even monopolize—the various forms of capital. Thus, domination should be seen not only in its usual (i.e., politico-economic) sense but also as a social and cultural contest, in which groups try to establish ideas about the respective value of different types of knowledge and activity and to administer these at a society-wide level. Not surprisingly, Bourdieu—like Veblen—was critical of the way in which the modern educational system supports this process as a kind of anti-democratic filter, a device that proclaims and cultivates certain kinds of skills at the same time that it stymies the efforts of most people to attain them (see Bourdieu and Passeron, 1977). Thus, repairing sentences or computer programs is deemed superior to fixing washing machines; skill at golf is better than skill at bowling; a thin body is preferable to a robust one.

As indicated above, people see the broader arrangement of culturally valued objects, resources, and states of being from somewhat different vantage points. These orientations Bourdieu describes by the term *habitus*. One of the great contributions of classic sociology is the explanation of how societal values becomes internalized in the minds and manners of individuals; however, Bourdieu's concept is more complicated than this. Like peasants who have worn the same clothing for years, people in general inhabit the distinctive cultural forms and styles to which they have become accustomed. Such formations include our values, goals, and psychological dispositions; the issues that concern us; our skills; our anticipations of pleasure; our self-understandings; our religious and political proclivities; indeed, our sense of what is possible and appropriate in the world. These orientations are not merely cognitive matters (questions of understanding and interpretation) but also senses of moral urgency; feelings of excitement, familiarity, and ease; and even levels of practical capability. Such dispositions have their origins in our families and in the social contexts of our raising. They are perpetuated by the series of social locations that is the life course. Human orientation is as much a set of practical feelings or assurances as it is a catalog of favored ideas. Moreover, action and interaction is less a result of carefully calculated decision-making than it is a sort of human inertia, a moving forward in the ways we feel to be right.

Bourdieu's book is about the rivalry of different occupational subcultures over matters of personal taste and style. In modern societies, these battles take place on many fronts, as there are myriads of smaller arenas or "fields," each with its own more or less public definitions of what is important and successful. For example, the fields of politics, religion, science, education, art, food, music, sport, and so on, are rather different things. These institutional arenas are themselves reducible to tremendous numbers of smaller fields, each with its own possibilities for personal expression. Thus, there are many different forms of intellectual work, sports, cuisine, popular music, medical practice, language styles, and so forth. Not surprisingly, people prefer settings within which they feel competent and socially accepted; a certain bar or restaurant is deemed to be a pleasant and congenial setting; another is not. Furthermore, these choices are driven by the entire history of our self-understandings, by the possibilities for friendship or social support in such settings, and by our economic capabilities.

Aesthetic choice is frequently a process of adjusting private vision to realistic social opportunities. Most of us, to use Bourdieu's phrase, make "virtues of our necessities" (pp. 372–396). If fishing from the bank of a river is what my friends and I can manage at this point in our lives, then we will savor those pleasures and speak of them to others. If we work long hours at an office or factory, then perhaps joking with comrades, playing cards at break, gossiping, or flirting may become the play-forms of relevance. As this book has tried to make plain, human beings have special abilities to construct and inhabit fabulous social worlds. In those settings we discover the nature of our own capabilities and experience the vicissitudes of social regard.

Such issues are displayed clearly in sports participation (pp. 210–225). Here one tends to choose favored activities from the limited menu of institutionalized or "ready-made" forms available in each society. Although these choices are determined to some extent by economic considerations, much more is due to "hidden entry requirements" such as family tradition, early training, obligatory styles of dress, and social-izing techniques. Furthermore, certain sports are understood as being associated with certain social classes historically. However, even when a sport crosses class lines in its appeal (as in the case of tennis), class-based approaches effectively differentiate the activity. Times and settings of play, equipment, coaching and support staff, connection to appurtenant social activities, manners of participants, and so on, mark the version as surely as one style of clothing is set off from another. In addition, par-ticipants' goals for the event, including desired outcomes for the body, may vary dramatically.

Thus working-class people, in Bourdieu's view, tend to favor sporting activities that emphasize strength, endurance, violence, sacrifice, and submission to collective order (as in team play). The body may be approached instrumentally or even roughly; energy, effort, and pain are sometimes acceptable aspects of the experience. In contrast, middle-class people tend to approach sports in more calculating and ascetic ways. Said differently, sports are often seen as opportunities to develop or perfect the body. Team sports at this level tend to be less important than individual activities, which provide structured opportunities for the display of solitary competence and measures of personal growth. This commitment to personal growth or even upward social mobility (along with the associated pattern of deferred gratification) recedes somewhat among the comfortably dominant groups. Gathered together in exclusive settings, upper-class people emphasize themes of fair play and conviviality as well as personal safety and relatively low levels of physical exertion. Gone now are most forms of physical or verbal violence and "anomic uses of the body," such as shouting and wild gestures (p. 217). Instead, participants support a more distanced or intellectualized view of sports that is consistent with their ability to control the many other elements of their lives. In that sense, the cool "aesthetic gaze" of philosophical discourse is in actuality a class-formation. Being disconnected from the grinding necessities of life, the dominant classes have the time, temperament, and training to regard the world in a curious but undemanding way.

Such an array of play-forms and approaches is surely the mark of a vital, complex society. However, among the malignancies of the class system is its determination to rate and grade the different forms, settings, and styles of play. Certain kinds of public amusement, musical and artistic taste, body type, and so on, are put forward as society-wide ideals; others are marked as disreputable alternatives or cheap imitations. Similarly, various social locales—cities, regions of the country, universities, theater districts, social clubs, restaurants, and so forth—are comprehended as being more prestigious or culturally central than others. Furthermore, in an era of mass communication and transportation, people can see more clearly what others have. Bourdieu thus develops the idea of "cultural goodwill," the acknowledgment by lower status groups that the standards and forms of behavior of the dominant group are the ideals for that society. Those who are disinclined to criticize the social order (itself an acquired skill) may conclude that their own activities are not just different from but also inferior to those of successful people.

Again, much of this is reminiscent of Simmel's arguments about the imposition of objectified forms and standards upon experience, the development of distinctive and logically coherent social circles, and the attempts of dominant groups to stabilize their relationships with subordinates. Society is marked by both centrifugal and centripetal tendencies. Groups desire that their identities should be coherent and independent of others; yet they are also drawn, like moths, to glittering social circles in which they will never be welcomed or flourish. Marginality and distance pertain. In that sense, working people play amiably enough with their friends in the social spaces that are their entitlement; but they see clearly the culture palaces of the upper-status groups and contemplate the pleasures found therein.

6 Erving Goffman on Play as Encounter

Few social scientists attain the celebrity of Erving Goffman. His first book, *The Presentation of Self in Everyday Life* (1959), crossed the traditional divide between academic and general readers and changed the way thousands of people thought about their lives. The contemporary world—at least in its middle-class, bureaucratic manifestation—was likened in those pages to a grand "con" or shell game. In Goffman's view, interpersonal exchanges could be seen as guarded forms of "impression-management." Like poker players concealing and then revealing their cards, people in every situation display information about themselves quite strategically. Maintaining a preferred image in public, "saving face," becomes the centerpiece of an endless series of interpersonal rituals in which the performances of others are evaluated for signs of authenticity or guile. In that sense, human conduct is reinterpreted as improvisational theater; communication becomes rhetoric.

Such images were part of a broad intellectual critique of 1950s Europe and America (see Bellah et al., 1991; Cantor, 1997). The postwar desire for security and order—expressed as a new uniformitarianism in business, family life, and political culture—had by that point lost some of its rationale. As the number of middle-class, educated people swelled and the leadership ranks thickened, the claims of the new bureaucrats (now recognized to be quite ordinary people like ourselves) were open to scrutiny. Conformity, in both its socialist and capitalist versions, was suspect. In that context, the intellectuals' assault on business and political culture included existentialism (a wide-ranging claim about the artificiality of meaning itself), soft versions of Marxism that questioned the psychological effects of consumerism, "absurdist" theater and literature, and a host of books from the sociological and psychological community about the dangers of middle-class life. We were becoming, it was claimed, a nation of "organization men" (Whyte, 1956); "cheerful robots" manipulated by a "power elite" (Mills, 1959); and rudderless, "other-directed" creatures hungry for the approval of our peers (Riesman, 1950). Indeed, the very "sanity" of the new society could be questioned (Fromm, 1955).

Goffman's work arose in this context (see Gonos, 1980). In an age marked by the increasing consumption of commercial products, television, and an ethic of advertising, people must become wary of the claims of others. However, because many do not yet see the nature or extent of these forces, the intellectual functions much as an artist or prophet who casts up jolting visions. Goffman's power as a writer derives from his use of what Lofland (1980, p. 25) has called a "perspective by incongruity." Unusual metaphors—of confidence games, casino workers, prisons, handicapped persons, and so on—were pushed deeply into the details of middle-class life. Readers were stunned by the levels of salesmanship and manipulation they found in those applications. Although there was as yet no groundswell for broad societal change, a look behind the scenes at the costuming and rehearsals of the new bureaucrats might afford one a small measure of freedom and self-direction. Realities that cannot be changed may at least be punctured. And in its darker, more Machiavellian application, understanding the props and procedures of others might help us to manipulate them.

Themes introduced in *The Presentation of Self* were developed by Goffman in another ten books over the next twenty-five years. His popularity among both academics and the general reading public is attributable not only to his choice of subject matter—themes related to the slips and errors of life, failures of communication, "spoiled" identity, and the management of emotions under these circumstances—but also to his writing style. Goffman combined a novelist's enthusiasm for the subtleties of experience with the categorizing mentality of a clinician. Each aspect of interpersonal life, or so it seems, is held up for a darkly humored, quasi-objective scrutiny that bridges the typical divisions between social science and art. To read any of his books is to find oneself behind the curtains of public life, to see the underpinnings of taken-for-granted reality.

Goffman's place in this volume derives from his understanding, perhaps deeper than any other modern social scientist, that interpersonal life is always, inevitably, a form of play. Like Simmel before him, he conveys the degree to which we are all actors playing an assortment of roles in the ongoing drama of everyday affairs. However, he also grasps the manner in which we play "at" these roles and "with" other people's sensibilities. Human behavior is a carefully regulated, but nevertheless desperate process of interpersonal confrontation, of move and counter-move. In the judgment of Geertz (1983, p. 24), nearly every piece of Goff-man's writing is dominated by a "game analogy." Goffman may well be famous for his dramaturgical view of society, but his real contribution is his description of social life as an information game.

This view of social reality is given full development in Goffman's (1969) book, *Strategic Interaction* (see also Manning, 1992; pp. 56–71). Because we cannot know directly the thoughts of others, we must make assumptions about their understandings and desires. The empirical basis for our "reading" of others is the expressions (a great range of information derived from their appearance and behavior) that they give off consciously and unconsciously. Interaction may be described as an "expression game," in which people provide clues—both about their understandings of the situation in which they find themselves and about their intentions to act in certain ways. To a large degree, human behavior is self-interested activity; and the ability to send and read expressions well is a power-ful weapon in getting one's way. In this general sense then, social life is played. Like canny adversaries in a court of law, people reveal and conceal, boast and cower, wheedle and cajole. Like players in a game, we make "moves" to cover our thoughts, to uncover the intentions of others, and even to give false clues to throw them off our trail. We do all this in full recognition of the norms governing the situation, the physical possibili-ties for hiding and revealing things, and the abilities of our audience to comprehend and evaluate our messages.

Beyond this sensitivity to the game-like qualities of social life, Goff-man occupies an honored place in this book because he brings together many of the traditions that have been important to the development of play studies. As Burns (1992, pp. 1–16) has demonstrated, this seemingly most idiosyncratic of writers (who rarely emphasized his obligations to others or even the connections to his own earlier work) was marked heav-ily by his own institutional exposures. Born in 1922, this best-known American sociologist was in fact a Canadian, the child of a working-class Jewish family in Manitoba. Undergraduate education at the University of Toronto and a year's work at the National Film Board of Canada cul-tivated a life-long sensitivity to social life as drama. Graduate study in sociology at the University of Chicago exposed him to that department's well-known traditions of symbolic interactionism (in which social life is viewed as the ongoing negotiation of personal identity) and ethnographic study. At Chicago, the subcultures of commonly ignored (and often "deviant") categories of people were analyzed by closely observing their behavior and by recording the language they used to describe their lives. Although always more the theorist than the empiricist in his inclinations, Goffman himself followed this format. At Chicago, Goffman was also exposed to the powerful anthropological viewpoint that social structure is largely an expression of culture, the patterning of material and symbolic resources available to people in society. Indeed, Collins (1988) has argued that Goffman's work should be seen in terms of its continuity with the Durkheimian tradition and not with symbolic interactionism. At any rate, this duality—that social life is not only an ever-negotiated, creative enterprise among self-interested individuals but also a reflection of preexisting symbolic and material frameworks—forms the dynamic tension that characterizes all of Goffman's writing.

Postgraduate study placed him at the National Institute for Mental Health in Maryland from 1954 to 1957. By posing as a hospital orderly, he developed his understandings of how various types of people become labeled and administered through "official" views of reality. Always his sensitivity was to the ways in which people resisted such efforts at control. If life was a kind of prison, then at least the inmates had a flourishing "underlife." In books like *Asylums* (1961a) and *Stigma* (1963), Goffman emphasized the extent to which all of us are potentially discreditable. To be in society is to be subject to administrative control. Even successful people at the center of society can, with only a slight mishap or two, find themselves at its margins.

As a professor, Goffman was centered at the University of California at Berkeley until 1968 and then at the University of Pennsylvania for the remainder of his career. At Berkeley, he was influenced by two traditions that have been important for play studies. The first of these, phenomenology, derives from the philosophical work of Edmund Husserl and Alfred Schutz and emphasizes the rational analysis of consciousness and verbal expression. The second, ethology, explores the social behavior of animals and considers the similarities of these patterns to human conduct. Upon his move to Pennsylvania, Goffman focused on the connection between language and social conduct. His final major works—*Frame Analysis* (1974) and *Forms of Talk* (1981) are assessments of these themes. Goffman died in 1982 at the age of sixty, with many admirers but no school of disciples.

In the following, I describe some of Goffman's contributions to the study of play and games. More specifically, I focus on three major themes: the treatment of games as "encounters"; the analysis of spontaneous involvement or "fun" in games; and the "frame analysis" of play. I conclude with some comments about the continuing significance of Goffman's work.

Games as Encounters

Goffman's book, *The Presentation of Self*, is fundamentally a description of the dramatic ploys individuals use to develop and sustain certain versions of themselves before others. By 1961, his interests had shifted to more thoroughly sociological analyses of interaction patterns. Such matters were explored in *Asylums* (1961a), a commentary on the social situation of mental patients and other inmates in "total institutions," and in a second book, *Encounters: Two Studies in the Sociology of Interaction* (1961b). This latter work relied on a new powerful metaphor of social life: the game.

For Goffman, an "encounter" is a social occurrence, a time when people orient to one another in a face-to-face way. More precisely, encounters entail the following elements: a "single visual and cognitive focus," a "mutual and preferential openness to communication," a "heightened mutual relevance of acts," and an "eye-to-eye ecological huddle" (Goffman, 1961b, p. 18). Encounters are social episodes, moments in space and time when flesh-and-blood individuals meet to conduct their affairs. For Goffman, such interpersonal meetings are the ultimate social reality, where the real work of the world is done.

Goffman's principal interest in encounters is the "single visual and cognitive focus" of the event. What keeps people orienting to one another? How do they determine what they will say and do? What sustains their "we rationale," the sense that they are sharing a moment together and merit one another's continued time and attention? Every sociologist puzzles about the "miracle of social order," that is, the fact that people more or less willingly enter into continuing arrangements with one another. For Goffman, encounters are the great test cases for human sociability. Like guests at one of Simmel's parties, each of us moves through the moments of life. A conversation with one person is started and then abandoned; the participants move in opposite directions and begin the dance anew.

As a metaphor to understand the great variety of human encounters, games "serve as a starting point" (p. 19). For Goffman, games are "world-building activities"; entrance into games connotes a willingness to adopt a restricted field of vision and to follow a specialized set of rules that bears only a marginal significance to the world beyond the event. In this regard, three types of rules are of critical importance.

The first type of norm Goffman terms "rules of irrelevance." Successful games depend on the placement of certain themes and issues outside the boundaries of consideration. To use his example, the expense of chess pieces or of the board itself is of absolutely no importance to the course of play. Similarly, the social status of players, including their previous competitive records, is of no pertinence once the game has begun. Players will use the same equipment and follow the same rules. In that sense, games feature selective inattention or disregard.

Excluding a wide range of issues means that others can come into focus more sharply. In that sense, games employ "realized resources"; that is, certain elements are defined as being "in play." A bottle cap becomes a checker in a board game; a tree, an out-of-bounds marker in a game of ball. Such objects no longer function in their previous sense. Just so, players take on game identities; people become right fielders in baseball, partners in bridge. As Goffman (pp. 19–20) explains: "A matrix of possible events and a cast of roles through whose enactment the events occur constitute together a field for fateful dramatic action, a plane of being, an engine of meaning, a world in itself, different from all other worlds except the ones generated when the same game is played at other times."

As we have seen, other commentators on play, including Huizinga and Simmel, have made similar observations. What distinguishes Goffman's analysis of games is his identification of a third set of norms, what he terms "transformation rules." Games, in Goffman's view, are not separated in clear, distinct ways from the other portions of life. Although participants cut games off from the rest of the world by applying the previous two categories of rules, games in fact have boundaries that are semi-permeable. Certain issues inevitably come through. Transformation rules are devices to deal with these potential interruptions or impediments to the course of play.

In that regard, the president of an organization probably will be accorded a certain degree of deference at the company softball game; women may be treated differently than men. When people inevitably lose their composure or otherwise insert their interests into the affair, there may be standard practices of teasing, consoling, or otherwise "pulling one aside" to restore the focus of the game. Injuries, arguments, changes in weather, phone calls reminding players of other duties, and so on, are all potentially game-breaking affairs. Successful games are encounters that somehow regain their direction and purpose. In other words, it is not enough to have an informal rule prohibiting the discussion of "business" during games of golf or tennis. There must also be practices that deal with such outside concerns when they inevitably arise and then allow the group to regain its shared focus.

At this point, it is important to note two somewhat unusual aspects of Goffman's treatment of games. The first is his desire *not* to separate games from other categories of activity. Instead he wishes to show the similarity between aspects of games and other forms of behavior. To make this point, he develops as an extended example Weber's famous model of bureaucracy. Bureaucracies—or indeed all organizations that attempt to keep people focused on a line of work—employ the same three types of rules described above.

A second unusual aspect of Goffman's approach is his ready acknowledgment of the limitations of games as metaphors for everyday affairs. Games, after all, are different from other portions of life in that games both simplify and exaggerate the themes they choose to address. Furthermore, they often follow a contest-format (embracing only certain aspects of human relationships) and are routinely contrasted with the supposedly more "serious" aspects of life. More pointedly, Goffman sets his own work against traditional "game theory" approaches (see Von Neumann and Morgenstern, 1944). Such theories, in Goffman's view, are too limited to be adequate explanations of human behavior. As he (1961b, pp. 34–35) explains, game theory tends to emphasize the rational calculations made by "sides" or "teams" as they pursue their "interest-identities" in quite narrowly defined contests. To that extent, game theory is about "players" whose task is to select from a possible set of "moves."

In contradistinction, Goffman sees his own work as a description of "gaming encounters." That is, he is interested in the social situation that surrounds the game. In games, people do more than "make moves"; they leave the table to go to the bathroom and answer the phone. They make jokes; they gossip; they try to coordinate the gaming encounter with the remainder of their lives. What intrigues Goffman then is not the role of people as players but rather as "participants"; he wishes to know about the broader set of expectations placed on them as persons who are playing a game. Hence, he is much more interested in the "table talk" than in the actual playing of the cards. In such ways, game playing is less an intellectual event (a question of making right and wrong moves) than a socio-emotional one (where people sustain their own and others' interest in the activity). As he (p. 37) concludes: "while it is as players that we can win, it is only as participants that we can get fun out of this winning."

Fun in Games

As indicated above, analyses of games and gaming commonly emphasize technical strategies for winning. Goffman's descriptions of "gaming
encounters" focus instead on success as social and emotional phenomena.
What is it that binds people together for these fleeting moments, that
makes them commit themselves so avidly to activities of such dubious
importance? As Goffman (p. 39) puts it: "Gaming encounters provide
us with fine examples of how a mutual activity can utterly engross its
participants, transforming them into worthy antagonists in spite of the
triviality of the game, great differences in social status, and the patent
claims of other realities."

This issue—people's level of involvement in their own activity—is
central to much of Goffman's writing. After all, it is one thing to understand cognitively what is expected of you in a social situation, it is quite
another to embrace those expectations enthusiastically. In that context,
Goffman (1961b, pp. 85–152) developed the concept of "role distance,"
the inability or unwillingness of individuals to commit themselves fully
to the obligations of social status. However, he also sees that people may
be distracted or upset by a variety of external events. For example, a person's attention may drift from the focus of the group because of the level
of stimulation. Too much stimulation—a flood of challenges that seem
too consequential for one's status outside the game—produces anxiety.
Too little stimulation results in boredom. In either case, one has slipped
from the "single visual and cognitive focus" that signifies engrossment
in the encounter.

Such matters may remind some readers of Csikszentmihalyi's (1975;
1990) well-known descriptions of "flow." Studying a wide variety of
human activities (chess, rock climbing, surgery, artistic creation), Csikszentmihalyi solicited statements from participants regarding the times
when they were engaged most fully in their own pursuits, when they
experienced the deepest, most intimate connections. A person in flow is
entranced by the necessities of the moment. Indeed, one's concentration
can be so deep that the interaction seems to defy conscious control. In
seeking explanations for this phenomenon, Csikszentmihalyi discovered
that flow was more likely to occur when the physical abilities of participants matched the objective difficulties of the situation. Thus, rock
climbers or skiers look for slopes of appropriate difficulty; chess or tennis players seek their equals. To be mismatched is to be threatened by
boredom or anxiety.

While Csikszentmihalyi emphasizes the role of physical challenges as determinants of involvement, Goffman focuses on the balancing of social skills and challenges. That is, "spontaneous involvement" in any line of activity depends on a kind of social matching, a mutuality of gestures that both stimulates and supports the participants. The opposite of this is a state of social awkwardness he (1961b, pp. 41–45) terms "tension." Tension, as used here, does not mean the quality of tenseness or uncertainty in play. Instead tension refers to a player's perception of discrepancy—between the world that one embraces spontaneously and the "world one is obliged to dwell in." To that degree, tension reflects a kind of social alienation, a feeling of apartness or objectification that occurs when one cannot accept the terms of his or her own involvement.

Interestingly, Goffman's analysis of social tension borrows elements from Freud's (1952) treatment of psychic tension. For Freud, personality was a kind of dark lake. However serene the surface, much—indeed a veritable life and death struggle—is happening below. At times, these elements rise suddenly and break the surface. For Goffman too, people may commit gaffs, slips, and boners that reflect unacknowledged feelings or uncertainties. Of course, for the sociologist, it is not the surface of conscious awareness that is broken but rather the world of social appearances. Although personal concerns provide much of the energy of social life, they must be introduced in skillful ways—or more precisely, in ways that respect the three kinds of rules described above. However understandable the impulse, simply blurting out, "How much money do you make anyway?" is (almost always) to violate rules of irrelevance. To insist that one simply cannot play with an inferior musical instrument or baseball glove is to violate rules of realized resources and to be a spoilsport in the bargain. Finally, people can respond awkwardly to the inevitable interruptions (both situational and personal) that threaten play. Failure to employ transformation rules skillfully ("I can't believe you just said that!") may well end the encounter.

When people's attention is diverted to peripheral matters, the "visual and cognitive focus" of the interaction is threatened. Two such diversions are self-consciousness and other-consciousness. To be preoccupied with personal characteristics or behavior is to be involved only marginally in the encounter. As stated above, interaction depends on the energy and inspiration that people bring to their affairs, but such essentially psychological matters are only occasionally the shared focus. Even in cases where they are (e.g., counseling sessions or intimate conversations between friends), there is still the danger of what Goffman (pp. 55–65) terms "flooding out." In this instance, our personal feelings—shock, fear, joy, embarrassment, boredom—have gotten the better of us. We burst forth with uncontrolled laughter, tears, expressions of disgust or outrage. Under such circumstances, the interaction must be paused to recognize the reaction, stabilized, and begun again after we have regained a kind of control.

Similarly, interaction can be marred by excessive social consciousness. Under these circumstances, we become preoccupied with the social framework, with the various customs that are being invoked or with the social jockeying of the participants. Such matters may be crucially important to the life of the encounter but they are rarely the focus. Even at distinctively "social" occasions, where the fads and foibles of other party-goers may be discussed, too much scrutiny or objectification of one's social setting is a distraction. As Simmel suggested, analyzing distant or "abstract" others at such affairs is one thing; analyzing your current companions is quite another.

To this degree, Goffman's essay on gaming encounters pursues different matters than *The Presentation of Self.* As the latter foregrounds themes of alienation and manipulation in self-experience, so the former seeks the possibilities for connecting more deeply and spontaneously with others. With this end in mind, Goffman considers a range of factors that lead to personal engrossment or even "euphoria." Some of these are stated directly; others are elements that may be inferred from his general approach.

As a factor in personal engrossment, the physical environment of the encounter is itself a determinant of involvement. As Goffman (p. 41) explains, gaming encounters tend to involve face-to-face confrontations. Putting two people across a table, or at arm's length, or in bed together is to place each in the other's gaze. Under such circumstances, very subtle monitoring and control can occur. Indeed, Goffman suggests that two persons may be better than one for maintaining psychological focus. Left to our own devices, attention may wander. The telling remark, gesture, or glance of another reminds us that we have strayed. Clearly, there is much to be said about the physical conditions that promote human connection; but regrettably he says no more here.

Like the physical environment, the cultural environment—the network of shared understandings and procedures—helps people maintain a public focus. As noted above, people are guided most effectively when there are clearly understood rules about matters deemed to be irrelevant, realized resources, and permissible transformations. Groups that know each other well—a small group of neighborhood kids, long-time poker buddies—tend to have these matters worked out. This is especially important in the case of transformation rules. Established groups will know their members' idiosyncrasies as well as the different kinds of interruptions that are likely to occur. Furthermore, the interruptions of one person may be managed differently than the interruptions of another. Every established group not only has a culture but also a history. People are kept in line by the application of this knowledge, and some members of the group are much more skillful enforcers than others.

It has been argued that there are "situational determinants" (both physical and cultural) that keep people focused. However, Goffman wishes to push the issue beyond mere questions of control and compliance. Instead, what causes people to commit themselves voluntarily to focused interaction, to find deep satisfaction in their endeavors? Again, he (pp. 66–67) finds gaming encounters to be perhaps the best examples of spontaneous or "easeful" interaction: "Not only are games selected and discarded on the basis of their ensuring euphoric engrossment, but, to ensure engrossment, they are also sometimes modified in a manner provided for within their rules, thus giving us a delicate tracer of what is needed to ensure euphoria." Goffman identifies a variety of factors that contribute to a sense of fun in gaming encounters. These factors or devices are grouped in two general categories: "uncertainty of outcome" and "sanctioned display."

UNCERTAINTY OF OUTCOME

Goffman notes that games hold people's attention because they are a kind of work in progress. Much of the pleasure comes from discovering or "settling" (by processes of personal intervention) the outcome. It follows then that keeping this outcome unknown until the very end of play will prolong people's attention. One device to accomplish this end is the "balancing of teams." Commonly this is done by the method of selection, for example, by choosing more or less equal sides; however, when equalizing opponents proves difficult, tenseness of play can be produced by "handicapping" (or otherwise weighting the challenges for each side). For example, more skilled players may have to play with fewer teammates or defend a bigger goal. Yet another device is "randomization," the introduction of luck or fate as a central element in the outcome. For example, in certain board or card games, young children and adults can compete on terms of virtual equality because luck is such an important part of the game. Indeed most games (chess being a conspicuous exception) employ luck in ways that help keep the powerful or skillful player at bay.

It should be noted that a premature knowledge of the outcome (e.g., a lopsided score or the awareness that a cheater is at work) is often a game-ending affair. By "skunk rules" or similar devices, players may be allowed to retire gracefully or otherwise save face. More frequently, they begin a new or modified version of the game (e.g., "pressing" or other double-or-nothing maneuvers when one has been beaten in golf).

However important uncertainty of outcome may be, by itself this factor is not enough to ensure engagement in the game. Goffman demonstrates this point with the example of flipping coins. Although a coin-flipping contest between two people typically will produce a tight game in which the status of participants rises and falls, it is likely to be boring or, at best inconsequential. Something else is needed. This other general factor Goffman terms "sanctioned display."

SANCTIONED DISPLAYS

Like other important thinkers on play, Goffman realizes that the most satisfying forms of experience are not separated completely from the wider world. Instead, successful games possess strategic or selective connections. A first type of connection is the employment of more general skills or values. As he (p. 69) explains, the most appealing games are those that grant people "an opportunity to exhibit attributes valued in the wider social world, such as dexterity, strength, knowledge, intelligence, courage, and self-control." To this degree, gaming encounters should be personally and socially "relevant."

Another type of connection is the use of "stakes." By putting something at risk—honor, money, future social opportunities—the participant makes evident his or her willingness to connect the play world to the world beyond. With stakes, people indicate to one another the "depth" at which they will play. However, in contrast to Geertz's (1972) well-known description of "deep play," Goffman argues that the most successful engrossment results from an "optimal" level of stakes. Setting the stakes too high results in anxiety; the mind runs off to matters beyond the event. Setting the stakes too low trivializes the affair. However, determining appropriate stakes is difficult if there are significant differences in the wealth or social status of the participants. Risking a thousand dollars means nothing to a rich person and everything to a poor one.

A related form of sanctioned display is the threat to physical safety. Arguably, there is no clearer indicator of personal commitment than putting one's life at risk. Again, gaming encounters are especially good examples of this, because people in games voluntarily accept physical risk. In descriptions that anticipate Csikszentmihalyi's work, Goffman again seeks a middle course between physical stakes set too high or too low. His example, the use of slope in children's slides or in skiing, is instructive. Activities that are too dangerous (or "steep") lose their playful quality. Activities without any risk rarely challenge the abilities of the participant. Encounters are enlivened by a sense of newness, creativity, and exploration. These qualities of personal risk-taking are magnified when they are incorporated into more public types of encounters. By taking risks in games, people dramatize their willingness to let others (either as opponents or as teammates) intercede in their physical well-being. Players bind themselves together in a common fate. As in the case of money bets, equivalent levels of physical risk seem to promote engrossment. For such reasons, boxing contests should equalize competitors by weight, equipment, and skill.

Sanctioned display can be seen again through the matching of social characteristics. Gaming encounters commonly gather together people of more or less equivalent social "worth." As Simmel noted, people of similar social class, profession, geographical region, and so forth, are more likely to have shared values or outlooks; furthermore, they may already know each other or share friendships. Under such circumstances, value-conflicts or requests for information about the participants are less likely to interrupt the event. Within a framework of general familiarity then, the encounter can be fine-tuned. And, as noted above, socially similar participants tend to have relatively equal amounts of social status (reputation in the community, opportunities for future social contacts, etc.) at risk. Not surprisingly, archrivals in sports tend to be socially similar. Mere facts of geography commonly separate the deadliest of enemies: two similarly sized public high schools from neighboring towns, for instance.

However, similarity is not everything. Indeed, too much familiarity, in Goffman's view, is boring. The exciting party or dance features more than ease of communication; also important is the prospect of intellectual stimulation and the possibility of making new social contacts. Partying with the "same old crowd" gets tiring; dinner conversations between long-established couples can be quiet.

Throughout his treatment of gaming encounters Goffman emphasizes the extent to which such events have boundaries that must be seen as "membranes" rather than as firmly established divisions. A certain level of separation from other events is necessary so that the group may develop and maintain a narrow focus. Too much separation threatens the activity with triviality and pointlessness. Too little separation floods the occasion with extraneous matters.

An example that brings together all these issues is the use of disguises in play. As physical elements, disguises are "realized resources," objects that help create the personas of players. Putting on a disguise signifies a willingness to play, or more precisely, to adapt one's behavior to the terms of the disguise. Thus, disguises are not merely physical but cultural artifacts, pathways for thought and action. However, the level of disguise is also crucial. As Goffman (p. 73) puts it, disguises "must check, but not stop, the flow of socially significant matters into the encounter." Stated differently, disguises are never mere boxes in which people hide. Rather, they function as screens that permit observers to see the generally human traits of the actor, allow inferences about his or her personal identity, and establish a context for the interpretation of character and action.

The successful or "fun" encounter, therefore, is one where people maintain simultaneously the sense of both connection and separation. Players in such settings have not merely abandoned their world but have it suspended, at it were, at arm's length. Elements from that wider world filter in and out. Crucially, the players themselves seem to control that ebb and flow. The rules of the play world are acknowledged but there is also the awareness that these rules hold players only lightly. People can either stop this world by quitting or can redirect it by changing the terms of their involvement. Feelings of uncertainty and self-discovery prevail. And the whole experience feels fresh because we know that the other, more enduring world is just beyond the door.

The Frame Analysis of Play

At the start of every social inquiry is the question posed by William James (1950): "What is it that is going on here?" This issue is of course a special problem for anthropologists. Behaviors understood one way in a certain society may be understood quite differently in another. However, interpreting behavior and events is difficult even within one's own society. Because human interaction is not "caused" but rather guided or developed by actors who are conscious of their own intentions, any given event possesses a multitude of possible interpretations. Activities that seem identical to the casual observer may be found on closer inspection to have quite different motives, norms, and meanings. Such discrepancies are the subject of Goffman's 1974 book, *Frame Analysis*.

In Goffman's world, human events are often not what they seem. Imagine coming across two people arguing loudly in a crowded shopping mall. Perhaps the argument started when one person bumped into the other. Was the initial bump intentional or was it an accident? Is the whole affair a joke that will, in a moment or two, have the participants and audience laughing? Is it a staged event, a scene from a movie, or some kind of store promotion? Is it a form of deception? (Maybe something is being stolen during the confusion.) Is it a test or initiation ceremony of some type? Do the two disputants understand the situation in the same way? (Perhaps one of the combatants is only pretending to be angry.) Does the gathering crowd of observers understand fully what is going on or at least have the same general view of it as the participants? Who is in the know and who is in the dark? Perhaps it is all a dream—or differently again, a daydream. What is it that is happening here?

How people define social situations is perhaps the central issue for symbolic interactionism, the sociological tradition that shaped much of Goffman's thinking. In this particular book, however, he wishes to make explicit the differences between that tradition and his own understandings of people's sense-making activity. Furthermore, Goffman wishes to distinguish his approach from an even more individualistic tradition, ethnomethodology.

One of the founders of symbolic interactionism, W. I. Thomas (see Collins, 1994, pp. 261–262), had claimed that reality is largely a matter of intersubjective definition. That is, if people decide that witches exist, then their behavior will be shaped by such beliefs. Pursuing that theme, symbolic interactionist writers have tended to emphasize the ways in which people develop and then agree to maintain various public understandings (see, e.g., Blumer, 1969). To that degree, human conduct is an ever-changing, creative process; ingenuity shapes the world. However, all this creativity is stabilized and given direction by symbols, the shared understandings of people. Armed with a knowledge of these symbols, even virtual strangers can communicate and develop relationships with one another. While ethnomethodologists agree that individuals actively shape the world, they question the extent to which people actually understand the symbols they use. We all operate with shared meanings, but the meanings themselves are neither very firm nor very clear. Reality for the ethnomethodologist is thus precarious, a veritable house of cards (see Garfinkel, 1967).

Goffman's *Frame Analysis* is a kind of anthropological response to these positions. In his view, the world—both in its material and symbolic dimensions—is much firmer than these other thinkers would have us believe. We are born into well-established patterns of ideas and artifacts that shape our apprehension of reality. People make meaning together, it is true, but they do not do it as they please. Behavior is rooted not only in situations that vary from moment but also in a broader cultural context. These cultural patterns take on special force when they are promoted actively by groups and organizations.

For Goffman, the number of "interpretive worlds" in which we operate is limited. Furthermore, the various contexts of interpretation—such as the dream, daydream, accident, mistake, misunderstanding, deception, joke, or game—are organized within culturally established patterns. Once we determine that an event is, for example, a "game" or a "joke," we have fairly clear ideas about how to proceed from that point on. For the sociologist the task is to enumerate and describe the major types of interpretive frameworks we employ. Seen in this light, *Frame Analysis* is a book about the "sociology of experience," a treatment of the ways in which cultural and situational factors guide people's interpretations of their own interactions.

As before, Goffman turns first to the world of play for examples of how social reality is constructed. During his years at Berkeley, Goffman was influenced by the ideas of anthropologist Gregory Bateson, particularly Bateson's comments on the "framing" of experience (see Bateson, 1972). During the early 1950s, Bateson observed animals in their cages at the Fleishacker Zoo in San Francisco. What impressed him was the way in which animals gave each other mutually understood signals that proclaimed how a set of actions should be interpreted. As he famously put it, a bite is no longer a "bite" when it's a "nip." Indeed, the nip is part of a wider set of signals that instruct the receiver that an action is to be seen as play and should be moved forward on those terms.

In Goffman's own terminology, play activities in animals are examples of the ways in which various behaviors can be placed into new "keys." Much as in music, the treatment of an issue may be shifted to slightly different grounds. Although the basic pattern remains much the same, there are certain adjustments that must be made for the whole affair to move ahead harmoniously. To that degree, play represents a kind of key-changing, in which a basic pattern (e.g., real fighting between animals) is modified.

Based on a review of the ethological literature, Goffman (1974, pp. 41–43) describes the major characteristics of play. In play, the "ordinary functions" of the activity are "blocked"; that is, play fighting replaces such goals as complete domination or even annihilation with other softer purposes. Indeed, the stronger party may even practice self-restraint to ensure a better match. Second, there is an "exaggeration of the expansiveness of some acts." The participants ritualize or dramatize their actions so as to make the nonserious implications of the event apparent. A third characteristic is the "interruption of sequences." That is, actions typically are not carried to their natural consequences (i.e., domination of the loser) but are instead stopped and started again. The fourth trait, repetitiveness, is consistent with the third. Much like Freud's (1957) descriptions of obsessive-compulsive disorders, actions are continually reworked—like knives being sharpened for purposes still unknown.

A fifth characteristic is voluntarism. The charm of play derives from the fact that either party can halt the operation. Yet another trait is role switching. In practices similar to the scenes of professional wrestling, animals alternate scenes of dominance and submission. Voluntarily, players experience advantage and disadvantage. A seventh characteristic is disconnection from the "external needs" of the participants. Behaviors often continue for long periods of time, indeed much longer than the real-life version of the activity. Clearly, some other (perhaps social) purpose is at work. This idea is given further expression in the eighth characteristic. Here Goffman claims that "social" play is preferred. That is, while animals play on their own, these practices usually give way when a potential playmate arrives. Lastly, play is marked by signs indicating the beginning and end of the playful period itself. However mysterious their nature or origins, shared understandings regulate the entire affair.

While Goffman's model clearly draws its inspiration from play fighting among animals, he does not intend its use to be limited in that way. Like animals, humans put on "play-faces." We also play in stylized, repetitive ways. In human play, the ends of actions are cut away from normal outcomes and purposes. We prize voluntarism and encourage a certain equality of opportunity among players. We are drawn to social settings. And most profoundly, we understand that the whole affair is guided by certain rules to which we must abide. To ignore these rules is to pull down the entire event. In other words, actions disrespectful of this context will be found to be incomprehensible or even threatening to others. The socially clumsy person may be left to play alone.

It should be emphasized that Goffman's (pp. 40–82) concept of the "key" implies that there is some more basic or well-established form of behavior to which this modified version refers. Again, to use his favorite example, play fighting draws its inspiration from "real" fighting. In this context, he identifies two basic forms of activity—the "natural framework" and the "social framework." Natural frameworks are accounts of events in the physical world; actions of this type are said to be "caused." Social frameworks, on the other hand, are accounts that comprehend the efforts of human intelligence to control action. Social behaviors thus should be termed "deeds" rather than "events"; they are pulled forward through the formulation and pursuit of goals rather than pushed ahead by blind forces. However, in both cases Goffman stresses the ways in which human beings collectively develop interpretations that make sense of the

world. Sometimes we mix the two basic frameworks or even add interpretations resting on ideas of supernatural forces. To return to our example, most people have some ideas about the nature of a fight, including
its possible causes, the likely course of the event, and the consequences
that may ensue. We can discuss the fight with other onlookers and even
anticipate what will happen next.

Goffman argues that there is an identifiable set of events and deeds
in the world of which we have socially shared understandings. Instead
of focusing on the literally endless ways in which actions could be interpreted, he stresses the more limited, practical (and socially organized) set
of explanations with which people operate. This is also his approach to
the study of keys, the various modifications of events and deeds. His cat-
egorization of keys includes five fundamental types: acts of make-believe,
contests, ceremonies, technical practices and re-doings (such as rehearsals, exhibits, and simulations), and re-groundings (actions performed for
unusual or nontraditional motives). For the current discussion, the most
important of these types are make-believe and contests.

MAKE-BELIEVE

Like other forms of play, make-believe is dominated by a sense that
nothing practical will come of the activity. Instead, satisfactions must
be found in the doing itself. Because there is no practical outcome, participants in make-believe must convince others that this world of short-
term satisfactions is a legitimate place to inhabit. Furthermore, they
must demonstrate that whatever happens is not necessarily to be taken
at face value but should be held at some remove. That is, a child who
pretends to be a mother for the purposes of a game does not take on that
role in its full range of consequences. Other children are asked to obey
the child-mother only because he or she is, within the moments of the
pretense, making some of the claims that mothers make in the broader
world. As there is no "real" reason to accept the actor in this role, the
whole event depends on the effectiveness of the performance and the
resulting compliance of the other actors. Engrossment (or the appearance of this) is everything. Potential participants who fail to recognize
the child-mother are "spoiling the fun." Because this sense of fun is the
principal rationale for what happens, the nay-sayers effectively destroy
the experience.

On the basis of this general understanding, Goffman addresses three
forms of make-believe: "playfulness," "fantasy or daydreaming," and
"dramatic scripting." The first of these, playfulness, refers primarily to
various forms of imaginative role play that sometimes interrupt the flow

of social interaction. Unfortunately, Goffman does not try to categorize the different situations that stimulate this type of playful interruption. He does, however, suggest that people allow themselves to play in this way when it is clear that their pretend behaviors cannot possibly be seen as "serious." To help make this point, he uses examples of the movie star Sophia Loren's "kissing" an airport employee through a plate glass window and of two boxers feigning readiness to fight at a weigh-in. Significantly, the public, formal nature of these two settings helps define the moment as clearly nonserious and provides safety for those who are acting out.

Throughout his treatment of framing, Goffman emphasizes the importance of limits. Often, these limits are socially shared ideas about taste or propriety; activities considered playful in one society or time period are ruled out-of-bounds in others. To support his point, Goffman uses examples of the imaginative mayhem of the upper-class gangs of eighteenth-century London or the antics surrounding public executions during those times. Playful posturing in one society is identified as cruelty, assault, and molestation in another. Furthermore, playfulness is contextual. Insult jokes about one's "mama" are acceptable when the butt of the joke is unknown to the teller or when the themes of the joke clearly do not apply. When the missiles hit too close to home, playfulness ends and seriousness begins. In these limited ways, Goffman peers into a world that every comedian knows intimately—where jokes and playful posturing depend for their success on the targets of the humor, the characteristics of the jokester, the situation surrounding the performance, and the manner in which they are told. In every case, rules of the greatest subtlety apply.

The two other forms of make-believe are quite different from playfulness. "Daydreaming" refers to activities that are typically private and spontaneous. Indeed, they are usually considered to be even less serious than night dreams, the latter being an acceptable topic of conversation. By contrast, "dramatic scripting" is oriented to the experiences of an audience rather than to those of the players. Commonly, these displays are worked out in elaborate detail and practiced for best effects. Such performances are, in Goffman's (p. 53) terms, "mock-ups of everyday life," highly formalized renditions of events that, if they occurred in real life, would be considered extremely spontaneous and improbable. However, even these have strict boundaries. To make this point, Goffman develops the example of pornography, the scripted public presentation of activities generally thought to be informal and intimate.

CONTESTS

For Goffman, the contest is a modified form of the fight, in which the latter activity has been ritualized and made safe. While fights in both animals and humans frequently occur for the clearest of reasons (e.g., to obtain territory, establish breeding rights, or mark status), contests typically develop for softer, purely symbolic reasons. As in the other discussions above, the establishment of proprieties or limits is critical. In this regard, Goffman traces the evolution of rules and equipment in boxing, devices to position that activity as a "sport" amidst changing standards of civility.

Having established the connection between fights and contests, Goffman admits that modern competitions seem to bear little relationship to the bloody battles of times past. Using hockey and tennis as examples, he acknowledges that the equipment and goals of those sports seem completely disconnected from survival issues. In his view, uncovering the historic or mythic roots of the rough-and-tumble games of children may be academically productive. However, most adult play has lost completely its connections to historically antecedent forms. Indeed, he (p. 57) wonders whether contests are no longer versions of once practical encounters but are instead "primary frameworks" in themselves.

For such reasons, Goffman posits a continuum between play and games. Play is typically a temporary transformation of some practical activity. An ordinary object suddenly becomes a "play-thing" and is abandoned just as quickly. Organized sports and games, on the other hand, are the products of formalization and institutionalization. Dominated by rules and instigated by controlling groups, sports and games find places within society on their own terms.

As noted above, Goffman's intention in *Frame Analysis* is to create a sociology of experience, to describe the major socio-cultural patterns that guide self understandings. Playfulness (like its more formal derivative, the game) is an example of such patterns. People at play can anticipate the beginnings and ends of the activity, its likely convolutions, and the predictable pleasures to be found within. Ultimately, the different keys are distinct modes of communication, channels that both construct and permit the expression of public sensibility.

But what if the participants fail to communicate with one another? What if one party deliberately misleads the other? Because so much of Goffman's sociology turns around the possibilities of information control or "spin" by people, it seems inevitable that he would turn his attention to this set of possibilities in *Frame Analysis* as well. Whereas the "key" is an idea based on shared understandings, the "fabrication" is Goffman's (pp. 83–123) term for those behavioral models built on blocked communication and deceit. However, even though one or more of the participants may be kept in the dark (or "contained") throughout the activity, the behavior itself typically follows a model that is thoroughly understandable to some of the participants, to observers who have been let in on the secret, and to those who may be called upon later to pass judgment on those who were involved.

Some of these deceptions are "benign"; that is, the deceiver is withholding information for relatively blameless reasons. Goffman includes here as types a variety of hoaxes done in the name of science or training, fabrications to test character, or other fictions perpetrated by parents for the good of their children. Such "white lies" are familiar enough; and we commonly look away or excuse hoaxes of this type. Other patterns Goffman terms "exploitative"; these include confidence games of various sorts and strategic manipulations by the military and police. His point is that human chicanery, even in its most devious and complicated renditions, tends to fall into fairly well-established patterns.

For our purposes, the most important category of benign fabrication is what Goffman (p. 88) calls "playful deceit." Here he considers a wide range of tricks and pranks under such categories as leg-pulling, practical jokes, and surprise parties. The principal feature of such jokes is the way in which a victim is kept "in the dark" for some period of time and then suddenly made to understand that another, fanciful definition of the situation has been in play. As creators of or participants in such events, we enjoy the sense of inclusion that comes from being in on the joke, the public exclusion and humiliation of the victim, and the spectacle of his or her reactions when the bubble is burst.

As always, Goffman emphasizes that these constructions have culturally defined limits. The joke should not be overly elaborate or continue for too long. It should not be harmful, that is, it should not cause any substantial reworking of the victim's self-understandings or relationships. Typically, witnesses should be present to help define the affair and make it less personal. Furthermore, observers tend to play carefully prescribed roles. If they participate too vigorously, it will seem that the group is "ganging up" on the victim. If the trick is entirely supportive or harmless (e.g., a surprise birthday party), enthusiastic collusion may be acceptable; otherwise, watchers should restrict themselves to "keeping a straight face" and reacting in a good-natured way when the mystery is revealed.

Goffman's treatment here suggests the extent to which a person may become a "play-thing" or otherwise be "put in play." Just as people juggle balls or words, so the intention of the players is not to destroy the object but to explore their own powers and experiences. Most forms of tricking and teasing try to reduce the status of the victim, both in their own eyes and in the view of the public. Cruel teasing wishes real harm, that is, deep emotional distress or a far-reaching loss of face. Subjecting the loved ones of people to public ridicule, damaging valued property, or causing the loss of jobs or friendships is a practical joke carried "too far." However, each group defines the latitude for permissible jokes. Playing "keep away" with a person's shoe may be funny in grade school but not in a corporate office. Joke guidelines vary not only by society but also by age, gender, ethnicity, geographic region, educational level, and so on. And of course, some people—and categories of people—are safer to attack than others.

Finally, Goffman (pp. 111–123) turns his attention to self-imposed fabrications. If people may deceive others for benign or exploitative reasons, they may also deceive themselves. Sometimes we become confused because of inadequate information or because of faulty, though well-intentioned, reasoning. Goffman refers to such states as "illusion." However, self-deception may also be the effect of distinctive physical conditions or more complex sources of wrong-headedness. Here he is thinking of such phenomena as dreams or other disassociated states like sleepwalking, psychotic delusions, hysteria, and trance-like states. At this latter point we leave the world of playful dalliance—represented by daydreams, musings, and the like—and enter the realms of compulsion.

As always, Goffman reminds us that human communication is a complicated matter. Confusions and misunderstandings may arise quite unintentionally or as the result of strategic design. Information about these designs and motives will be shared among some actors but not others. Indeed, people rarely expect to have full knowledge of another's thoughts or intentions. For example, in the "contest," deception—in the form of hidden strategies, fakes, or feints—is an expected part of the game. Some participants (typically teammates) are in on the plot; others are not. To push the argument to its furthest point, people may not even have complete information about their own desires and designs. As the Freudians claim, the conflicts of life occur as much within ourselves as between ourselves and the world at large.

Sometimes these misunderstandings—and the scramble of adjustments they cause—are designed to produce pleasure in participants and observers. Human beings are puzzle-makers. We doodle, fantasize, jest, and scheme. We cast up possibilities and relish the chaos that results. We enjoy "roughing up" real-life victims (the butts of jokes, the losers of games) and then helping them back up when the game is over. At such times, information games become forms of play. However, even well-intentioned efforts to play sometimes escape control. Boundaries are crossed; harm is done. This spectacle of things falling apart never surprises Goffman. After all, we are as much the prisoners of situations as we are the masters of them.

Implications of Goffman's Thought for the Study of Play

Goffman's work brings together many of the concerns of the symbolic interactionist tradition. How are definitions of the situation constructed? Who controls those processes? How does social interaction begin, unfold, and end? Do actors have different kinds and levels of commitment to an event? What happens when there is disagreement or misunderstanding? How is personal identity and experience related to social behavior? The analysis of such matters is the contribution of this tradition to the study of play.

In Goffman's case, only some of these issues are addressed well. As a number of critics have claimed (see Lofland, 1980; Williams, 1988), Goffman's analysis of interaction tends to have a surprisingly static quality. That is, his work seems ultimately to be a categorizing or typifying endeavor. Readers are presented with types of phenomena, modes of relating, sets of causes, forms of experience, and so forth. Rarely are they provided with descriptions of how social phenomena begin, rise to prominence, and disappear. Put differently, Goffman's concepts brilliantly catch people "in the act" but less effectively capture the comings and goings of life itself. In that same vein, Goffman's takes on human beings and their activities always seem somewhat distant and objectified. Although we sometimes hear the language of his subjects as they talk about their lives, for the most part we get the perspective of the theorist. Examples from literature, movies, newspapers, and advertisements are used to assemble compelling descriptions of human predicaments. As we are startled by the insights of the great novelist or poet, so we admire Goffman's formulations.

Other critics (see Gouldner, 1970, pp. 378–390; Garfinkel, 1967, p. 174) have argued that Goffman fails to confront the political dimensions of social life. That is, although Goffman is rightly famous for his descriptions of the ordinary person's confrontations with an increasingly bureaucratized world and for his portraits of stigmatized and otherwise disadvantaged people, he says little about the working identities and machinations of the powerful. And, of course, as a theorist who emphasizes micro-sociological issues, he is thought to neglect the broader structures of power and privilege so central to the Marxian tradition. As the recipient of many of Simmel's intellectual gifts, it is not surprising that Goffman should also inherit his criticisms.

Nevertheless, Goffman's approaches are extremely important for the study of play. Chief among these contributions is his general insight that play is not some minor, easily compartmentalized phenomenon but rather a mode of experience that undergirds all of human existence. Like Huizinga before him, Goffman recognized that play lies just beneath the surface of our lives together. Frequently, it exists only as a latent possibility; at other times, it bursts through the surface claiming the entire moment for itself. On such occasions, life moves into a different key.

Another contribution to play scholarship is Goffman's descriptions of the way in which play itself is situational or contextual. Again, in his view, play activities must not be analyzed as a series of isolated events. Rather, play activities are deeply social "encounters," occasions when people develop a distinctive type of connection to the other parts of their lives. For Goffman, play exists largely as a commentary on ordinary life. Routine skills, values, and responsibilities are seemingly set aside, only to be taken up again in frequently artificial or exaggerated ways. Ordinary affairs are decorated, mimicked, and mocked—chopped into little pieces and savored for the qualities discovered by this process.

All of Goffman's sociological writing examines this tension between the emerging structures of the moment and the more enduring patterns and statuses of the wider world. Individuals are "players" but they are also "participants" in ways that recognize their broader identities; play activities may be spheres unto themselves, but they draw sustenance from the macrocosm around them. In that sense, the play world is a kind of bubble, whose surface can easily be de-formed, penetrated, and burst. His treatment of the norms used to accomplish this separation (rules about matters held to be irrelevant and about realized resources) is a worthy contribution. Even more significant are his depictions of transformation rules. By focusing on the ways in which people deal with external concerns, Goffman helps us see how the bubble is repaired, from the inside, over and over again.

This anthropological sensitivity to cultural norms is expressed also in his ideas about the importance of limits in expressive life. Societies, communities, organizations, categories of groups and persons, all have their standards of what is intelligent, tasteful, and just. As he emphasizes, even the transitory moments of life are "framed" by a complex of rules and ideas that make action within that context comprehensible. Such frameworks are cultural artifacts, preestablished patterns that permit the formulation and evaluation of experience.

Goffman's analysis of "fun" in games illustrates not only the importance of limits but also the precious tension that exists between these inner and outer worlds. Declaring an activity to be "fun" or (rather differently) to be "funny" is acknowledging first that the activity has stayed in bounds—that it is appropriate for the setting at hand. The player who disregards or dramatically exceeds these limits quickly turns the affair into something else—a form of defilement, damage, or disrespect. Furthermore, while fun is stimulated by the tenseness that comes from uncertainty of outcome, Goffman's more general emphasis is on the terms surrounding that uncertainty. "Tension," in that sense, refers to the quality of connection between the play world and its environment. Play is made fun by the feeling that participants have been set free from the claims of the world. However, it is "sweetened" by external matters: threats to physical safety, monetary bets, affronts to personal honor, and so on. Too little connection to the outside world encourages a certain aimlessness that wanders into boredom. Too much connection focuses the mind on external affairs; play becomes work. Goffman's claims about the relationship between these external attachments and the depth of engagement in the event itself merit further study.

Goffman also points to important matters with his accounts of the different roles that people play in encounters. After all, what is play for the golfer is work for the caddy. In a much profounder sense, people are always differentially located. In every situation, we are divided not only by our statuses and personal histories but also by the kinds of commitments, concerns, and information that we possess. Social relationships are fundamentally collisions between these circles of personal worth and order. Goffman's greatness derives from his ability to describe the social marginality or "distance" (see Goffman, 1961b, pp. 85–152) that modern people sense about their own involvements. Like characters in a contemporary novel, all of us exist on the edges of our own experiences with others.

In the end, Goffman should be praised for the clarity and comprehensiveness of his ideas. More clearly than other modern sociologists, he envisioned play as a laboratory for the study of voluntary connections between people. He understood the extent to which all social life has game-like qualities without surrendering to the simplistic notion that games are adequate models for the full range of human expression. His extension of Bateson's concept of framing—including the idea of key— captures the extent to which play and games exist as quasi-independent, comprehensible structures for the organization of human experience. In that sense, he wedded an anthropologist's understanding of culture to the social and psychological analyses for which he is best known. Through his work, one learns that social encounters feature an ever-changing balance between the claims of the moment and those of the wider world, that participants bring into play multiple aspects of their identities. Social life is an endless process of becoming clear about which sort of reality will pertain in any one encounter—understanding what lines of action can be taken and what claims for the self can be made.

Birrell on Sport as Ritual

In an important essay, Susan Birrell (1981) has applied and extended Goffman's understandings of interaction rituals to the study of modern sport. Emphasizing initially the link between Goffman's work and Durkheim's treatment of religious ritual, she develops models that suggest the extent to which symbolic events are negotiations of personal identity in public settings. She explores the theme of sport as character drama and indicates how ritualistic and playful themes combine in sporting activities.

As noted previously, Durkheim highlighted the extent to which rituals—and especially religious rituals—are formal enactments of idealized social order. People participate in such events so that they may feel deeply the importance of society to their lives and understand the distinctive set of beliefs that their society supports. For such reasons, society strongly encourages its members to join together in these ways; images of duty and self-discipline prevail. Critical elements in these processes of public respect are sacred symbols—concrete words, deeds, and objects that bridge the gap between ordinary existence and abstract ideals.

Birrell's writing makes explicit the connections between this approach and Goffman's studies of day-to-day interaction rituals. Whereas Durkheim was concerned with the symbolic idealization of society, Goffman was preoccupied with the idealization of individual selves. Indeed, his work suggests the extent to which individuals themselves may be seen as living symbols, concrete embodiments of society's ideals about what a person should be and do. Much of his writing (see, e.g., Goffman, 1956; 1967) addresses the extent to which people either respect or disrespect each other in socially defined ways. Rituals of "deference" are actions that acknowledge the quasi-sacred status of the other; rituals of "demeanor" are attempts to shore up or otherwise make visible one's own reputability. In addition to his emphases on individuals as "sacred symbols" and on the rituals of everyday life, Goffman departs from Durkheim in another way. For Goffman, rituals are less a "laying on" of moral order than a matter for interpersonal negotiation. In this latter process, public order is both affirmed and re-created.

To Birrell, sporting events are occasions to test and display personal status. Citing Goffman's (1967) essay, "Where the Action Is," she suggests the importance of sports as "action situations," settings in which the unpredictable nature of the outcome forces people to reveal their commitments and self-understandings. Such situations are critical occasions for the testing and display of "character." Her essay explores the way in which four themes frequently associated with character—courage, gameness, integrity, and composure—are evaluated by sports observers. By studying the demeanor of sports participants we learn that character (and public reputation) is not simply conferred but rather won through personal effort. In that light, the most admirable sportspeople are those "charismatic" heroes who demonstrate how an ideal self can still triumph over the difficulties of a contentious world. By contrast, villains and other moral weaklings are those who abandon public ideals, who succumb to private and profane fascinations.

In such ways, sport should be understood as a meeting place of moral order and private interest. Moreover, this negotiation of personal identity (Birrell, 1981, pp. 363–364) is a dialectical process, a type of spiraling interchange between individual prerogative and cultural form. In their capacities as interaction rituals, sports help people acknowledge one another's importance and their common debts to society. As playful contests, these same events allow people to challenge the status of others and in that process to evaluate their own demeanor in times of stress.

In this particular essay, Birrell analyzes personal experience in the fashion of Simmel or Goffman; that is, she spells out the possibilities of a distinctive type of social situation (sport) for the display of character in general. However, much of her subsequent writing (see, e.g., Birrell and Cole, 1994) focuses on issues that Goffman did not address fully. One of these issues is the extent to which gender is a cultural "logic" that opens and closes opportunities for the people who are so categorized. This logic not only transcribes the social situations where men and women operate but also extends into the deepest regions of selfhood and sense of well-being. Returning to the theme of sport, Birrell (1983) describes how female athletes experience quite different sets of opportunities and face different character and identity issues than their male counterparts. Males typically have strong (and even life-long) systems of cultural and social support for sports participation. Parents typically encourage them; schools provide opportunities; ready playmates are at hand; time and resources become available; coaches embrace them; significant others give permission to go play. For girls, these cultural and social permissions are not only somewhat different from the outset but dwindle over the life course. Moreover, the logic of the sporting world may be set up to oppose the prevailing framework for femininity, thereby causing females to make a complicated series of adjustments, re-definitions, and creative assertions unknown to males (see Cahn, 1994; Festle, 1996). At any rate, a one-size-fits-all understanding of ritual actors will not do. Differently defined and situated people will go through the ritual process in different ways and will encounter profoundly different effects when they reemerge in the broader society.

Goffman, it may be recalled, has been criticized for his failure to connect identity ceremonies to wider issues of social structure. In Goffman's work, people are shown interacting from positions of social advantage and disadvantage, but too little is said about the vast institutional and organizational arrangements that limit the meaningful options of those involved. Like many feminist researchers, Birrell (1988) moved away from studies of individual categories of actors—a "women-in-sport" approach—to studies of the social patterns that frame all categories—a "gender-in-sport" approach. To take this more clearly sociological or relational line of thought is to address how these patterns have changed historically and how they vary from one social unit (society, community, institutional setting, social class, age group, etc.) to another. Moreover, to shift from cultural to social matters is to find oneself in the wheelhouse of the modern political economy, to gaze at those very matters of power and privilege that Huizinga so fastidiously avoided (see Birrell and Richter, 1987; Birrell and Theberge, 1994). Such issues are considered in the section that follows.

The Play of Gender: Feminist Studies of Sport

As noted previously, social science research commonly focuses on the general question: Who (i.e., what categories of persons, groups, and organizations) does what kinds of things in what ways under what conditions and for what reasons? However, human behavior is almost never a "natural" or unregulated affair but is instead a spectacle of public permissions and resistances, assertions and compliance. Who one is and what one does are inevitably bound up with patterns of social structure that reach downward from the widest frameworks of society. As Durkheim would have it, we are at every moment both constrained and enabled by our involvement in society. In that sense, the most microcosmic matters of personal experience and daily life are connected to the great issues and organizations of the day. Culture, power, and selfhood intersect (see Hargreaves, 1994).

Few fields of study illustrate these issues better than gender studies. And sport, as Willis (1982) claims, seems an especially apt place to study gender just because it is so often thought to be separate from the more enduring claims and commitments of the social world. As noted in the first chapter, play in its idealized form is characterized by qualities of separation and transformation. In play, people are allowed to be "themselves" and from that vantage point can explore a host of customarily forbidden possibilities. Feminist scholars of sport argue that such a description of play—at least in its application to the real world—is incomplete or even false (see Hall, 1996; Messner and Sabo, 1990; Costa and Gurthrie, 1994). The sporting world—from its simplest and most informal manifestations to the pyrotechnical displays of big-time sport—is marked deeply by themes and influences of the wider society. Moreover, players are hardly natural or free. Instead, they enter the sporting ground with the same socio-cultural baggage they carry about in other portions of life. In sport, we are treated—and treat ourselves—in ways that are not so different from our routine social involvements.

As might be anticipated, feminist theorists and researchers have been the champions of gender scholarship. Although feminist thought is united by its commitment to social justice for historically disadvantaged categories of people and by its special sensitivity to the status of women, that commitment is expressed in many different schools of thought and styles of work (see Boutilier and SanGiovanni, 1983; Hall, 1990; Costa and Guthrie, 1994). In that light, "liberal" approaches (focusing on enhanced access of women to sporting opportunities and resources) are contrasted to neo-Marxist emphases on the patterning of gender relations in capitalist societies, "radical" commentaries on the impact of patriarchy in so many social domains, "cultural" approaches that stress the connections between public meaning systems and private agency, and even more visionary attempts to reconceive gender in a more equitable and humane world.

How do sporting events function as gender ceremonies? One way to organize these issues is to consider them in terms of a distinction between social differentiation, social inequality, and social stratification. Social differentiation refers to the ways in which groups and organizations categorize individuals and then enact procedures to see that these differences are maintained. Three profoundly important examples of this process are sex, gender, and sexual orientation. As Hall (1990; 1996) has emphasized, the biological and socio-cultural differences between human beings are extremely complicated. Nevertheless, a great range of societies employ a binary or polarizing approach in which male-female, masculine-feminine, and heterosexual-homosexual distinctions are defined in quite narrow and mutually exclusive ways. Typically, these conceptual schemes are set forward as public ideals, with the result that only some members of society are able to attain them. Those who realize the standards best are held out as "models" for the majority; while the majority themselves seek to maintain their standing as "normal" people. The remaining members of the population are marked as deviants, people to be reformed or set aside.

These dichotomies are also wrapped together so that only masculine male heterosexuals and feminine female heterosexuals enjoy favored status; other combinations are considered somewhat perverse or unnatural. As Hall (1996) has shown, sport—another quite complicated matter—also has been defined in this narrow and bifurcated way. Although sport in its reality features nearly endless varieties of physical capability and expression, "real" sport in many societies is defined as a set of competitive events stressing individual achievement, ascetic control, aggression, speed, and explosive strength. It is not coincidental that these qualities are also central to the stylized masculinity promoted in these same societies. Thus sport (defined in this specialized way) is frequently understood to be a "male preserve" (Theberge, 1994) or "men's cultural center" (Kidd, 1990). In these breeding grounds, the participation of "heterosexual-masculine" males is solicited earnestly. Males of other dispositions are encouraged to improve or watch. Included in this educational process is the labeling of unsuccessful players as homosexual, feminine, or even female. Even more problematic is the participation of females. With the qualities of "real" sport set forth as they are, women of all types may find themselves labeled as second-class performers, moved to supporting roles, or otherwise marginalized as "intruders" (Bolin and Granskog, 2003). Oddly, lack of athletic success for females may pose less of a problem for gender identification than too much success. Women and girls who are "too good" at sports may find themselves marked as homosexual, declared masculine, or even inspected to see that they are indeed female (see Cahn, 1994).

At one level, it is possible to study these matters simply as different formats for cultural expression. For example, females may be said to confront different value-complexes, opportunity sets, socialization procedures, and definitions of self. Thus Greendorfer (1983) has summarized some of the research on childhood socialization practices. Historically, boys have been exposed primarily to a limited range of toys labeled as masculine, encouraged by both parents to play actively, and discouraged by their fathers from cross-typed (i.e., feminine) or cross-sexed play. Boys frequently play outdoors and in somewhat larger groups with multiple roles. Their activities often feature adjustable rules and possibilities for skills development. Such elements allow them to explore patterns of dispute settlement and leadership formation. Girls historically have been encouraged to play indoors, in smaller groups, and in activities emphasizing turn-taking or solitary repetitive tasks. Rules may be few and quite explicit, thereby limiting possibilities for negotiation and skills development. Through the course of childhood, parental support (especially from fathers) for "rough-and-tumble" play declines.

As Greendorfer notes, such patterns are largely the result of cultural belief systems that continue to change as each generation redefines the meaning of gender. However, narrowly defined gender roles are still powerfully established; and "effective" socialization means that vast numbers of each sex will prefer the somewhat standardized vision of identity, activity, and experience held out to each group. For example, some females (and fewer males) may well declare the contemporary version of sport to be pointless, silly, or even socially harmful and opt instead for differently structured forms of physical endeavor. Other athletically committed girls and women may choose sports that focus on grace, balance, flexibility, and poise—qualities commonly thought to be part of the feminine value complex. Still others may try to recast sporting activity in their own styles and terms. However, it should be noted that individuals who are quite successful within these narrowly defined roles—possessors of Bourdieu's (see chapter 5) cultural, symbolic, and physical forms of capital—sometimes resist the efforts of less traditional people to alter those arrangements.

Again, the historic link between sport and gender can be evaluated simply as a species of cultural pluralism. That is, males and females are tracked in somewhat different ways in societies. The consequences of that tracking system are legitimate matters for scholarly concern. In that context, one can raise questions about the usefulness of having masculinity and femininity defined so narrowly and about the rationale for having certain values included in one gender set and not another. Masculinity and femininity complexes can be evaluated for their respective strengths and weaknesses. Even more problematic is the justification for having a "two-worlds" approach amidst the complexities of an advanced industrial society. The role of media in proffering (and to some degree, standardizing) gender visions can be analyzed. More generally, debate can focus on whether these gender complexes should be expanded, modified, or removed entirely.

However, feminist scholarship typically moves beyond issues of social differentiation to issues of social inequality (see Boutilier and San-Giovanni, 1983, pp. 93–130). In this latter sense, gender roles are seen not only as opportunities for personal expression but also as frameworks that regulate people's access to wealth, power, prestige, and knowledge—that is, to the valued resources of society. As it does for other marginalized groups, "separate" commonly means "unequal." Routinely, dominant groups select the choicer morsels of the social and cultural array; subordinate groups get what remains. Such matters are brought to a head when there are only two categories of people and when these two categories are expected to live together on the most intimate of terms.

In this light, sporting activity is not a trivial affair but an important conduit to what is valued in societies. At one level, this means access to Bourdieu's physical capital—working resources that include health, fitness, appearance, physical skills, bodily assurance, and so on. However, equally important is access to symbolic capital—capabilities expressed in character, personality, and anticipations of social regard. As Birrell argues, sporting events are ceremonial in this critical way. In sports, people can test their physical and psychological capabilities against others. In spectator sports, these tests and displays are made public. When communities choose to support male rather than female participants or link sport with masculine values, the effects are enduring and profound. Sports feature the interaction of selected categories of people on selected terms. When the whole affair is segregated by sex (and by other, less decisive variables), the boundaries for the development and use of social resources are drawn inward.

Feminist scholarship has described how these patterns of restriction vary historically (see Mangan and Park, 1987; Wimbush, 1989; Hargreaves, 1994) and cross-culturally (see Hargreaves, 2000). In that light, some of the earlier beliefs and constraints have been removed; participation levels of girls and women in sports have risen. Progress—or its opposite—can be measured in terms of the accomplishments of famous sportswomen or by collections of aggregate data on the sporting activities of subcategories of girls and women. Studying the ways in which different kinds of people make their way through the sporting world is critically important. Millions of potential athletes never begin their journeys through sport, others drop out quickly, and the rest achieve athletic histories of every description. Without summaries of such activity, social science is merely anecdote.

Nevertheless, to focus on inequality in the terms above is to see social life as an aggregation of individual behavior. Clearly, some people play some games for some periods of their lives or obtain other positions in the athletic world; others do not. That data can be grouped or averaged. By this process, differences between people appear to be incremental or scattered. Furthermore, this approach takes as given the system within which people operate and instead concentrates on ways to empower individuals to succeed in those terms. By such lights, human inequality is shown to be subtle and complicated. However true all this may be, an inequality focus is different from a view of gender as an element of social stratification.

The concept of social stratification entails the understanding that individuals and groups are organized into (more or less) socially stable levels or strata. These levels are patterned (existing as coherent forms connected to other types of social structure), constant (enduring over time in more or less the same fashion), and legitimated by ideology (see Heller, 1985). To occupy a certain strata is to see minor personal differences obliterated. Instead, people become members of a community of shared circumstance. Members find themselves drawn together into characteristic patterns of interaction and communicate with one another about similar life problems and chances. As Weber's and Bourdieu's work makes clear, industrial societies tend to emphasize occupational levels; however, levels of authority, knowledge/education, and social prestige are important as well. The modern class system combines these elements in complicated ways. Although there are opportunities for different kinds of social mobility, the positions that individuals occupy are themselves relatively stable. Because of that stability, people can "locate" one another, assign rights and responsibilities with assurance, and extend appropriate levels of deference. Finally, the entire pattern of ranking is justified by belief systems that articulate the strata and explain why current residents hold their spots. Not surprisingly, the holders of the best positions are often the most energetic in the creation and defense of these justifications. However, such "hegemonic" processes are also made possible by the "complicity of the disadvantaged" (Theberge and Birrell, 1994, p. 327).

As neo-Marxist feminists have emphasized (see Costa and Guthrie, 1994, pp. 235–252), gender is connected closely to patterns of economic stratification. To the extent that a person is unable to support herself economically, certain patterns of dependency are enforced. However, radical feminism has argued that gender is an ordering of its own sort. In social institutions of every type—family life, healthcare, politics, education, economics, science, and even recreation—relatively autonomous conceptions of gender inequality are worked into the assignment of positions and the patterning of relations. In that sense, social life is less a collective agreement of diverse but well-meaning individuals than it is a common encounter with clearly articulated idea systems, which are enforced powerfully at every level of social structure.

As proponents of social justice, feminist scholars of sport are interested not only in describing and criticizing problematic aspects of modern gender relations but also in developing strategies for social and cultural change (see Hall, 1996; Birrell and Theberge, 1994). Such strategies may include the invasion of customarily male sports, with the result that the public meanings of these sports may be reworked. An interesting example of this is the entrance of women into the male-dominated sport of body-building (see Bolin, 1992; Gilroy, 1997). As Bordo (1993) has argued, females historically have confronted stereotypes that seek to objectify and pacify them. Female body-builders counter those ideas by actively "sculpting" physiques that effectively embody such masculine virtues as great strength and large, sharply defined muscles. Furthermore, women lifters participate in the mixed culture of the weight-room. However, female bodybuilders also confront the ideals of "cosmetic femininity"—a pressure to be smooth and sleek, to wear feminine hairstyles and flashy posing attire, and to otherwise stay close to societal ideals for the female form. Indeed, the process of posing itself (especially the elaborately choreographed routine before the audience) is an extreme form of objectification or public "gaze." Hence female bodybuilders operate in the ambiguous or liminal space opened by the dimorphic gender system, both playing at these ideals and being controlled by them.

Other feminist prescriptions include the encouragement of cross-sexed and cross-typed play, new policy commitments by communities and schools, changes in the sporting media's treatment of gender, and the development (and in some cases, reclamation) of leadership positions in the sporting world. More radical visions include changes in the nature of sport itself. That is, although modern societies typically glorify male sports performers and the so-called masculine value complex, there is no inherent reason why sporting activities can not embrace more fully traditionally "feminine" themes such as cooperation, nurturance, balance, flexibility, fine motor skills, and social awareness. Males and females can participate jointly. Such themes as primacy of winning, elitism of skill, hostility to opponents, and physical endangerment can be reduced (Birrell and Richter, 1987). Individuals can be encouraged to create rather than enact established forms. Gender categories can be explored and expanded. Such changes can be honored rather than demeaned.

To some extent, such arguments try to return play to its guiding theme, the discovery and testing of human possibility. In effect, they challenge the nature of the contest format—the very shape of the event and the range of issues and rewards at stake. Perhaps, contestive styles of play should be mixed with more cooperative, integrative patterns. Clearly, there are many possible forms and styles of physical expression that can be celebrated in societies. The final chapter explores the nature of play and connects that form to three other, critically important modes of human relationship.

7 *Play as Human Expression*

In describing the status of contemporary play studies, Sutton-Smith (2004) has recalled the fable of the blind men and the elephant. In that story, several sightless men are asked to inspect the massive beast. Some touch only the elephant's side and declare its possessor to be a wall; others feel the tail and claim it as a rope. Still others embrace the legs and imagine themselves in the presence of trees. Those who touch only the trunk, tusks, or ears provide similarly narrow accounts. In the story, the men are blamed not for the shortness of their vision but for their failures to be more enterprising in their exploration of the entire animal and to communicate those findings to one another. Play scholars, or so it seems, work in similarly isolated ways.

The current book has argued that, at the very least, we should add another—sociological—set of observers to the collection of researchers inspecting the elephant. In saying this, I do not claim any special superiority for the sociological perspective. Rather, sociological thinking is merely one more set of sensitivities that should be incorporated into a wider understanding of play. More provocative perhaps is my argument that the elephant of play can be understood most effectively—and perhaps only understood at all—by comparing it to other, not entirely dissimilar, species of animals. In this context, work, ritual, and communitas have been introduced as those monkeys, tigers, and bears.

However useful these approaches may be, it should be acknowledged that play continues to be a remarkably difficult creature to capture and inspect. Like the fabled elephant, play has many unusual aspects, each fascinating in its way. That scholars should spend their careers mapping just one of these dimensions is not surprising. Moreover, play is an especially evanescent creature. It can appear suddenly at the edge of consciousness and then disappear without notice. Just as quickly, it can turn into other forms of behavior. And play is spectacular in its range of objects and settings. Play can be a moment of quiet reflection or an occasion for public hilarity. It can feature the most careful kinds of scrutiny or be wildly thoughtless. And playing with bats and balls seems somehow different from the play of the mind or the practical joke or the pun or the flirtatious glance or the castle made of blocks (see Sutton-Smith, 1997; 2001).

Such difficulties having been noted, this concluding chapter sets forth a more general view of play as a distinctive mode of human relationship. This formulation is followed by an attempt to spell out some of the connections of play to those personal and social contexts that stand beyond it. The foundations for this synthesis are the ideas of the classic thinkers presented in the previous chapters. To frame the issue in this way is to return to the set of concerns raised by Huizinga himself: What is the nature of play and what is its significance in society?

Huizinga Revisited

Huizinga, it may be recalled from chapter 1, identified play as a "well-defined quality of action" or "special form of activity" marked by five defining traits (Huizinga, 1955, p. 4). Those traits were play's voluntary nature, its difference from ordinary or "real" life, its qualities of seclusion and limitation, its combination of order and disorder, and its connection to secrecy. Understood in this way, play manifests itself as a celebration of human capability, when "an influx of mind breaks down the absolute determinism of the cosmos" (Huizinga, 1955, p. 3). Although many of the sociological thinkers presented in the previous chapters seem to contradict this view—by emphasizing the effects of cultural form, public obligation, and social consequence on expressive behavior—I do not think such considerations negate or otherwise weaken Huizinga's fundamental insights. On the one hand, the sociological contribution should be understood as a specification of the conditions under which playful behaviors occur. On the other hand, the classic sociologists help us to see play in a more abstract and complex way—as a quality of relationship that people have with one another and with the conditions of their lives.

To begin, Huizinga's decision to define play as a special form or quality of action seems well founded. As I have argued elsewhere (Henricks, 1999), play can with some justification be seen as a set of cultural forms that guide activity (e.g., playing rules for checkers or golf), as a distinctive quality of personal experience (e.g., pleasure or excitement), or even as a set of private orientations that players bring to these endeavors (e.g., creative or disruptive fascinations of every type). By focusing on play as activity, Huizinga allowed himself (and later researchers) to ask: What are the cultural forms that seem to facilitate playful interaction? What are the various kinds of experiences that people have in these settings? What curiosities, propensities, and motives bring them to the playground? As Simmel (1971, pp. 23–35) explained, to hold up one aspect of the world as form—in this case, behavior or activity—is to bring all the other elements in as "contents" that inform or specify such behaviors. However, Huizinga himself was not always consistent in viewing play as a form of relationship. That is, comments on the "spirit" or orientation of players, pertinent cultural frameworks enabling play, or even the quality of the experience itself are offered throughout his book.

Although I have chosen to adopt Huizinga's definition of play as a theoretical baseline from which to proceed, I do not claim here that his approach is entirely adequate or correct. As noted previously, Huizinga emphasizes the social contest rather than other forms of playful activity. He caters to the world view of European, upper-status males. He supports the Western preoccupation with creativity and self-assertion but curiously ignores the more private expressions of play. Every page of his book seems resigned to the prospect of public rivalry and related forms of confrontation. Huizinga's players are at bottom warriors, who fling insults, poems, songs, missiles, scholarly ideas, and tennis balls at one another's heads.

Is Huizinga yet another blind man, who has felt the elephant's tusks and declared their bearer to be a fighting machine? Certainly, one must wonder whether Huizinga's *agonistic* view of play can embrace the delicate tracings of the artist, wild runs down the canyon river, imaginative pretense by children, bets cast at the casino or track, the suspended animation of the bungee cord, the lover's dance, and so forth. Perhaps play is too wild and various to be captured in this way.

As stated above, I do believe that Huizinga's conception addresses the fundamental qualities of play. However, I also believe that key elements of that model need to be clarified and interrelated. Moreover, his model needs to be generalized so that it applies more easily to a broad range of playful activities. In that spirit, I examine first the differences between play and what I have called its "opposites"—ritual, work, and communitas—as patterns of expressive behavior. This is followed by an analysis of play as a distinctive pattern of interaction.

Play as Expressive Behavior

As indicated above, Huizinga (1955, p. 4) himself seems to have been torn between seeing play as a "well-defined quality of action" and as a "special form of activity." Although this difference in terminology seems quite modest, it reveals a shift in perspective that is important to explore here. In the former case, play is presented as an action or behavior of individuals. Such people "play" tennis and checkers or "play" with one another. Not surprisingly, this viewpoint has been championed by academic psychology. By such lights, behavior is thought to be the expression of individual disposition, concern, and sensibility. And play, as one species of behavior, is thought to be especially dependent on these sources.

This theme has been addressed by Lieberman (1977) under the rubric of "playfulness," or what she calls the "play element in play." Successful players, in her view, bring something special to their encounters. Through their energy, wit, creativity, spontaneity, and general enterprise, they make play happen. Play in that sense is a "cognitive style," a commitment to transpose circumstances of any sort into opportunities for play.

Although Huizinga eschewed psychological approaches, he recognized that play is dependent on the motives and satisfactions of players. When these cognitive, emotional, and even spiritual commitments are withdrawn, it makes little sense to claim that play exists. However, he also aspired to see play in a more objective way, as a category of activity identifiable on its own terms. In this sense, he adopted the perspective of Simmel and the other sociological thinkers. That tradition invites the question: Does play—as a pattern of interaction—have a logic or "geometry" that differentiates it from other forms of human connection?

To return to the former perspective, it does seem that play is a distinctive form of human expression. People at play approach their environments differently than people engaged in work, ritual, or communitas. In that context, I contend that a playful orientation is characterized by a distinctive pattern of response to two dimensions of personal relating. The first dimension concerns the "stance" or orientation of individuals toward the conditions of their existence. In that sense, play will be described as a *transformative* (rather than *conformitive*) style of subjective expression. The second dimension concerns the role of personal experience in the management of behavior. In this context, play will be defined as *consummatory* (rather than *instrumental*) behavior. In combination, these responses create a fabric of behavior that differentiates play from the other three types.

PLAY AS TRANSFORMATION

In *Homo Ludens* play is said to be an occasion for voluntarism (combining freedom and will) and creativity. To play is to take on the world, to take it apart, and frequently to build it anew. So understood, play for Huizinga is a protest against determinism, a claim that humans need not merely endure existential conditions but can reform these according to their own desires and insights. For such reasons, play—especially in its protected formal settings—is thought to be the engine of history.

Although he longed for the aesthetic wonderment of earlier centuries, Huizinga's view of play is marked by the optimism of the Enlightenment and by the romantic sensibility of the century that followed. Released from customary restraints, humans can fashion beautiful new forms. Order-building activity is thus the natural proclivity, even birthright, of us all. Having acknowledged this view, I do not think that transformation—as the act of confronting and changing the forms and patterns of the world—need always be painted in such rosy hues. In most general terms, to play is to interrupt the flow of events, to seize themes from those and other settings, and to apprehend these themes in distinctive ways. In this process, order-making or "creativity" (really only a judgment about the merits of certain actions and outcomes) is perhaps no more informative or entertaining than behaviors we usually term disruptive.

To state the matter in quite pejorative terms, play represents a scheming or manipulative stance of subjects toward external objects and patterns. It may be argued that viewing play in this fashion—as the imposition of human will upon the world—betrays a deeply dualistic approach to knowledge and experience. In such a viewpoint, subjects are said to oppose the objects of their apprehension. Players create and then feed off the divisions they establish. However, I contend that such processes of separation and reconnection are crucial elements in personal awareness. Moreover, play is merely one mode of reconnection. As will be seen, there are other—equally important—ways of encountering the conditions of life.

If play represents a project in opposition and control, in what ways are these transformative desires expressed? I would cite at least four types of control (see also Henricks, 1999). First is the subject's *control of access* to the play sphere itself. As Huizinga (1955, p. 7) emphasized, play tends to be relatively voluntaristic. Players routinely have some degree of control over when they start their behavior and when they end it. Although Goffman (1961b) describes the various ways in which people help one another stay within the play setting (through uses of his so-called transformation rules), there is still the sense that players have a right to leave should more pressing matters intervene. In such ways, people decide to play.

A second type of control is the *ability to initiate action sequences*. Once inside the play sphere, people assert themselves by starting the various moments of action. As card players take turns dealing, bidding, drawing, and revealing their cards, so players of every type step forward to begin the action anew. Even in activities like gambling or bungee jumping (where the fate of the participant is dominated by external factors), there is a playful beginning. People signify their readiness and then jump, cast, pull, or throw themselves into the void. As we tell others, "It's your play."

Yet another type of control is the *ability to control the activity* once begun. Many occasions have relatively voluntary beginnings; we sign up for activities and then consign ourselves to a chain of events. Play seems different in that participants retain a general sense of being in control, of managing their affairs. When people manipulate small objects for the sheer pleasure of seeing the results of that activity—as when they throw popcorn kernels at a bowl—the world seems truly their own. When the objects and issues at play are impossibly formidable—like the mountains and seas confronted by the great adventurers—issues of control may shift to smaller matters (e.g., physical or emotional aspects of the self) that can be controlled. Whatever the obstacles, play celebrates the abilities of people to defy and manage their surroundings. To "play with" an object is to experience the satisfactions of trying to control it.

A final type of control is the *ability to interrupt action sequences*. As will be developed later, play tends to have a fitful quality. Actions frequently start and stop, start and stop again. Disruption, improbability, and surprise are critical elements. Much of this unpredictable quality comes from the players themselves. In play, people are granted a certain license to confound and tease, to stop the objects of play "in their tracks" or otherwise disrupt their routines. Whether this impish quality is a version of ourselves wishing to escape or simply an expectation (as the sociologists would have it) of the play role itself, it seems clear that play activities commonly feature a mysterious, less-than-forthcoming approach to life. Like characters in Goffman's books, players frequently defy (and are allowed to defy) the best-laid plans of others. Participants routinely bluff and feint, ridicule and shame, claim seriousness and then deny it a moment later. In such ways grander, more public logics are confounded.

How much control is needed for a behavior to qualify as play? Clearly, the more or less "voluntary" decision to abandon oneself to an uncontrollable chain of events—in the manner of Simmel's adventurer—is different from the careful manipulations of a board game or building project. As noted above, some postmodern writers (see Hans, 1981; Kuchler, 1994) have taken the former view—that play is a willing dive into an almost chaotic universe that is itself "at play." Likewise, students of traditional societies (see Handelman, 1990) have emphasized the extent to which players may embrace social and cultural patterns that vary widely in their degrees of orderliness. Although a decision of this type is always somewhat arbitrary, I tend to use the term play to describe those behaviors that feature a relatively high degree of manipulation or resistance by participants. Behaviors that emphasize the entry of people into wider realms of order are described instead as ritual or communitas.

This preference for a more "activist" model of play is perhaps reminiscent of the psychologist Piaget's (1962) attempts to define play as a form of "assimilation," the project of imposing psychic and behavioral order on reality. For Piaget, play is an activity through which young children develop personal frameworks for dealing with the world. Although the bulk of human experience is a balancing act between processes of accommodation (personal adjustment to the forms and demands of external reality) and assimilation (the fitting of those realities into one's own forms and demands), play represents an exaggerated version of the latter mode. Playful children subject objects of the world to their own sensory-motor and conceptual patterns. In "reproductive play," these actions are repeated for the sheer pleasure of mastery. Play becomes a kind of exercise or practice. More complicated is "symbolic play." As children mature, their internal schemas become more firmly established, and at some point these patterns become the foci for purely internal or imaginary interactions. In symbolic play, children take the world into their minds and otherwise control the signifying or symbol-making processes. A stick becomes a truck, another child a fireman. In such ways, people luxuriate in their ability to render the world in their own terms, to subordinate it to egocentric demands.

For Piaget, play is primarily a practice of imposing and (through the results of that process) modifying personal form. However, to see play primarily as a project of mastery or control—as a preening of the psyche's newfound powers—is to miss the other side of the transformative impulse. That is, to transform is not only to stop the world and make it submit to one's demands but also to de-form or alter those processes. In that sense, players wish not only to strengthen their own structures for addressing life but also to watch life adjust to them, to see what it does when provoked. Thus, although the desire for cognitive mastery is one important element in play, the behavior also features more complicated emotional and relational components.

In that regard, few people would claim that play is equivalent to acts of noticing and apprehending something or to processes of mental or physical exploration, in which objects are inspected merely to discern their features. Under such circumstances, the world is indeed controlled and manipulated and the ego is able to reaffirm its own powers and judgments. But the relationship feels dispassionate and static. Nor do simple acts like drinking a cup of milk seem particularly playful. In that example, a portion of the world is taken up and manipulated to suit one's purposes. There is considerable pleasure in performing this complicated task and in experiencing the milk's flavor. Although practices of this type must have been amazing adventures at some point in our childhoods they no longer possess these qualities. Still, as Ortega (2003) explains, it seems wrong to associate play primarily with some early "egocentric" stage of personal development or to argue that play ultimately must surrender to the more "balanced" pattern of cognitive maturity exhibited by adults.

For his part, Huizinga (1955, pp. 46–75) takes the somewhat different position that play is essentially an attempt to *engage* the world, to pull other people or objects into special patterns of communication or interaction. In his perspective, manipulation and exploration are not equivalents of play. Moreover, just because play is a quest for engagement, this project seems different from the desire to destroy objects or otherwise end relationships with them. The playful orientation is not so much a quest for control as an invitation to the world to enter a pattern of confrontation and rivalry. In that context, sheer manipulation—or even "winning"—becomes less important than the interaction process itself. Thus, such matters are not only the fascinations of children but the most fundamental commitments of adults as well.

PLAY AS CONSUMMATION

As noted above, Huizinga's definition of play foregrounds the themes of seclusion and limitation, disconnection from real or ordinary life, and commitment to secrecy. Such traits, to my mind, are merely specifications of a more general desire of players to separate their endeavor from other life activities. Furthermore, this quality of separation is closely connected to the idea that play is relatively self-contained, that it allows people to experience a sense of completion within the space-time frame of the activity itself. For this reason, I use the term "consummation" to describe this combination of exclusivity and internal focus.

In *Homo Ludens* these qualities of exclusivity and focus are described in several different ways. The first of these is the *separation from external consequences*. As Huizinga (p. 9) notes, play is usually separated from the material "interests" or consequences of the world. Furthermore, players typically seek no fixed resolutions of social affairs. When play does lead to such results (e.g., a sandcastle or a new ordering of winner and loser in a game), there is commonly the sense that these creations have little status beyond the event itself. Products are frequently destroyed or abandoned or, at any rate, are of little importance to those outside the play event. Fundamentally, play is a celebration of process rather than product, a place where activity itself becomes the touchstone for personal reflection and self-assessment.

A closely related matter is the *separation from external purposes*. As functionalist theory (see Merton, 1957, pp. 19–84) has made plain, consequences are different from purposes. The practices of individuals and social organizations have multiple effects on society; only some of these effects are intended consciously by the practitioners themselves. It is useful then to distinguish the consequences of a behavior from its abiding rationale. In its simplest versions, play's rationale is the production of certain forms of experience among participants. However, many playful activities have purposes (e.g., finding the exit of a maze, winning a race) that are pursued with tremendous intensity. However, even here those end-states are meaningful only within the context of the event itself. Reaching the top of a mountain first is a profound experience only when one considers the difficulties and limitations confronted by the climbers. Getting there first by means of a helicopter is an entirely different matter. In such ways, accomplishment is locked into the event and is not transferable beyond its boundaries.

This commitment to eventfulness is also supported by the *employment of distinctive cultural elements*. Although playful behavior can burst through the fabric of everyday life at any point, that moment frequently vanishes just as quickly. As Goffman (1961b) points out, the play bubble—that pattern of mutual recognition by individuals that they are players—is quite fragile. Players must develop (often quite quickly) a host of constitutive norms—"rules about realized resources," "rules of irrelevance," and "transformation rules." This acceptance of the play sphere as a legitimate place to spend one's time is afforded also by a set of visual cues. People put on socially recognized "play faces" and otherwise adopt the manner and personality of players. A new definition of "time" (or at least pointed disregard for official versions of that concept) is acknowledged. Curious costumes and theatrical accessories may be employed. Space is claimed and then reorganized. By such processes, play is stabilized and made coherent.

A final element is the extent to which players become conscious that they are at play. This *separation by awareness* is, in essence, the recognition by participants that something new is afoot and that there should be a commitment by them to move the action ahead on those terms. As Bateson (1971) notes, animal species seem to know when they are at play. They acknowledge their willingness to participate and then communicate just as clearly that they have had enough. The fact that there are frequently disagreements among players about who should play, when to play, how to play, and so forth, only makes more evident the extent to which play is a matter of conscious construction.

Finally, this awareness that people have chosen to set themselves apart in a curiously elaborate (and perhaps trivial) activity encourages a sense of secrecy (see Huizinga, 1955, pp. 12–13). To play privately or publicly is, often, to "steal time" from more pressing endeavors—and in the process to upset the normal standards for what is important. What seems foolish to outsiders can sometimes only be appreciated within the arcane logic of the event. Insiders recognize that they have gathered together in something unusual and to that degree stand against the world.

Students of play may disagree about the degrees and types of separation that are defining elements of play events. My view is that perhaps only the first two themes—separation by purpose and by consequence—are defining aspects of a playful orientation. To some extent, human activities of every type—the workday, the lover's spat, the church service, the evening meal—are separated or bounded. How else are people to make sense of the world, to know when one set of behaviors ends and another begins? We all use distinctive codes and artifacts so that we can operate in different settings. For example, going to work for many people means putting on special clothing, arriving at a certain time, showing a badge at the gate, taking one's position in a curiously configured building, and so forth. Likewise, few activities are separated more carefully from ordinary affairs than sacred rituals. Indeed, much of the power of these rituals derives from the sense that their guiding symbols and practices seem fantastical and remote.

A related issue is the separation by awareness, the sense that one is in a setting quite different from ordinary affairs or, at least, from other possible settings. Such awareness, in my view, is only the perceptual equivalent of eventfulness itself. That is, people are also aware that they are on the job, in the shower, doing the laundry, and so on. Huizinga and the other proponents of play have been right to insist that play can be a little world of its own type, a special zone where people conduct themselves in distinctive ways. However, like Bateson's monkeys, we not only put on play-faces but faces appropriate to doing work, making love, giving advice, brushing teeth, and so forth. Life is a sequence of behaviors and we are aware when we move from one to the next.

What does seem distinctive about play is the degree to which the characteristic rationale for the activity—its subjectively comprehended reasons for existence—is contained or restricted within the activity itself. To play is to acknowledge that this restricted sphere is a legitimate place to operate, that people can passionately pursue objectives here without interference or condemnation from other spheres. There will be personal or social consequences for what occurs—be these consequences public embarrassment, experiences of success or failure, feelings of animosity, or understandings of allegiance or support; however, these consequences are for the most part kept "in the room."

Saying that play is focused on event-generated awareness and understandings still does not capture precisely the orientation of players or the spirit of play. After all, many activities (taking a bath, going to a movie, walking in the rain) are attempts to find satisfying experience but we do not think of them as play. And other activities have event-driven goals (filling in a crossword puzzle, completing an exercise regimen, singing the lyrics to a song) but again do not seem particularly playful in spirit. It seems critical then to see play as transformative not only in an objective or external way but also in subjective or emotional terms. That is, just as players seek reactions from the world by their assertive behavior, so they provoke their own emotional reactions.

This viewpoint—of play as a pattern of intra-psychic assertion and adjustment—has been developed by Sutton-Smith (2003). In that approach, play is thought to be a type of intersection between the more rational, neocortical aspects of the psyche and older, more organically generated emotions. Thus the various forms of play are attempts to call out and control such universally recognized emotions as happiness, surprise, sadness, anger, disgust, and fear. In play, we reacquaint ourselves with these fundamental aspects of our nature at the same time that we reenforce our abilities to keep them in check. Again, the playful project is not only to stir up these monsters inside us but also to see how well we react to them and whether we can control their powers.

Sutton-Smith's approach also addresses the question of what kinds of emotional reactions are pertinent to play. Although play is commonly thought to be a land of happy surprises, clearly the activity can be onerous and mean-spirited as well. However exhilarating or anxiety-producing the wave of sensations, it does seem that play is satisfying in that players find some pleasure in their abilities to confront and manage these issues. Critically then, players not only register and respond to their own sensations but seek them out in an active way. On the basis of such satisfactions, play is sustained.

To say all this is only to claim that play is a deeply phenomenological as well as behavioral affair, a process of cognitive awareness and assessment of the self in action. Private experience is ultimately a balancing or coordination of moments of assertion and reflection. We commit ourselves to actions in the world and survey the effects of those actions. At times, consciousness is directed inward, at our own processes of sensation and conception. In such ways, we are able to objectify our own selves not only as objects in the world but also as subjects. Like people gazing into a series of endlessly reflecting mirrors, we watch ourselves in the act of watching—and become conscious of consciousness itself.

Play is consummatory then in the sense that players desire moments of emotional and cognitive completion. We apprehend ourselves in the midst of action, evaluate the satisfactions of certain behavioral and emotional positions, and assert ourselves again. But play is much more than a carefully monitored process of watching and adjusting to the happenings of the world. Rather, players dance between the rational and nonrational realms of experience. We find ourselves slipping in and out of control; emotion catches us off-guard and nearly overwhelms us. As Huizinga (1955, p. 2) put it, the essence of play lies in this curious "power of maddening."

Play Compared to Other Forms of Expressive Behavior

To this point, I have argued that the term "play" should not be applied to every type of behavior that is bounded, spirited, and emotionally satisfying. Other forms of behavior display many of these same traits. Instead, play is to be distinguished by its special combination of the themes of transformation and consummation. These distinctive qualities can be shown most easily by means of a typology.

The first axis of the diagram suggests the polarity between the *transformative* orientation described above and its opposite, the *conformitive* mode. Play and work are identified as transformative enterprises, ritual and communitas as conformitive ones. The second axis describes the rationale of the participants. Play and communitas share the *consumma-*

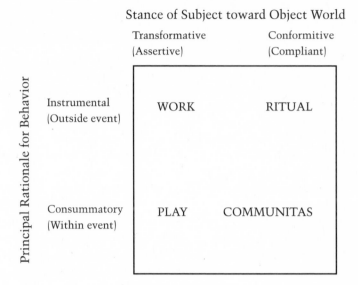

Figure 1. Modes of Expressive Behavior

tory position, within which psychological and behavioral states become the guiding ends of action. At the opposite pole is *instrumentalism*, the extent to which ends are elements of wider fields of action. Although these four modes of individual orientation are presented in ideal-typical terms, boundary lines between the types have not been drawn. Although some personal behaviors approximate these four stations, many more are combinations of these themes; and others feature alternations from one of these orientations to another.

PLAY AND WORK AS RIVAL FORMS
OF TRANSFORMATION

So far, attention has been placed on play as a transformative mode of encounter. The impulse to oppose and control is also exhibited in the other great transformative mode of relationship—work. As may be recalled from chapter 2, Marx's view of labor echoes themes from Huizinga. On the basis of their needs and interests, humans confront and shape the world. The products we create are ultimately mirrors of our own personal abilities and qualities. We refashion the world so that we may learn about it and in the bargain, discover ourselves. For Marx as for Huizinga, this transformative activity is a kind of human birthright. People should initiate, control, and otherwise reap the satisfactions of their renderings.

As indicated in the figure, work differs from play in that the former emphasizes products and outcomes. Creative labor thus acquires a broader (or at least more public) meaning than creative play. Things are made and take their places in the world. Services are performed; life opportunities are changed. In such ways, work is consequential. Play, on the other hand, speaks primarily in symbolic and experiential terms to those caught in the moments of creation.

As play is the consummatory mode of transformation, so work is its instrumental equivalent. Players affirm that they are willing to live inside the boundaries of events and, as part of that process, to acknowledge only the present. Like Simmel's adventurers, players proclaim that there is only one thing in the world that matters—and that thing is happening now. By contrast, work typically overruns boundaries. Work is thought to be "serious" or important, something more for adults than for children. Work is consequential; work is purposive. People "make" themselves work in a way that rarely applies to play. Frequently, work is viewed as a kind of routine, a necessary element in the business of living. At worst, it is drudgery. As in the biblical curse of Adam, work is the acknowledgment that life has fallen into ordinariness.

However, this negative view of work is only a selective way of saying that work is connected to wider patterns of personal and public life. Work, or at least certain aspects of it, may well be enjoyable; still, its principal rationale is the provision of goods and services for those outside the work setting. Work focuses on products or outcomes. Workers live in the future. As Weber (1958b, pp. 155–183) warned, modern societies have made a fetish of instrumentalism. In such settings, activity becomes worthwhile only when it leads to something better.

It would be wrong to see work simply as economic activity. Clearly, most of the business of living must be considered work. People do household chores, wash the car, buy groceries, make dinner, and take the kids to soccer practice less for the inherent satisfaction of performing those tasks than for the end-states they achieve. All of these actions have transformative elements. People move and remove objects, take things apart, put them back together again, select and combine endlessly. As in the case of play, such practices are impositions of will, attempts to render the world according to private conceptions of what it should be.

All of this Marx understood well. Indeed, his conception of creative labor is really a critique of the narrow, capitalist interpretation of work.

For Marx, labor is the vehicle by which people express their nature. But it is also the means by which they integrate the different portions of their lives and reenforce their connections to others. In that sense, labor is less the productive activity of industrial workers than the general way in which people provide for themselves and their communities. Marx's workers create things with their hands and minds; those creations take on objective status in the world. Just as these products reflect the abilities of their makers, so they serve the needs of their possessors. What is crucial in this entire process is that the created object has meaning in a wider world beyond the event in which it was created. In that sense, works of art speak not only to creators in the moments of their making but ultimately to wider audiences quite innocent of those processes.

RITUAL AND COMMUNITAS AS CONFORMITIVE MODES OF ORIENTATION

A quite different path to knowing and experience is to yield to the forces of the world. That path—represented by ritual and communitas—is termed the *conformitive* mode of experience. To say that this approach emphasizes conformity or yielding is not to claim that participants in such events are somehow passive or indifferent. Quite the contrary, con-formitive activity is equally an act of will and frequently demands the most far-reaching kinds of effort and reorientation by those involved. If the transformative quest is to have the world adjust to the schemes of individuals, then the conformitive project requests the opposite relationship. Participants rush to these latter events so that they may expand and complete themselves. More clearly than play and work then, conformitive events are transformations of the self.

Not surprisingly, sociology and anthropology have somewhat more to say about ritual and communitas than about their transformative cousins. After all, both disciplines fundamentally challenge an individualistic view of life. That is, representatives from these fields tend to claim that there are supra-individual realities that transcend or otherwise frame personal behavior. Anthropology of course is the great champion of the culture concept, the idea that there are long-established patterns of information and artifact shared by the members of society. In such a view, private experience is guided—and even constituted—by collective products.

For its part, sociology argues that there are patterns of interpersonal relationship posed between the realms of individuality and culture. Social bodies, it is argued, have structures that guide—and make possible—human encounters of every type. Like culture, such patterns are abstractions that transcend the activities of their living members and frequently survive them after their deaths. Whatever the metaphysical status of its subject matter, sociology insists that structures like groups, societies, social classes, and roles are entities that people recognize and sustain and that influence the character of their lives. All this is only to say, as Durkheim did, that society is not some aggregate of psychological impulses but instead a great collective project that makes possible the decision-making—and the very impulses—of those individuals found within its boundaries.

All of the social scientists discussed in the preceding chapters emphasize the indebtedness of the individual to social and cultural form. Even the young Marx, as a champion of the transformative project, argues that our nature is constituted by our involvement with others. To have distinctively "human" sensibilities, one needs the ideas, language, and cooperation of a wider community. To take another case, Weber's sociology is based on a view that individuals find their visions of life (and the motivation to pursue those visions) from socially sponsored value-complexes. For his part, Durkheim is the evangelist of the societal perspective, a prophet who believed that social structures and norms are the architecture of freedom. More than all the others, Simmel seems fascinated by abstract forms of every type; his sociology reflects both our dependence on these forms and our curious approach-avoidance relationship to them. And Goffman, however scheming his characters may seem, is at the end a portraitist of social rituals. However maleficent its structures and customs, society is ultimately a tremendous public monument, the work of generations.

In this context, rituals are expressions of the conformitive, instrumental mode of orientation. As argued in the preceding chapters, rituals are entries into symbolic and social form. To enter the ritual mode one must recognize first that there are significant models of belief and behavior that stand beyond the individual. These models may be compelling in cognitive, moral, or aesthetic ways; the most powerful and appealing ones combine these elements. In every case, such models are framings of possibility, idealized visions of what life can be.

As Durkheim and the social anthropologists indicated, some of these models are presented as being of special importance to the members of society and are propped up by a variety of sanctifying procedures. "Sacred" ideals and acts are often reserved for special, difficult-to-access places and imputed to have origins in special, long-ago times. Highly trained or qualified custodians may be appointed to guard these sites and to officiate at the ceremonies contained therein. Furthermore, such events routinely are tinged with ideas of hierarchy. As Durkheim (1965) stressed, sacred matters are commonly thought to be transcendent—not only in the degree of their abstraction but also in the sense that they are superior to other sectors of society.

Conformitive events are fundamentally exercises in public obligation and responsibility. However, participation here is not equivalent to forced subordination or servility. Rather, to conform or comply in these settings is to recognize the worthiness of the claims of others and to willingly adapt one's behavior in these terms. Such claims may be found in the kinds of sacred models discussed above or in such routine equivalents as the policies of organizations, the values of a family, or the requirements of the physical world. To that extent, conformitive action is reminiscent of Piaget's (1962) treatment of accommodation, that psychological readiness to imitate and reproduce external forms.

Just as play is not confined to the activities of playgrounds or designated institutional spheres like sport, so ritual is a much broader concept than the sacred events mentioned by Durkheim or even the identity ceremonies central to Goffman's writing. Like Marx's labor, ritual is a more general pattern of human expression. For each of us, daily life is filled with dozens of ritualized activities. Some of these—like opening a door for someone to show respect or shaking hands in stipulated ways—are social; others—like the morning preparations of the self for the day—are personal. In any case, people adopt a ritualized orientation when they follow predetermined conceptions of a pattern of action to achieve identified external ends.

Like work, rituals are defined here as instrumental activities. Rituals help us communicate with others, accomplish tasks with less effort, save energy for other pursuits, focus on narrow aspects of a situation, and so forth. If the more superficial forms of ritual make life run more smoothly, the more eventful, serious forms profoundly challenge and change the self. By aspiring to difficult models, people frequently develop skills and qualities of character. They substitute new life strategies for older ones. They gain respect for other people and groups. In the most sacred rituals, initiates walk away from the event as newly constituted persons. In such ways, rituals connect the portions of life.

A final type of orientation is communitas—the conformitive, consummatory mode of expression. Like ritual, communitas commonly features social or symbolic immersion. However, also like ritual, it can feature the most complicated kinds of participation in natural, supernatural, or psychic realms of order as well (see Schechner, 1988; Spariosu, 1989). People allow themselves to be swept away, covered over, lost in form. In such ways, communitas is a stepping away from the distinctive patterns and schemes of the individual. This is done not for instrumental reasons—preparing oneself for some future state of affairs or accomplishing long-term goals of the group—but for the satisfactions inherent in participation itself. In communitas we give ourselves up and in the process discover new dimensions of our being.

It should be noted that modern Western societies—with their individualistic, rights-oriented, instrumental casts—have been deeply ambivalent about communitas. At the social level at least, such willing surrenders of self quickly produce images of communism, fascism, cults, and tribalism. Even immersions into religion, nationality, and family are thought to be appropriate only in degree. Anything more smells of fanaticism. Certainly, Huizinga (1955, pp. 195–213) was deeply disturbed by the attempts of the totalitarian governments of his time to take over and control public ceremonies and, in so doing, to countermand traditional forms of self-assertion.

However, it is important to separate the obeisance to symbolic and social form from those patterns of force and fraud used by authoritarian governments. Indeed, this was Durkheim's intellectual project. For Durkheim, with his rabbinical and small-town roots, the willing immersion of people into patterns of collective life is precisely the way in which the sphere of individuality is protected and expanded (see Giddens, 1972). People who participate in the collective product of language have a tremendous arsenal of conceptual and communicative resources at their disposal. So armed, individuals are more thoughtful, focused, and assured than they would be on their own. Moreover, they feel themselves to be more powerful. Private thought seems stronger when couched as collective wisdom, private speech is louder with a chorus of supporting voices.

Although he termed his subject matter the "play-form" of association, Simmel's (1971, pp. 127–140) essay on sociability should also be understood as one of the great commentaries on communitas. Although Simmel's party-goers laugh and flirt, tease and cajole in playful ways, the major theme of his description is the importance of group identity and normative order for those proceedings. In Simmel's play-form of association it is the second part of this compound term that claims his attention.

Again, Simmel's emphasis on the ways in which personal expression is restricted in sociability seems critical. Pointedly, revelers must not attempt to insert their own interests or preoccupations too deeply into the affair. Instead, balls and parties feature stylized, quasi-personal versions of people. Good hosts (and guests) recognize the importance of all the other attendees and sacrifice their own interests in this regard. Skillful manners, including tact—the ability to help others maintain an idealized identity—are paramount. In such ways, Simmel's essay evokes comparisons to Goffman's (1967) commentaries on "face-work" and "rituals of deference and demeanor." However, Goffman's writing focuses more directly on themes of individual identity and on the benefits of keeping up appearances in the world at large. Simmel's work focuses instead on the value of interpersonal connection or, even more abstractly, the logical requirements of the social form to which everyone is committed.

As noted above, sociability entails no purposes beyond the event itself. To repeat Simmel's (1950a, p. 45) contention, the "aim is nothing but the success of the sociable moment and, at most, a memory of it." Such themes, it seems to me, are central rationales for such events as festivals, pageants, parades, fairs, picnics, public dramas, musical performances, displays of visual art, and spectatorship at sporting events. On such occasions, a good portion of the pleasure comes from being part of the crowd and from witnessing others perform and mingle. Although spectators may be confined to designated seats and otherwise accept a host of restrictions for their behavior, attendance is not passivity. Like Simmel's party-goers, spectators create these moments together. At ball games, for example, programs and souvenirs are purchased, hot dogs eaten, feet stomped, umpires booed. There is an anthem to be sung, a "seventh-inning stretch" to be made, and quasi-obligatory participation in "the wave." However playful the various cheers, jeers, and gestures may be, there is a still a sense that the crowd is enacting honored forms of behavior.

Although perhaps the most frequent rationale for communitas (and for play) is "having a good time," such events have broader repercussions for personal and collective self-understanding. Through opposition and manipulation of the object world, players learn its strong and weak points, the places where they can assert themselves most effectively. In communitas, people submit themselves to the forms and powers of the world and reevaluate their own status as objects in that way. To attend a sophisticated performance of music or dance is frequently to be stunned by the capabilities of the performers and, more generally, by the capacities of human beings. In a way that play does not match, communitas provides its participants with soaring, expansive feelings.

Any discourse on the subject of communitas should include some comments on the nature of love. As Marx's concept of labor is an idealized version of work, so love occupies that status for communitas. In general parlance at least, love is connected closely to ideas about profound levels of sharing, responsibility, fellow feeling, doing for others, and so forth. Although the objects of love (another person, country, God, a cherished pet, etc.) may vary, the underlying theme of all love is the voluntary sacrifice of oneself for the concerns of another. Moreover, to be "in love" is to find oneself suddenly immersed, to feel oneself twisted and surprised by the powers of relationship. In addition, one can be in love with the idea or cultural form of love. As the old joke has it, a romantic is someone who goes to a restaurant where violins are playing and orders a table for one. However, even this immersion in the settings and ideals of love is a modest form of personal expansion. A much more significant project is love itself. To love actively in the world is to commit oneself deeply to another and to the wider relationship built on that foundation. To the extent that lovers pursue no ambitions beyond this pattern of mutual support, communitas reigns. All this notwithstanding, love should not be confused with self-denial or purely altruistic behavior. As Fromm (1956) stressed, to love is also to seek support and strength, and in the process to expand the boundaries of self-regard.

Normally, communitas features a commitment to both social and cultural form. Groups typically support (and to some extent are defined by) distinctive cultural patterns (beliefs, norms, valued artifacts, etc.). To enter a group wholeheartedly is to internalize these cultural elements. It may be recalled, though, that Durkheim's (1965, pp. 420–428) concept of collective effervescence suggests the extent to which the experience of sheer sociality itself can overwhelm the commitment to any particular set of ideas and values. In great moments of collective festivity, people feel themselves caught up and carried along in a surge of public energy. Under such conditions, social and cultural order split apart, radical ideas emerge, and collective fascination acquires the weight of moral imperative.

This sense of disconnection from institutionalized cultural understandings and placements is also a theme of Turner's (1969) treatment of communitas. In Turner's rites of passage, initiates sometimes find themselves huddled together in isolated huts, deprived of their old places in the world and not yet in receipt of new ones. In such betwixt-and-between moments, the power of brotherhood or sisterhood is profound. To be socially dead—to stand naked with others in a common grave—is to reevaluate one's position in the world. For Durkheim, this commitment to collectivity itself was the true center for people's transcendent yearnings. The symbolic forms we cherish are merely adumbrations on this theme.

Play as Interaction

It has been argued to this point that play—and its companion forms—
are dependent on the willing commitment of individuals. But personal
disposition is only one ingredient in the production of behavior. Who
has not put on his or her best "play face" only to have that invitation
rejected? Similarly, people may tease, flirt, or joke and see their efforts
fall flat. For play to occur—and be sustained—players must have an object
(be it a person or some other form) that somehow responds in satisfying
ways. Seen in that light, play is less a behavioral strategy of individuals than a complicated interaction or dialogue *between* people and the
conditions of their lives. As Biesty (2003) puts it, play is a "formative"
process, a sudden leap into a situation that produces a distinctive quality of experience.

To see play as an activity or interaction (rather than as a behavior) is
to shift from a psychological to a sociological perspective. In this latter
regard, the focus is placed on patterns of interchange, of which individual
behaviors are merely one component. Such patterns of interconnection, it
is argued, can be studied more or less objectively as phenomena in their
own right. An extreme version of this approach would require that scholars study play without consulting the motives, experiences, and desires
of the players themselves. Within those restrictions they would look for
some characteristic pattern of interaction that differentiates play from
other activities. It may strike the reader that this is precisely the set of
limitations that scientists encounter when studying the play of animals
(see Fagen, 1981).

Although the common vision of interaction tends to be one in which
two beings are committed equally to communicating with one another,
often this is not the case. In other words, interaction can be quite "imbal-
anced." Participants may vary dramatically in their degree of interest in
sustaining the interaction, their motives, and their ability to influence
the course of action. In that light, consider a cat "playing" with a mouse.
Although the cat could quickly kill the mouse, it does not do so. Moreover, the cat does not merely control or manipulate the mouse. Instead,
it captures the mouse and then releases it, opens up avenues for escape
and closes these off. Frequently, it will injure the mouse to hamper its
mobility. What is cruel play to human observers (and not play at all to
the mouse) is an exercise in the meaning of predation, an interchange
of skills between cat and mouse in a specific environmental context. A
dead mouse, as an object to bat about, may provide only a few moments
of fun; a mouse that is too vigorous—and thus escapes—no fun at all.

As a form of interaction, human play is not so different. Typically people play with or against the objects of the world. We juggle balls, make puns, invent silly dances, and stand on one leg for as long as possible. Sometimes we take on human opponents in games like chess or tennis. We try to defy the limitations of our bodies, the laws of gravity, rules of grammar, and lady luck. In every case, there is a sense in which people objectify forces and forms and then assert themselves against these elements.

But, as noted above, play is less a quest for complete control than a distinctive dialectical relationship, a pattern of call-and-response between people and objects. Sometimes these forms and forces—like the mountains, seas, and winds—are indifferent to us. Still they are worthy adversaries whose facets present us with an ever-changing array of difficulties. At other times, we force the world into movement; we bounce basketballs, hit golf shots, and cast dice. Differently again, we contend with animated creatures who test their wills against our own. In every case, play seems to be an activity where people engage the world through confrontation. Initial acts of assertion are followed by adjustment to the effects of these behaviors; these adjustments are the touchstones for further assertions. Even schoolyard bullies pick their targets with an eye to the physical and emotional resistance they will encounter.

For Huizinga then, play was especially a social phenomenon, an interchange between relatively well-matched and equally committed actors. Furthermore, such meetings tended to be oppositional or confrontational in nature. Playful confrontations, though, seem to be distinguished from other confrontations by a certain spirit or character. As he (Huizinga, 1955, pp. 5–7) pointed out, play is curiously connected to laughter, surprise, and mystery. Typically in play events, it is unknown how things will develop or end. Indeed, much of the pleasure comes from being astounded by all the actions and reactions. A rock is slipperier than anticipated, a run of bad luck almost impossible to comprehend. For such reasons, play activities often exhibit a jumpy, arhythmic quality.

When living creatures play against one another, there is all the confusion of not knowing the intentions of the opponent. As stated above, bluffing and feinting are standard practices. Moreover, players are frequently given some license to act spontaneously, to upset the order of things. In short, play is ruled by a spirit of freshness or novelty, a sense that things have not occurred in quite this way before. As in a game of cards, every hand is somehow different. So too is the exchange of wagers and the processes of concealing and revealing the cards. We find ourselves surprised not only by the behavior of our companions but also by our own emotional outbursts. Play is fascinating to the degree that it draws us into the unpredictability of relationship and explores our reactions to it.

In keeping with Simmel's ambition to develop a "geometry" of human relations, these matters have been described graphically below. Once, again, the figure contrasts play with work, ritual, and communitas. However, in this instance, the focus is on these phenomena as patterns of interaction. The horizontal axis in the figure focuses on "pattern of engagement" and represents the tension between *contestive* and *integrative* activities. Contestive activities explore the meanings of difference and opposition; integrative activities explore cooperation and union. Play and work are seen as contestive forms; ritual and communitas as integrative endeavors. Again, these differences are matters of degree or are reflective of the aspect of a relationship that is under consideration. Thus, ritual and communitas may use moments of opposition and challenge—or may plunge individuals into deep experiences of isolation and chaos; ultimately, though, these events focus on the totality or unity that has been discovered through this process. Finally, it should be emphasized that all four patterns are attempts to build relationships and thus are to be distinguished from patterns of withdrawal and non-engagement.

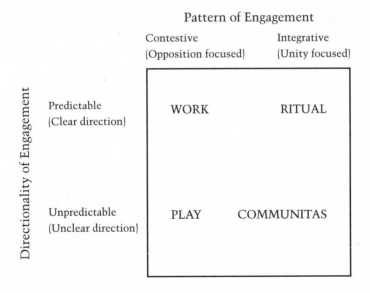

Figure 2. *Modes of Human Interaction*

The vertical axis focuses on the linearity or "directionality" of relationship. In this context, some activities are characterized as relatively *predictable;* that is, the sequence and outcome of the activity is more or less clearly ordained or understood. Work and ritual are seen as examples of this mode. Alternately, some activities—here, play and communitas—are viewed as much more *unpredictable* in rhythm and direction. To return to a theme developed earlier, "spontaneity" is not only a willful, mischievous quality that players bring to their play but also a characteristic of the interaction itself. Both play and communitas feature unexpected happenings, and participants must be ready to adjust their behavior quickly.

Seen in this light, work reemerges as a *contestive* but largely *predictable* activity. Because workers are aware typically of the end-states they wish to reach, their behavior tends to be orderly or systematic. Principles related to efficacy (goal-attainment) and efficiency (best uses of means) are frequently developed and followed. Certainly, work may stall or move in counterproductive directions, but there is an expectation that participants will regroup or otherwise return to the proper path. In contradistinction to play, work tends to be a cumulative or value-added enterprise.

Even more pointedly, work is guided by visions of completion and rest. Although work itself is a form of engagement—an exercise in addressing and responding to reality's forms and forces—workers anticipate that their activity will result in some relatively static product or form. Curiously then, work is a pattern of engagement that seeks resolution or even non-engagement as its appropriate end. Ultimately, our cat kills the mouse—and does so in a "workmanlike" way. In the same sense, the artist finishes the painting, hangs it on the wall, and regards it in its completed form.

As noted above, a large portion of human activity should be seen as work. Just meeting the physical requirements of our bodies is a ceaseless pursuit and imposes a rhythm and regimen to life. Work is frequently a repetitive or routinized affair. Most days are filled with a familiar series of self-imposed tasks; it makes a certain sense to dispose of these in the most efficient (and repeatable) ways possible. People brush their teeth and drink their coffee in characteristic fashion.

Like work, ritual is also an orderly endeavor. However, ritual is *integrative* rather than contestive in spirit; ritualized activities emphasize joining and supporting. In social rituals, participants try to firm up their connections to others and to the public understanding of their identities. They do this not by setting their own terms (as in play) but by fitting themselves to established frameworks for who they should be. Even in rituals of a most strictly personal nature, the events serve to link the different moments of life and to reenforce the various dimensions of identity. By harnessing our impulses within these stable forms, we allow ourselves to be identified (both by ourselves and by others) and on those terms make our way within the world.

Some of the orderliness of rituals is attributable to the role of the past in these events. Compared to other time frames, the past represents a firmer set of possibilities. Whatever our propensities to embroider past events, there remains a sense that these matters have concluded and are beyond intervention. Past events can be held up as solid or true exemplars of what humans, nature, or the gods can be and do. Indeed, the past lives among us primarily as a set of idealized memories and artifacts, curious distillations from the tremendous complexity of life. This conceptual edifice is typically a dominating force in rituals. Hence, ritual is commonly serious and orderly. People are attentive to the requests of those about them (and above them); self-consciousness becomes a public matter. Ritualized actions tend to have a predictable, even scripted quality; initiates move through a series of stages toward anticipated outcomes.

Another aspect of the past is critical to ritual as well. Commonly, rituals are thought to be repetitive events, or more precisely, actions that repeatedly follow established forms. Repetition inscribes themes into personal and public life. Each cutting re-opens (and deepens) the channel for individual movement. Symbolic events, as Durkheim (1965, pp. 216–272) maintained, may well be occasions to jolt or reawaken people to the importance of these forms; however, sometimes sheer repetition itself carries people forward. Like footsteps fitted to the worn places in cathedral stairs, behavior falls into patterns that are difficult to resist. Through repetition, ideas that were once fresh and striking become habits of mind.

For such reasons, ritual is perhaps the most orderly of the four forms of activity. On the one hand, ritual "seeks" order in that it asks its practitioners to attach themselves to transcendent forms and codes. On the other, ritual "follows" order in that the activity moves through clearly demarcated stages and processes. To participate in ritual is to be part of something that transports us through the minutiae of life. In the most sublime rituals, we participate in eternity.

How different this sounds from the manners and sensibilities of play. Play is characteristically buoyant and disrespectful, and players are indulgent in the broadest sense of that term. Committed to living in the present, players insert their interests and enthusiasms wherever possible. Within the boundaries of the event itself, action typically dances and darts. We demolish our carefully constructed castle of blocks and are fascinated by the clatter of its collapse.

In contrast, rituals are preoccupied with the maintenance of order rather than with its dissolution. While oppositional or contestive elements are sometimes built into rituals—as sets of challenges or ordeals expressed through actions and vows—these tests tend to be comprehended as intra-personal challenges. That is, it is the self (with all its distractions and weaknesses) that must be overcome. And during occasions of ritualized combat, it is rarely the structure or symbolic framework of society itself that is disputed but rather the rightful place of specific individuals and groups within that order. Indeed, by fighting (or even dying) in such settings, warriors reaffirm the majesty of society and its authority to make such claims on its members.

Finally, communitas expresses the *integrative, unpredictable* mode of relationship. As in the case of play, activities like fairs and festivals tend to have an energetic, spontaneous quality. Laughter and high spirits prevail. People wander about, going from one part of the grounds to another, discovering curious sensations at every point. There are exotic sights to be seen, foods to be eaten, rides to be taken. Moreover, the experience is somehow confusing. At times, we become lost in the crowd or in the maze-like corridors of the grounds. People of every description wander by. Barkers reach out to claim our attention. The world it seems is a hubbub (see Bahktin, 1981).

Moreover, the present reasserts itself in communitas. Events like parties or fairs seem to have only loosely established beginnings and ends. Participants come and go at will, spread themselves about the setting, and spill over its boundaries. Little activities within the larger event are stationed beside one another (or follow one another, as in a parade) without apparent reason. We make our way through this carnival-like environment, resisting the appeals of some and acceding to others. Almost by chance we find ourselves in certain settings and miss others entirely. We climb aboard the mechanical conveyances at fairs or enter conversational circles at parties hardly knowing what the sensations will be. In such ways, communitas should be understood as an adventure in the meaning of form.

However, communitas differs from the adventurousness of play. Players are active; they seek out the world and turn it about to test their own powers. In contrast, participants in communitas encounter the world in softer, more receptive ways. At fairs and spectator events, experience is a matter of seeing and "sampling" sometimes packaged offerings. We partake of these thrills and spills and leave the setting with an altered understanding of what the world can offer.

The reader may be struck by the similarity of communitas to the postmodern treatment of culture described in chapter 4 (see also Rosenau, 1992; Hans, 1981; Kuchler, 1994; Spariosu, 1989). In those accounts, contemporary culture is conceived not as a unified, systematic framework but rather as an almost chaotic swirling of images and artifacts. Like spectators at a fireworks display, modern people are subjected to a tremendous barrage of pictures and noises, semi-intelligible claims and counterclaims. Behind the fireworks there is no central operator or guiding set of meanings. Rather, reality is essentially a brightly colored present; superficiality, fragmentation, and tangibility prevail.

However, even in this view communitas is at bottom an integrative matter. In radical postmodernism, people are encouraged to immerse themselves in the pool of semi-meanings and artifacts, to accept and operate on those terms (see Henricks, 2001). In less radical versions, people acknowledge their connections to limited sets of others and move their understandings ahead in these ways. Amidst all the buzzing and swirling—and superficial chaos—of festive gatherings then, there is still a curious sense of togetherness. People understand themselves to be part of a "crowd" or "event" and organize their enjoyment in those terms. In such ways the small is fitted to the large, the concerns of individuals to the developing patterns of collectivity that surge around them.

It is important to remember that these different patterns of interaction intertwine in the real-life events of the world. As noted above, rituals may have their contestive moments. Likewise, play events may have ritualized portions (frequently at the beginning and end) where officials declare terms of engagement and ultimate resolutions (see Sutton-Smith, 1997, pp. 91–126, on play and communal identity). For most people, routine work activities feel as much like acts of ritual and communitas (i.e., the fitting of oneself to external patterns and demands) as they seem to be opportunities for creativity and control. In the manner of Simmel then, the intention here is to identify the principal themes of events or, failing that, to indicate which aspects of events seem to be organized in which ways.

It is the misfortune of the social scientist that reality should be so complicated. Nevertheless, real people in the moments of their lives discern these matters clearly enough. Indeed, the thesis of this chapter—that play, communitas, work, and ritual are different forms of behavior marked by characteristic rationales and styles of expression—is something of a commonplace. For its part, play represents the testing, teasing, impish style of relating. With ears perked, we poke at the world to discover its possibilities for novelty and amusement. Communitas represents that softer, more receptive mode. For these few moments, let us savor the pleasures and excitements proffered to us by the world. By contrast, workers do not meander and mingle but gather their resolve and move ahead. However energetic and calculated their renderings, they live less in the present than in the vision of things to come. Finally, ritualists walk soberly in the pathways of what has gone before. The journey may be demanding and enthralling, but the destination—those altered placements in the realms of order—is the ultimate prize. As Goffman argued, it may take us a few moments to comprehend the character of a situation and other people's dispositions within it. Nevertheless, we "frame" these settings quickly enough and adjust our behaviors accordingly. A player's role is different than the role of a worker or a ritualist. Like speakers of a language who cannot articulate the rules of grammar, we comprehend these different forms with a fascinating depth and subtlety of knowledge; and we move the action ahead in the appropriate ways.

The Social Organization of Play

Can lightning be captured in a jar? Fundamentally, play is little more than externalized whim—a rebellion of consciousness against the forms and forces of the world. Players take it upon themselves to tease or taunt reality. That altered relationship produces a flood of sensations. Players stay connected to the extent that these sensations continue to amuse or satisfy. Suddenly satisfactions decline, interests shift, and the play moment is gone.

How can an activity so evanescent and unpredictable be worked into the fabric of societies? And why should societies choose to make this happen? Such questions, it may be recalled, were the very issues that Huizinga confronted. He wanted to emphasize play's inherent value and protect its status in society. However, he did not wish to make play submit to other regimens and forms—or to have it be explained as "functional" in those terms. Moreover, he understood that harnessing play to other social imperatives may well turn play into something else, or at the very least, deprive it of the qualities of spontaneity and creativity that make it distinctive.

The following section discusses three ways in which social groups and organizations try to capture or stabilize play. It should not surprise the reader that Huizinga anticipated all three. As he (1955, p. 13) claimed, play in its more socially developed forms often appears as a "contest for something" and as a "display of something" that is valued more generally in society. As a "contest for something," play is often directed toward the range of material incentives and consequences normally associated with work. As a "display of something," play is reinterpreted in a broader symbolic context—and in the process frequently becomes ritualized. It is even more common that play materializes as an "experience of something," as an entry into (and communication with) social and cultural form. In this last instance, play becomes mixed with the themes of communitas.

PLAY AS AN EXPERIENCE OF FORM

As noted above, playful behavior is ultimately an antinomian enterprise, a protest against orders and orderliness. As ragings against externally imposed routine, these little bursts of creativity are surely important to the participants themselves. But living so willfully in the moment has its limitations. Without some abstract framework or structure, people cannot link their own activities systematically or evaluate them comparatively. Thus, behavior is merely something that starts and stops. Just as thoroughgoing formlessness destroys a cumulative experience of life, so it makes communication between people exceedingly difficult. People need established pathways to one another, if only to argue and compete.

The relationship of play to form is a kind of paradox that many writers have noted (see Gruneau, 1980; Loy, 1982; Sutton-Smith and Kelly-Byrne, 1984b). Play may well be a rebellion against form, an attempt to disrupt or countermand external patterns. But forms themselves are necessary, as elements to identify and oppose and as channels of communication. Play is distinguished by its curious combinations of order and disorder, by its acceptance of certain rules and regimes at the very time that it assaults others.

As Huizinga, Caillois (1961), and others (see Levy, 1978) have noted, play is often packaged in symbolic form. Probably the best examples of this packaging are "games." Although games can be understood as specialized activities of individuals and groups, they are considered here as cultural forms—as integrated patternings of rules, roles, and material implements that permit a distinctive range of "moves." The enactment of these moves in turn creates patterns of relationship—advantage and disadvantage, coalition and rivalry, victory and loss—during the event. Thus, to embrace the framework of a game is to reinterpret one's standing in a new (and frequently quite comprehensive) system of meaning.

These meaning systems effectively control the inherent volatility of play, including its strong tendencies toward individuation. As Durkheim (1964b) points out, sheer egocentricity is not a firm basis for social relationship. Human interaction and communication depend on shared normative frameworks. Only by recognizing the degree to which ongoing relationships are based on patterns of trust and support can people plan and implement strategies of action. As claimed above then, games tend to be contestive rather than purely oppositional formats. Game rules coordinate and manage private initiative; they specify terms of engagement and procedures to reach conclusion or disengagement. In such ways, games give play the very qualities of linearity or directionality it typically lacks. Although players grow tired or otherwise wish to quit, they are discouraged from doing so by definitions of what a completed game means and by the expectation that they finish. Such matters are especially important when two or more people play together; but they also encourage players of "solitaire" or its variants to find resolution.

The distinctive meaning system of the game also transcribes the objects and settings of play. Under these terms, experience can become "exotic" or "ecstatic." Moreover, these orderings of time and space help turn what is merely a behavior or process into an "event," an activity that is bounded and complete. Game forms not only encourage a distinctive set of behaviors but also extend those behaviors through their duller or less engaging moments.

The power of game forms to shape play behavior is magnified dramatically when these forms become institutionalized (see Loy, 1968). Knowledge of game rules, equipment, playing spaces, performers, and history is incorporated into a wide range of social settings and otherwise becomes part of public consciousness. Once games have been institutionalized, people can more easily describe their own play experiences to others and invite them to play. If games participation is valued, they can trade off the "symbolic capital" obtained through their skills and successes in such endeavors. They can participate knowingly in public discussions of "big games" and use game metaphors in other conversations. Indeed, games participation and observation can become a socially respectable way to spend personal or family time.

These observations only reiterate Goffman's point that games themselves are set into wider normative contexts. Such norms include ideas about the place and importance of games in society. Games are frequently associated with certain times of day, are anticipated to take certain amounts of time, and occur in certain spaces. Participants may be allowed to dress, touch, or otherwise express themselves in distinctive ways in games. Some games may be considered more culturally important than others or be deemed appropriate only for certain social categories (e.g., young children, men, or wealthy people). Some game events survive all but the most serious forms of interruption; others have little status and can be ended at any time. As Goffman maintained, we are not merely "players" but "people," who deal with a broader societal ethic about the propriety and implications of play.

As the classic sociologists argued, institutionalized play-forms feature comprehensive cultural "logics." These systems of meaning extend beyond the playing rules themselves to the wider contexts within which the game is understood. These distinctive logics make it much more likely that certain behaviors and experiences will occur here than in differently structured events. At one level, this means that societies and their groups may encourage certain game forms rather than others. Somewhat differently, groups fit a particular game form to their own histories and value complexes; they adopt their own styles of play. Previous chapters have indicated in small ways the complicated relationship of game preferences to the social characteristics of sponsoring groups and organizations. Veblen, recall, was fascinated by the sporting customs of the business elite; the school of British cultural studies explored the playful interpretations of working-class people. And Bourdieu was curious about the expressive choices of every class-fraction. Such choices should be seen as the opening and closing of doors for aesthetic opportunity. As Weber's study of music makes plain, the more rational, systematic approach of the West created a wonderful range of new possibilities for artists, composers, conductors, and audiences. However, it also led people away from improvisational, informal styles of play.

The level of commitment to rules and orderliness in games may vary historically and cross-culturally. Elias's work on the civilizing process suggests that there was not only a new "content" for public manners (i.e., a different set of rules) in recent centuries but also a heightened commitment to internalizing and using such rules in society at large. This commitment to public civility or mannerliness is consistent with social situations in which highly placed people acknowledge their connections to—and even their dependence on—diverse and widely separated categories of others. To emphasize these shared connections, experiences, and patterns of respect is to push play in the direction of communitas. In that light, playful elements are considered less important than "sportsmanship" and fellow feeling. As in the selection of play-forms themselves, styles of play and mannerliness itself can be controlled ruthlessly by the dominant groups or be left to the discretion of the players. As was shown in the case of gender, these apparently opposite approaches become entangled in "socially influenced" patterns of choice.

However interesting these variations in expressive form, the more fundamental point should be reiterated here. As Simmel argued, people at every moment of their lives confront formal arrangements—whether these be at the personal, social, or cultural level. Life itself is an interplay of forms, a process of entering and withdrawing, of shaping and being shaped by what stands beyond. Even play—that most fitful and sponta-neous type of behavior—lives amidst the patterns of the world. More-over, as Durkheim suggested, our being shaped (and even constituted) by these symbolic arrangements is not a condition to be mourned. Instead, humans find purpose and direction for life through formal encounters and even develop their sense of self in precisely these terms. Crucially also, our voluntary commitment to the social forms of communitas gives us qualities of strength, energy, and inspiration that we would otherwise lack.

PLAY AS A CONTEST FOR SOMETHING

Much of the fun or happiness of play comes from being with others, from sharing moments of mutual commitment and support. As in Simmel's essay on fashion, in play-as-communitas the ambition of the player is not to stand "apart" but to stand "out." In that sense, players endorse the web of group affiliations, the overall pattern for interaction. What they seek are only the most modest movements of self within those settings—the triumph of the well-played card, the clever remark, the knowing glance. On such occasions, we reaffirm both our valued social connections with others and our special place inside the social circle.

For Simmel, who had experienced his share of marginality, the plea-sures of sociability were sublime. For Goffman, the satisfactions of social inclusion—in play or elsewhere—are not enough. In Goffman's (1961b) world, social engagement is fragile or problematic. Preoccupied as they are with personal status—both in their own eyes and before others—indi-viduals foist their own interests and insecurities onto others. Moreover, despite their best (most sociable) intentions, they find that they have trouble staying focused on the matters at hand. Minds wander, boredom intercedes, and interruptions become welcomed rather than discour-aged. As indicated in the previous chapter, Goffman argues that people must be "held in" through the skillful use of a variety of rules, including transformation rules (that deal with interruptions when they do occur). Rules for the selection of sides and for the conduct of play may help to structure a "good game," one that is more likely to be engaging. Still, all this may not be enough. Games may require appropriately determined "stakes."

Although Huizinga recognized the value of symbolic prizes or rewards for players, he was much less supportive of material (especially monetary) incentives. Goffman had no such reservations. Certainly, players may be motivated by Bourdieu's "symbolic capital," the accrual and dispensation of social regard. However, monetary transactions—through payment for participation or through gambling—may also "sweeten the deal." Also, such rewards can be given either to the individual or to the team as a whole. Typically, these awards are connected to the overall outcome of the event. Thus people—as partisans—keep focused on an ending that is structured to be as unpredictable or mysterious as possible.

To the extent that players pursue outcomes and rewards, play may start to resemble its instrumental equivalent, work. Again, the purest forms of play encourage people to indulge themselves psychologically in processes of creativity. Workers aspire to finish the job and to experience its utility. Play-as-work entails this focus on end-pleasure. Indeed, just because the prospect of success is so uncertain in play—often, one of the participants is guaranteed to lose—there may be extreme emphasis on such work-like matters as preparation, control of performance, and strategic calculation.

At an individual level, this more instrumental approach is illustrated by the conversion of play into exercise. Exercise can be understood as the conscious employment of repetitive activity to develop personal skills and qualities that are useful in other settings. To take examples from physical activity, a few sit-ups or a lap around the track may be a satisfying diversion, a reacquaintance with the human body in motion. A few laps or sit-ups later, displeasure dominates, and other patterns of psychological adjustment are called into service. Ascetically inclined types push on because they want to improve their appearance, avoid future health problems, prepare for other forms of physical activity, and so on. In addition, a work-like manner is sometimes adopted. People become serious and systematic, counting out and recording repetitions. They survey the effects of their work by getting out the measuring tape, standing on the scale, and looking into the mirror. Not satisfied with the results, they consult the advice of knowledgeable others. In each instance, the meaning of "satisfaction" shifts from the momentary pleasure of the activity itself to a (hopefully) admiring regard for the job just completed or the person one has become. In the process, play's unpredictable quality has been sacrificed for the mental determination and technical efficiency of work. In contradistinction to Piaget, I have argued that playful behaviors lose their defining character when they are "reproduced" in repetitious ways.

It will be remembered that Huizinga very much opposed the utilitarian spirit and cult of efficiency that marked the industrial age. But he was interested less in the personal uses of play than in its social applications. Like Weber, Huizinga feared the reign of bureaucratic organizations and technocratic approaches. Under such conditions, play itself was being transformed into a perversion of itself, a device to earn money for sponsors. For him, professional play—with its monetary incentives, leagues, formal associations, rule by officials, and training regimens—was anathema. Play under such circumstances had "stiffened into seriousness" (see Huizinga, 1955, p. 199). And the traits he prized—such qualities as freedom, spontaneity, joy, creativity, mystery—had been reduced to matters of secondary importance.

PLAY AS A DISPLAY OF SOMETHING

As Goffman (1967) argues, much of human interaction can be understood as a series of "rituals" in which people construct and manage their public identities. By putting on an appropriate "face," adopting a telling stance and manner, looking in the proper directions, wearing certain clothing, spouting the right words with the right tone of voice, and so forth, people effectively say "yes" to a distinctive vision of social or cultural life and to their idealized placement within that order. Frequently also, rituals are processes of mutual acknowledgment. By displaying ourselves to others under publicly established terms, we effectively "name" ourselves and then carry those names into the other settings of our lives.

By contrast, communitas and play are understood typically to be pleasant interludes, escapes from such concerns. A night at the opera or in a lover's embrace, an afternoon spent bowling or in the park, are little indulgences, escapades focusing on the experiences of the participants themselves. As Stone (1955) has noted, all this changes when play is given wider public meaning, when it becomes display. When play activities are interpreted as symbolic events—as representations of broader identities and issues—those activities acquire a new weight and bearing. Indeed, they take on many of the features of rituals.

As dramatic spectacles, play activities may be laden with a range of meanings that influence the life opportunities of participants. As has been shown, public play events are frequently occasions where individuals (and groups) make accountings of themselves before others. The participation of these players (now seen as "performers") may be interpreted as indicators of personal quality in a much broader sense. What people play and how they play it become markers of public identity. It may be recalled that this was the emphasis of Veblen's argument about the leisure class. The "conspicuousness" of a leisure form was more important than the inherent satisfactions of the activity.

In play-as-ritual, special attention may be given to the criteria by which participants are chosen. Because the playful contest is now thought to be socially significant, only certain categories of people may be allowed to play. Historically, males have tended to have more access to play activities and more attention has been placed on the quality and results of their participation. However, issues of age, social class, religion, occupational background, nationality, community affiliation, and so on, have been quite important as well. As in religious ritual, certain types of people are placed in the spotlight and others are relegated to spectatorship or other supporting roles.

Those admitted to the play circle may find themselves subjected to much scrutiny regarding the quality of performance. As in ritual, officials make certain that rules are observed carefully. In sports where officials are frequently absent or distant—as in golf or tennis—participants are expected to self-administer the rules in the most scrupulous ways. Willing conformity to those rules is central to the idea of sportsmanship and is interpreted as a mark of character more generally. Furthermore, there are expectations regarding the intensity of emotional commitment by performers. Not uncommonly, participants are expected to play hard as well as fairly, even after reasonable hope of victory is gone. Thus, players are evaluated not only on the basis of "professional" virtues—effectiveness and efficiency—but also with regard to such "amateur" matters as love of the game, sportsmanship, and broader qualities of judgment and decorum.

In summary, play-as-ritual is symbolically consequential for identity in wider social circles. By playing well—or poorly—players make statements about their psychological and social qualities. Success in this sense is important not only for the self-concept of the players themselves but also for the communities that help define them. Moreover, games sometimes define entire communities. In the massively publicized and attended contests between nations, communities, and universities, bragging rights for the collectivity as a whole rise and fall with the outcome.

As in ritual, play under these circumstances loses much of its light-hearted and casual air. People who know they are being watched behave differently. When they know the outcome is important, they behave differently again. Themes of responsibility and discipline rise in prominence. Officials and managers are employed. Team spirit and cooperation are central. Victory—accomplished in the proper way—is synonymous with glory; defeat wears the trappings of shame.

Conclusions

What is the proper function of play in society? Should it be affiliated with the other activities described above? For his part, Huizinga seems to have accepted the linkage of play to ritual and communitas. In that spirit, he approved of the play-festival-rite complex of earlier times. In *Homo Ludens*, play typically appears not only as a contest but also as social and symbolic participation. In the public settings that were Huizinga's primary interest, players feel each other out before watchful others. For all their rantings and showings off, the contestants somehow reaffirm their regard for one another and for the collective frameworks that make these spectacles possible.

It strikes me as very significant that Huizinga did not emphasize individual play or intimate play or the play of children in his accounts. After all, such matters are tremendously important in the building of people's lives and the maintenance of societies. Although Huizinga (1955, p. 47) tended to dismiss such issues as culturally unimportant, I think that he recognized that play can only come into its most complicated manifestations and deepest fulfillment when it is connected to significant societal themes. Moreover, play must be rescued from its own self-indulgent and antinomian tendencies by institutionalizing its more spectacular versions on the important cultural stages of society. In such ways, play stays as important for adults as it is for children.

Huizinga's unwillingness to connect play and work is more difficult to understand. Of course, some of this antipathy is the expression of his aristocratic, idealist sensibilities. From that perspective, play should be about symbolic or even spiritual explorations and outcomes rather than equivalent processes in the material world. The style or aesthetic resonance of an age was, for Huizinga, more important than its subsistence patterns or administrative policies. Aristocrats and peasants (and traditional peoples) supposedly understand quality-of-life issues in this broader way; middle-class city dwellers do not. Thus, in its modern guise, work has become a single-minded fascination with the future. By contrast, play always acknowledges the wonderful complexity of the past, even as it toys with past patterns. When people sell off or otherwise surrender their cultural birthright for the sake of some narrowly focused, financially rewarded pursuit, they lose their connection not only to the past but also to the present and future as well.

This viewpoint having been acknowledged, I see no reason to separate so strictly the material incentives and consequences of play from the symbolic ones. Play is appropriately concerned with the propagation of ideas and values just as it legitimately explores material creation and reward. Values development is important but so is the development of physical skill. Contests can be "for" or "about" different kinds of things. That is, play can be supported or sanctioned by society (and by all manner of groups and organizations within it) in different ways.

What does seem critical is that play not lose its distinctive character and contributions through this institutionalization process. Although Huizinga did not develop these two themes at length, his (1955, pp. 204–213) description of the twin dangers of "false play" and "puerilism" should be remembered here. "False play" is that perversion of human creativity that occurs when organizations take over and manage play for their own ends. Although the activities appear to be dynamically interactive and emotionally engaging, the participants themselves are not really in control—or are in control only in quite modest ways. Play's transformative quality is actually overridden by stylized conformity. In the worst cases, relative freedom of choice and action gives way to compulsory (or even compulsive) behaviors.

Although Huizinga did not acknowledge their work, the contributions of the critical theorists (see Horkheimer and Adorno, 1972; Jay, 1973) should be revisited here. In their view, expressive life, or even the experience of personhood itself, has become objectified. This objectification process—epitomized in the practices of modern advertising—occurs at the most private levels of desire and goal-formulation. Like many tangible products, experience has become a commodity to be bought and sold. Cultural experiences, from the sublime to the profane, are produced, marketed, and consumed like cornflakes. As experience has become somewhat standardized, so also have the possibilities for personal creativity been diminished. People can still express themselves as they desire but the social settings for such expression have been altered and the pathways to cultural prominence have been taken over almost entirely. What people want and how they should want it have become matters for bureaucratic fabrication. Such worries about the cultural insignificance of personal and interpersonal expression in modern societies are guiding concerns of *Homo Ludens.*

Puerilism is a different matter. For Huizinga, puerilism was a style of adolescent barbarism that had become prominent in the Northern Europe of his time. As he saw it, this rah-rah spirit—based on a predilection for crude sensation and clubby sentimentality—was inappropriate and even dangerous for adults. While one can dismiss Huizinga's concern as the wan protest of an aesthete trapped in a decadent age, his broader point is quite important. That point, in my view, is that play may well be child-like in many of its aspects but that it must not be childish. Although Huizinga demonstrated the degree to which play should be connected to the traditions of societies, play should not be "regressive" (see Henricks, 1988). To regress is to try to return (always in selective ways) to earlier stages of personal or social development. Some level of return to these stages is valuable, but to pretend that some narrow aspect of childhood or the Middle Ages is a foundation for adult life in the modern world is a formidable lie. Life is not a soccer match or fraternity party or game of tag. Even for a traditionalist like Huizinga, play must confront squarely the challenges of the modern world. In that sense, play is always looking ahead as well as behind, an engine of "progress" as well as a commentary on where we have been.

To summarize, false play reveals the perversion of play—and aesthetic experience more generally—by large modern states and organizations. Puerilism is the specter of play succumbing to small, self-proclaiming factions. In Nazism, these two themes became the aesthetic underpin-nings of a broader process that caused the death of millions of people, including Huizinga himself.

If play can be turned and twisted so easily to serve the best or worst of purposes, what is its proper station in society? Following Huizinga—and using Simmel's metaphor—I would argue that adult play must be recognized as an important aspect of human life and then maintained at a strategic "distance" from other institutionalized patterns and practices. As Simmel recognized so well, it is in that tension-filled space between connection and disconnection that play lives. Like freedom itself, play is an inquiry into the meaning of marginality. In play people are con-nected to interesting social themes and processes at the very time that they are disconnected from them. Players are both themselves and not themselves, inside society and outside its boundaries at the same time.

Of these two aspects, disconnection is perhaps the easier to describe. Players typically are permitted a certain freedom from interference. Indi-viduals are allowed a certain selfish indulgence; other social claims and processes are put on hold. Although play is frequently mixed with other types of activities and thus linked to external consequences, players maintain a strong sense of living in the moment. Moreover, players are able to concoct and put into operation their own personal and social schemes that contrast sharply with those of the wider society. As has been said throughout this book, players make the world anew.

However, play is not simply disconnection or separation or independence. The essence of the ideas of marginality and distance is that people stay connected even as they find themselves separated. To play is to know there is a wider world—with all its obligations and complexities—just beyond the gates of the playground. Furthermore, this wider world is needed to give play its sense of urgency and meaning. From those external settings, people import the frequently contradictory values and challenges of their times as well as their own more general issues about personal functioning. Such matters may be practiced or affirmed in play or they may be countermanded or inverted by new forms (see Handelman, 1998). However, in almost every case, players "regard" the world about them and then use the objects of those visions as elements of their play.

Curiously, play can be disabled by excessive degrees of either connection or disconnection. In the first instance, societal themes and claims can overwhelm play. Informal play can be declared trivial and stopped. Alternately, managing organizations can put forth their own versions of the activity and then dictate the terms by which people participate. External concerns and consequences make the resulting activity heavy and repetitive. Choice becomes obligation and then compulsion. The very soul of the activity, the celebration of people's abilities to confront the conditions of their lives, is gone.

But too little connection to societal themes makes play, at least from a social viewpoint, pointless and shallow. Without interesting or important cultural issues, "stakes" of some pertinence, and a commitment by others that affirms the enterprise, play is only egocentric indulgence. However assertive they proclaim themselves to be, people are trapped in an endless loop between the changing conditions of the moment and their own sensations. Unbounded play realizes Durkheim's worst fears about anarchy and individuation.

As Huizinga argued then, societies need to reaffirm the value of a playful spirit in populations of all ages. Times and places should be protected for individually sponsored play; groups and organizations should build legitimate play opportunities into their routines. To do this is to do more than signify the critical importance of personal experience as an aspect of public well-being. Play is an opportunity for people to try out the implications of cultural and social possibilities without enduring consequence or reproach. Play allows people to understand life in both its material and symbolic context and to discover the appropriate limits of their powers. It makes people confront the relationship between private and public interest and thus reacquaints them with the meaning of social order. Play gathers together the emotional, cognitive, and moral dimensions of existence into sharply distilled moments. In such ways, human capacity is diversified and thickened, and societies themselves are made stronger.

REFERENCES

Adams, B., and Sydie, R. A. (2001). *Sociological theory.* Thousand Oaks, CA: Sage.

Allison, H. (2001). *Kant's theory of taste: A reading of the critique of aesthetic judgment.* Cambridge: Cambridge University Press.

Alpert, H. (1965). Durkheim's theory of ritual. In R. Nisbet (Ed.), *Emile Durkheim* (pp. 137–141). Englewood Cliffs, NJ: Prentice-Hall.

Aycock, A. (1998). Owning up: Bourdieu and commodified play in the USCF chess catalogue. In M. Duncan, G. Chick, and A. Aycock (Eds.), *Diversions and divergences in fields of play: Play and culture studies,* 1 (pp. 253–274). Greenwich, CT: Ablex.

Bahktin, M. (1981). *The dialogic imagination.* Austin: University of Texas Press.

Bateson, G. (1971). The message: This is play. In R. E. Herron and B. Sutton-Smith (Eds.), *Child's play* (pp. 261–269). New York: Wiley.

Bateson, G. (1972). *Steps to an ecology of mind.* New York: Ballantine Books.

Baudrillard, J. (1983). *Simulations.* New York: Semiotext.

Beamish, R. (2002). Karl Marx's enduring legacy for the sociology of sport. In J. Maguire and K. Young (Eds.). *Theory, sport, and society* (pp. 25–40). New York: JAI.

Bellah, R. (1965). Durkheim and history. In R. Nisbet, *Emile Durkheim, with selected essays* (pp. 153–176). Englewood Cliffs, NJ: Prentice-Hall.

Bellah, R. (1967). Civil Religion in America. *Daedalus,* 96: 1–21.

Bellah, R. et al. (1985). *Habits of the heart: Individualism and commitment in American life.* Berkeley: University of California Press.

Bellah, R. et al. (1991). *The good society.* New York: Alfred Knopf.

Bendix, R. (1960). *Max Weber: An intellectual portrait.* Garden City, NY: Doubleday.

Berlin, I. (1963). *Karl Marx: His life and environment.* New York: Oxford University Press.

Berlyne, D. (1960). *Conflict, arousal, and curiosity.* New York: McGraw-Hill.

Bertens, H. (1995). *The idea of the postmodern: A history.* New York: Routledge.

Biesty, P. (2003). Where is play? In D. Lytle (Ed.). *Play and educational theory and practice: Play and culture studies,* 5 (pp. 44–55). Westport, CT: Praeger.

Birrell, S. (1981). Sport as ritual: Interpretations from Durkheim to Goffman. *Social forces,* 60: 354–376.

Birrell, S. (1983). Psychological dimensions of female athletic participation. In M. Boutilier and L. SanGiovanni (Eds.), *The sporting woman* (pp. 48–91). Champaign, IL: Human Kinetics.

Birrell, S. (1988). Discourses on the gender/sport relationship: From women in sport to gender relations. *Exercise and sport science reviews*, 16: 459–502.

Birrell, S., and Cole, C. (Eds.). (1994). *Women, sport, and culture*. Champaign, IL: Human Kinetics.

Birrell, S., and Richter, D. (1987). Is a diamond forever?: Feminist transformations of sport. *Women's studies international forum*, 10: 395–409.

Birrell, S., and Theberge, N. (1994). Feminist resistance and transformation in sport. In D. Costa and S. Guthrie (Eds.), *Women and sport: Interdisciplinary perspectives* (pp. 361–376). Champaign, IL: Human Kinetics.

Blumer, H. (1969). *Symbolic interactionism: Perspective and method*. Englewood Cliffs, NJ: Prentice-Hall.

Bohannon, P. (1960). *Conscience Collective* and Culture. In E. Durkheim et al., *Essays on sociology and philosophy* (pp. 77–96). K. Wolff (Ed.). New York: Harper Torchbooks.

Bolin, A. (1992). Vandalized vanity: Feminine physiques betrayed and portrayed. In F. E. Mascia-Lees and P. Sharpe (Eds.), *Tattoo, torture, mutilation, and adornment* (pp. 79–90). Albany: State University of New York Press.

Bolin, A., and Granskog, J. (Eds.). (2003). *Athletic intruders: Ethnographic research on women, culture, and exercise*. Albany: State University of New York Press.

Boorstin, D. (1962). *The image: A guide to pseudo-events in America*. New York: Harper Colophon.

Bordo, S. (1993). *Unbearable weight: Feminism, western culture, and the body*. Berkeley: University of California Press.

Bottomore, T. (1964). Introduction. In K. Marx, *Selected writings in sociology and social philosophy* (pp. 1–48). T. Bottomore (Ed.). New York: McGraw-Hill.

Bourdieu, P. (1984). *Distinction: A social critique of the judgement of taste*. R. Nice (Trans.). Cambridge: Harvard University Press.

Bourdieu, P. (1993). *The field of cultural production: Essays on art and literature*. New York: Columbia University Press.

Bourdieu, P., and Passeron, J. (1977). *Reproduction in education, society, and culture*. London: Sage.

Boutilier, M., and SanGiovanni, L. (Eds.). (1983). *The sporting woman*. Champaign, IL: Human Kinetics.

Brantlinger, P. (1990). *Crusoe's footprints: Cultural studies in Britain and America*. New York: Routledge.

Brohm, J. (1978). *Sport: A prison of measured time*. London: Ink Links.

Brubaker, R. (1984). *The limits of rationality: An essay on the social and moral thought of Max Weber*. London: George Allen and Unwin.

Bruner, J. S., Jolly, A., and Sylva, K. (1976). *Play—its role in evolution and development*. New York: Basic Books.

Burns, T. (1992). *Erving Goffman*. New York: Routledge.

Cahn, S. (1994). *Coming on strong: Gender and sexuality in twentieth-century women's sports*. New York: Free Press.

Caillois, R. (1961). *Man, play, and games*. New York: Free Press.

Cantelon, H., and Ingham, G. (2002). Max Weber and the sociology of sport. In J. Maguire and K. Young (Eds.), *Theory, sport, and society* (pp. 63–81). New York: JAI.

Cantor, N. (1997). *The American century*. New York: Harper Collins.

Chick, G. (2001). What is play for? Sexual selection and the evolution of play. In S. Reifel (Ed.), *Theory: In context and out: Play and culture studies, 3* (pp. 3–25). Westport, CT: Ablex.

Christie, J. (Ed). (1991). *Play and early literacy development*. Albany: State University of New York Press.

Clark, T. (1973). *Prophets and patrons: The French university and the emergence of the social sciences*. Cambridge: Harvard University Press.

Coakley, J. (1996a). Play group versus organized competitive team: A comparison. In D. Eitzen (Ed.), *Sport in contemporary society: An anthology*, 5th ed. (pp. 53–61). New York: St. Martin's.

Coakley, J. (1996b). Sport in society: An inspiration or an opiate? In D. Eitzen (Ed.), *Sport in contemporary society: An anthology*, 5th ed. (pp. 32–49). New York: St. Martin's.

Coleman, J. (1961). *The adolescent society*. New York: Free Press.

Colie, R. (1964). Johan Huizinga and the task of cultural history. *American Historical Review*, 47: 607–630.

Collins, R. (1986). *Max Weber: A skeleton key*. Beverly Hills, CA: Sage.

Collins, R. (1988). Theoretical continuities in Goffman's work. In P. Drew and A. Wooton (Eds.), *Exploring the interaction order* (pp. 41–63). Boston: Northeastern University Press.

Collins, R. (1994). *Four sociological traditions*. New York: Oxford University Press.

Collins, R., and Makowsky, M. (1993). *The discovery of society*, 5th ed. New York: McGraw-Hill.

Comaroff, J., and Comaroff, J. (1993). *Modernity and its malcontents: Ritual and power in postcolonial Africa*. Chicago: University of Chicago Press.

Coser, L. (1960). Durkheim's conservatism and its implications for his sociological theory. In E. Durkheim et al., *Essays on sociology and philosophy* (pp. 211–232). K. Wolff (Ed.). New York: Harper Torchbooks.

Coser, L. (1965) Georg Simmel. In L. Coser (Ed.), *Georg Simmel* (pp. 1–28). Englewood Cliffs, NJ: Prentice-Hall.

Coser, L. (1977). *Masters of sociological thought*, 2d ed. San Diego, CA: Harcourt, Brace, Jovanovich.

Costa, M., and Guthrie, S. (Eds.). (1994). *Women and sport: Interdisciplinary perspectives*. Champaign, IL: Human Kinetics.

Cox, H. (1969). *The feast of fools: A theological essay on festivity and fantasy*. New York: Harper and Row.

Csikszentmihalyi, C. (1975). *Beyond boredom and anxiety*. San Francisco: Jossey-Bass.

Csikszentmihalyi, C. (1990). *Flow: The psychology of optimal experience*. New York: Harper and Row.

Curry, T., and Jiobu, R. (1984). *Sports: A social perspective*. Englewood Cliffs, NJ: Prentice-Hall.

Daly, G. (1999). Marxism and post-modernity. In A Gamble, D. Marsh, and T. Tant (Eds.), *Marxism and social science* (pp. 61–84). Champaign: University of Illinois Press.

Denzin, N. (1977). *Childhood socialization*. San Francisco: Jossey-Bass.

Derrida, J. (1981). *Positions*. Chicago: University of Chicago Press.

Doty, W. (1986). *The study of myth and ritual*. Tuscaloosa: University of Alabama Press.

Douglas, Mary. (1960). *Purity and Danger*. New York: Praeger.

Duncan, M. (1988). Play discourse and the rhetorical turn: A semiological analysis of *Homo Ludens*. *Play and culture*, 1: 28–42.

Dunning, E. (1988). *The roots of football hooliganism: An historical and sociological study*. London: Routledge and Kegan Paul.

During, S. (1993). Introduction. In S. During (Ed.), *The cultural studies reader* (pp. 1–28). London: Routledge.

Durkheim, E. (1951). *Suicide: A study in sociology*. New York: Free Press.

Durkheim, E. (1960). The dualism of human nature and its social conditions. In E. Durkheim et al., *Essays on sociology and philosophy* (pp. 325–340). K. Wolff (Ed.). New York: Harper Torchbooks.

Durkheim, E. (1961). *Moral education: A study in the theory and application of the sociology of education*. New York: Free Press.

Durkheim, E. (1964a). *The division of labor in society*. New York: Free Press.

Durkheim, E. (1964b). *The rules of sociological method*. New York: Free Press.

Durkheim, E. (1965). *The elementary forms of the religious life*. New York: Free Press.

Durkheim, E. (1972): *Emile Durkheim: Selected writings*. A. Giddens (Ed.). New York: Cambridge University Press.

Durkheim, E., and Mauss, M. (1963). *Primitive classification*. Chicago: University of Chicago Press.

Edwards, H. (1973). *Sociology of sport*. Homewood, IL: Dorsey.

Edwards, H. (1984). The collegiate arms race: Origins and implications of the "Rule 48" controversy. *Journal of sport and social issues*, 8: 4–22.

Ehrman, J. (1968). *Homo Ludens* revisited. *Yale French Studies*, 41: 31–57.

Elias, N. (1996). *The Germans: Power struggles and the development of habitus in the nineteenth and twentieth centuries*. Cambridge: Polity Press.

Elias, N. (2000). *The civilizing process: Sociogenetic and psychogenetic investigations*, rev. ed. E. Dunning, J. Goudsblom, and S. Mennell (Eds.). E. Jephcott (Trans.). Maldon, MA: Blackwell.

Elias, N., and Dunning, E. (1986). *The quest for excitement: Sport and leisure in the civilizing process*. Oxford: Basil Blackwell.

Ellis, M. (1973). *Why people play*. Englewood Cliffs, NJ: Prentice-Hall.

Engels, F. (1986). *The origin of the family, private property, and the state*. New York: Penguin.

Erikson, E. (1950). *Childhood and society*. New York: Norton.

Erikson, E. (1977). *Toys and reasons*. New York: W. W. Norton.

Fagen, R. (1981). *Animal play behavior*. New York: Oxford University Press.

Fernandez, R. (2003). *Mappers of society: The lives, times, and legacies of the great sociologists*. Westport, CT: Praeger.

Festle. M. J. (1996). *Playing nice: Politics and apologies in women's sports*. New York: Columbia University Press.

Fine, G. (1983). *Shared fantasy: Role-playing games as social worlds*. Chicago: University of Chicago Press.

Foucault, M. (1979). *Discipline and punish*. Harmondsworth, England: Penguin.

Freud, S. (1938). *The basic writings of Sigmund Freud.* A. A. Brill (Ed.). New York: Modern Library.

Freud, S. (1952). *A general introduction to psychoanalysis.* New York: Washington Square.

Freud, S. (1957). Beyond the pleasure principle. In J. Rickman (Ed.). *A general selection from the works of Sigmund Freud* (pp. 141–168). Garden City, NY: Doubleday Anchor Books.

Freud. S. (1958). *On creativity and the unconscious: Papers on the psychology of art, literature, love, and religion.* B. Nelson (Ed.). New York: Harper and Row.

Freud, S. (1962). *Civilization and its discontents.* New York: W. W. Norton.

Freund, J. (1969). *The sociology of Max Weber.* New York: Vintage Books.

Frey, J., and Eitzen, D. (1991) Sport and society. *Annual review of sociology,* 17: 503–522.

Frisby, D. (1981). *Sociological impressionism: A reassessment of Georg Simmel's social theory.* London: Heinemann.

Frisby, D. (1984). *Georg Simmel.* London: Tavistock.

Fromm, E. (1955). *The sane society.* New York: Holt, Rinehart, and Winston.

Fromm, E. (1956). *The art of loving.* New York: Harper and Row.

Fromm, E. (1999). *Marx's concept of man.* New York: Continuum.

Fustel de Coulanges, N. (1980). *The ancient city.* Baltimore: Johns Hopkins.

Gamble, A. (1999). Why bother with Marxism? In A. Gamble, D. Marsh, and T. Tant (Eds.), *Marxism and social science* (pp. 1–8). Urbana: University of Illinois Press.

Garfinkel, H. (1967). *Studies in ethnomethodology.* New York: Prentice-Hall.

Geertz, C. (1972). Deep play: Notes on the Balinese cockfight. *Daedalus,* 101: 1–28.

Geertz, C. (1973). *The interpretation of cultures: Selected essays.* New York: Basic books.

Geertz, C. (1983). *Local knowledge.* New York: Basic Books.

Gerth, H., and Mills, C. W. (1958). Introduction: The man and his work. In M. Weber, *From Max Weber: Essays in sociology.* C. W. Mills and H. Gerth (Trans. and Eds.). New York: Oxford University Press.

Geyl, P. (1963). Huizinga as accuser of his age. *History and theory,* 2: 231–262.

Giddens, A. (1972). Introduction: Durkheim's writings in sociology and social philosophy. In E. Durkheim, *Emile Durkheim: Selected writings* (pp. 1–50). A. Giddens (Ed). New York: Cambridge University Press.

Giddens, A. (1978). *Emile Durkheim.* New York: Penguin.

Gilroy, S. (1997). Working on the body: Links between physical activity and social power. In G. Clarke (Ed.), *Researching women and sport* (pp. 96–112). London: Macmillan.

Goffman, E. (1956). The nature of deference and demeanor. *American anthropologist,* 58: 473–502.

Goffman, E. (1959). *The presentation of self in everyday life.* Garden City, NY: Doubleday.

Goffman, E. (1961a). *Asylums.* Garden City, NY: Doubleday.

Goffman, E. (1961b) *Encounters: Two studies in the sociology of interaction.* Indianapolis: Bobbs-Merrill.

Goffman, E. (1963). *Stigma: Notes on the management of spoiled identity.* Englewood Cliffs, NJ: Prentice-Hall.

Goffman, E. (1967). *Interaction ritual: Essays on face-to-face behavior.* Garden City, NY: Doubleday Anchor.

Goffman, E. (1969). *Strategic interaction.* Philadelphia: University of Pennsylvania Press.

Goffman, E. (1974). *Frame analysis: An essay on the organization of experience.* New York: Harper Colophon.

Goffman, E. (1981). *Forms of talk.* Oxford: Basil Blackwell.

Gonos, G. (1980). The class position of Goffman's sociology. In J. Ditton (Ed.), *The view from Goffman* (pp. 134–169). New York: St. Martin's.

Gouldner, A. (1970). *The coming crisis of western sociology.* New York: Avon Books.

Greendorfer, S. (1983). Gender role stereotypes in early childhood socialization. In G. Cohen (Ed.), *Women in sport: Issues and controversies* (pp. 3–14). Newbury Park, CA: Sage.

Gruneau, R. (1980). Freedom and constraint: The paradoxes of play, games, and sports. *Journal of sport history,* 7: 68–85.

Gruneau, R. (1983). *Class, sports, and social development.* Amherst: University of Massachusetts Press.

Guttmann, A. (1978). *From ritual to record: The nature of modern sports.* New York: Columbia University Press.

Hall, M. A. (1990). How should we theorize gender in the context of sport? In M. Messner and D. Sabo (Eds.), *Sport, men, and the gender order* (pp. 223–240). Champaign, IL: Human Kinetics.

Hall, M. A. (1996). *Feminism and sporting bodies: Essays on theory and practice.* Champaign, IL; Human Kinetics.

Handelman, D. (1990). *Models and mirrors: Toward an anthropology of public events.* New York: Cambridge.

Handelman, D. (1992). Passage to play: Paradox and process. *Play and culture,* 5: 1–19.

Handelman, D. (1998). *Models and mirrors: Toward an anthropology of public events.* New York: Berghahn Books.

Hans, J. (1981). *The play of the world.* Amherst: University of Massachusetts Press.

Hargreaves, J. (1994). *Sporting females: Critical issues in the history and sociology of women's sports.* New York: Routledge.

Hargreaves, J. (2000). *Heroines of sport: The politics of difference and identity.* New York: Routledge.

Harris, M. (1974). *Cows, pigs, wars, and witches.* New York: Vintage.

Hegel, G. (1977). *Phenomenology of spirit.* Oxford: Clarendon.

Held, D. (1980). *Introduction to critical theory: Horkheimer to Habermas.* Berkeley: University of California Press.

Heller, C. (Ed.). (1985). *Sructured social inequality: A reader in comparative social stratification.* New York: Macmillan.

Henricks, T. (1983). Toward a general theory of alienation. *Sociological inquiry,* 53:3: 200–221.

Henricks, T. (1988). Social science meets Updike: The passion for sport as personal regression. *Aethlon: The journal of sport literature,* 2: 131–146.

Henricks, T. (1991). *Disputed pleasures: Sport and society in preindustrial England.* New York: Greenwood Press.

Henricks, T. (1999). Play as ascending meaning: Implications of a general model of play. In S. Reifel (Ed.), *Play and culture studies 2: Play contexts revisited* (pp. 257–277). Stamford, CT: Ablex.

Henricks, T. (2001). Play and postmodernism. In S. Reifel (Ed.), *Theory in context and out: Play and culture studies 3* (pp. 51–72). Westport, CT: Ablex.

Henricks, T. (2002). Huizinga's contributions to play studies: A reappraisal. In J. Roopnarine (Ed.), *Conceptual, social-cognitive, and contextual issues in the fields of play: Play and culture studies, 4* (pp. 23–52). Westport, CT: Ablex.

Hinkle, R. (1960). Durkheim in American sociology. In E. Durkheim et al., *Essays on sociology and philosophy* (pp. 267–295). K. Wolff (Ed.). New York: Harper Torchbooks.

Hoch, P. (1972). *Rip off the big game: The exploitation of sports by the power elite.* Garden City, NY: Doubleday Anchor.

Horkheimer, M., and Adorno, T. (1972). *Dialectic of enlightenment.* New York: Herder and Herder.

Huizinga, J. (1936). *In the shadow of tomorrow.* New York: W. W. Norton.

Huizinga, J. (1954). *The waning of the middle ages.* Garden City, NY: Doubleday Anchor.

Huizinga, J. (1955). *Homo ludens: A study of the play-element in culture.* Boston: Beacon.

James, W. (1950). *Principles of psychology*, vol. 2. (pp. 283–324). New York: Dover Publications.

Jameson, F. (1991). *Postmodernism, or, the cultural logic of late capitalism.* Durham, NC: Duke University Press.

Jarvie, G., and Maguire, J. (1994). *Sport and leisure in social thought.* New York: Routledge.

Jay, M. (1973). *The dialectical imagination: A history of the Frankfurt School and the Institute for Social Research, 1923–1950.* Boston: Little, Brown.

Judd, D., and Fainstein, S. (1999). *The tourist's city.* New Haven, CT: Yale University Press.

Kant, I. (1968). *Critique of Judgment.* H. Bernard (Trans.). NY: Hafner Publishing.

Kasler, D. (1989). *Max Weber: An introduction to his life and work.* P. Hurd (Trans.). Chicago: University of Chicago Press.

Kidd, B. (1990). The men's cultural centre: Sports and the dynamics of women's oppression / men's repression. In M. Messner and D. Sabo (Eds.), *Sport, men, and the gender order: Critical feminist perspectives* (pp. 31–44). Champaign, IL: Human Kinetics.

Klugman, E., and Smilansky, S (Eds.). (1990). *Children's play and learning: Perspectives and policy implications.* New York: Teacher's College Press.

Krieken, R. (1998). *Norbert Elias.* New York: Routledge.

Kuchler, T. (1994). *Postmodern gaming: Heidegger, Duchamp, Derrida.* New York: Peter Lang.

Lancy, D., and Tindall, B. (Eds.). (1976). *The anthropological study of play: Problems and prospects.* Cornwall, NY: Leisure Press.

Lefebvre, H. (1969). *The sociology of Marx.* N. Gutterman (Trans.). New York: Vintage.

Levi-Strauss, C. (1967). *Structural anthropology.* Garden City, NY: Doubleday Anchor.

Levine, D. (1971). Introduction. In G. Simmel, *On individuality and social forms* (pp. ix–lxv). D. Levine (Ed.). Chicago: University of Chicago Press.

Levine, D. (1981). Rationality and freedom: Weber and beyond. *Sociological inquiry*, 51: 5–25.

Levine, P. (1986). *A. G. Spalding and the rise of baseball: The promise of American sport*. New York: Oxford University Press.

Levy, J. (1978). *Play behavior*. New York: John Wiley and Sons.

Lewis, G. (1980). *Days shining of red: An essay on the understanding of ritual*. Cambridge: Cambridge University Press.

Lieberman, J. (1977). *Playfulness: Its relation to imagination and creativity*. New York: Academic Press.

Lin, S-H., and Reifel, S. (1999). Context and meanings in Taiwanese kindergarten play. In S. Reifel (Ed.), *Play contexts revisited: Play and culture studies, 2* (pp. 151–176). Greenwich, CT: Ablex.

Loewith, K. (1970). Weber's interpretation of the bourgeois-capitalistic world in terms of the guiding principle of rationalization. In D. Wrong (Ed.), *Max Weber* (pp. 101–122). Englewood Cliffs, NJ: Prentice-Hall.

Lofland, J. (1980). Early Goffman: Style, structure, substance, soul. In J. Ditton (Ed.), *The view from Goffman* (pp. 24–51). New York: St. Martin's.

Loy, J. (1968). The Nature of sport: A definitional effort. *Quest monographs*, 10: 1–15.

Loy, J. (Ed.). (1982). *The paradoxes of play*. West Point, NY: Leisure Press.

Loy, J., and Booth, D. (2002). Emile Durkheim, structural functionalism, and the sociology of sport. In J. Maguire and K. Young (Eds.), *Theory, sport, and society* (pp. 41–62). New York: JAI.

Lugones, M. (1987). "Playfulness, world-traveling, and loving perception." *Hypatia*, 2: 3–19.

Lukes, S. (1985). *Emile Durkheim: His life and work*. Stanford, CA: Stanford University Press.

Luschen, G. (1967). The interdependence of sport and culture. *International review of sport sociology*, 2: 127–139.

MacAloon, J. (Ed.). (1984). *Rite, drama, festival, spectacle: Rehearsals toward a theory of cultural performance*. Philadelphia: Institute for the Study of Human Issues.

Maguire, J., and Young, K. (Eds.). (2002). *Theory, sport, and society*. New York: JAI.

Malcolmson, R. (1973). *Popular recreations in English society: 1700–1850*. Cambridge: Cambridge University Press.

Malinowski, B. (1948). *Magic, science, religion, and other essays*. Glencoe, IL: Free Press.

Mandel, E. (1975). *Late capitalism*. London: New Left Books.

Mandel, E., and G. Novack. (1970). *The Marxist theory of alienation*. New York: Pathfinder Press.

Mangan, J. A., and Park, R. (Eds.). (1987). *From fair sex to feminism: Women in the industrial and postindustrial eras*. London: Frank Cass.

Manning, P. (1992). *Erving Goffman and modern sociology*. Stanford, CA: Stanford University Press.

Marcuse, H. (1941). *Reason and revolution*. New York: Oxford University Press.

Marcuse, H. (1964). *One-dimensional man.* Boston: Beacon Press.

Marling, K. (Ed.). (1997). *Designing Disney's theme parks: The architecture of reassurance.* Montreal: Canadien Centre for Architecture.

Martindale, D. et al. (1958). Introduction: Max Weber's sociology of music. In M. Weber, *The rational and social foundations of music* (pp. xi–lii). Carbondale: Southern Illinois University Press.

Marx, K. (1964). *Selected writings in sociology and social philosophy.* T. Bottomore (Ed. and Trans.). New York: McGraw-Hill.

Marx, K. (1972). Alienation and social classes. In R. Tucker (Ed.), *The Marx-Engels reader* (pp. 104–106). New York: Norton.

Marx, K. (1995). *The poverty of philosophy.* H. Quelch (Trans.). New York: Prometheus Books.

Marx, K. (1999). Economic and philosophical manuscripts. T. Bottomore (Trans.). In E. Fromm, *Marx's concept of man* (pp. 87–196). New York: Continuum.

Marx, K., and Engels, F. (1959). *Basic writings on politics and philosophy.* L. Feuer (Ed.). Garden City, NY: Doubleday Anchor.

Mennell, S. (1992). *Norbert Elias: An introduction.* Cambridge, MA: Blackwell.

Mennell, S., and Goudsblom, J. (Eds.). (1998). *Norbert Elias on civilization, power, and knowledge.* Chicago: University of Chicago Press.

Mergen, B. (Ed). (1986). *Cultural dimensions of play, games, and sports.* Champaign, IL: Human Kinetics.

Merton, R. (1957). *Social theory and social structure.* Glencoe, IL: Free Press.

Merton, R. (1967). *On theoretical sociology.* New York: Free Press.

Messner, M., and Sabo, D. (Eds.). (1990). *Sport, men, and the gender order: Critical feminist perspectives.* Champaign, IL: Human Kinetics.

Mills, C. W. (1959). *The power elite.* New York: Oxford University Press.

Mitzman, A. (1969). *The iron cage: An historical interpretation of Max Weber.* New York: Grosset and Dunlap.

Morgan, L. H. (2000). *Ancient society.* Cambridge: Harvard University Press.

Murchland, B. (1971). *The age of alienation.* New York: Random House.

Nagel, M. (1998). Play in culture and the jargon of primordiality: A critique of *Homo Ludens. Play and culture studies,* 1: 19–30.

Neyer, J. (1960). Individualism and socialism in Durkheim. In E. Durkheim et al., *Essays on sociology and philosophy* (pp. 32–76). K. Wolff (Ed.). New York: Harper Torchbooks.

Nisbet, R. 1965. *Emile Durkheim, with selected essays.* Englewood Cliffs, NJ: Prentice-Hall.

Nisbet, R. (1966). *The sociological tradition.* New York: Basic Books.

Norget, K. (2000). Ritual. In R. Scupin (Ed.), *Religion and culture: An anthropological perspective* (pp. 80–105). Englewood Cliffs, NJ: Prentice-Hall.

Opie, I., and Opie, P. (1959). *The lore and language of schoolchildren.* New York: Oxford University Press.

Opie, I., and Opie, P. (1969). *Children's games in the street and playground.* New York: Oxford University Press.

Ortega, R. (2003). Play, activity, and thought: Reflections on Piaget's and Vygotsky's theories. In D. Lytle (Ed.), *Play and educational theory and practice: Play and culture studies,* 5 (pp. 99–116). Westport, CT: Praeger.

Pampel, F. (2000). *Sociological lives and ideas: An introduction to the classical theorists.* New York: Worth.

Parsons, T. (1968). *The structure of social action,* 2 vols. New York: Free Press.

Parsons, T. (1971). *The system of modern societies.* Englewood Cliffs, NJ: Prentice-Hall.

Parsons, T. (1974). The life and work of Emile Durkheim. In E. Durkheim, *Sociology and philosophy* (pp. xliii–lxx). New York: Free Press.

Pescolido, B., and Rubin, B. (2000). The web of group-affiliations revisited: Social life, postmodernism, and sociology. *American sociological review,* 65: 52–76.

Piaget, J. (1962). *Play, dreams, and imitation in childhood.* New York: Norton.

Pierce, A. (1960). Durkheim and functionalism. In E. Durkheim et al., *Essays on sociology and philosophy* (pp. 154–169). K. Wolff (Ed.). New York: Harper Torchbooks.

Plumb, J. (1973). *The commercialization of pleasure in eighteenth-century England.* Reading, England: University of Reading Press.

Poggi, G. (1993). *Money and the modern mind: Georg Simmel and the philosophy of money.* Berekely: University of California Press.

Radcliffe-Brown, A. R. (1972). *Structure and function in primitive society.* Glencoe, IL: Free Press.

Rappaport, R. (1968). *Pigs for ancestors: Ritual in the ecology of a New Guinea people.* New Haven, CT: Yale University Press.

Reifel, S. (Ed.). (1999). *Play contexts revisited: Play and culture studies, 2.* Greenwich, CT: Ablex.

Richter, M. (1960). Durkheim's politics and political theory. In E. Durkheim et al., *Essays on sociology and philosophy* (pp. 170–210). K. Wolff (Ed.). New York: Harper Torchbooks.

Riesman, D. (with Denney, R., and Glazer, N.). (1950). *The lonely crowd: A study in the changing American character.* New Haven, CT: Yale University Press.

Rigauer, B. (1981). *Work and sport.* A. Guttmann (Trans.). New York: Columbia University Press.

Ritzer, G. (1983). *Sociological theory.* New York: Alfred A. Knopf.

Ritzer, G. (1994). *The McDonaldization of society.* Newbury Park, CA: Pine Forge Press.

Rogers, C., and J. Sawyers. (1995). *Play in the lives of young children.* Washington, D.C.: National Association for the Education of Young Children.

Roopnarine, J., Johnson, J., and Hooper, F. (1994). *Children's play in diverse cultures.* Albany: State University of New York Press.

Rosenau, P. (1992). *Post-modernism and the social sciences: Insights, inroads, intrusions.* Princeton, NJ: Princeton University Press.

Rossiter, C. (1960). *Marxism: The view from America.* New York: Harcourt, Brace, and World.

Roszak, T. (1972). Forbidden games. In M. Hart (Ed.)., *Sport in the socio-cultural process* (pp. 91–104). Dubuque, IA: William C. Brown.

Rubin, K. (Ed.). (1980). *Children's play.* San Francisco: Jossey-Bass.

Rubin, K., Fein, G., and Vandenberg, B. (1983). Play. In E. K. Heatherington (Ed.), *Handbook of child psychology, vol. 4: Socialization, personality and social development.* New York: Wiley.

Sage, G. (1990). *Power and ideology in American sport: A critical perspective.* Champaign, IL: Human Kinetics.

Sartre, J. (1956). *Being and nothingness: A phenomenological essay on ontology.* H. Barnes (Trans.). New York: Citadel Press.

Schechner, R. (1988). Playing. *Play and culture*, 1: 3–27.

Schiller, H. (1989). *Culture, inc.* Oxford: Oxford University Press.

Sica, A. (2000). Rationalization and culture. In S. Turner (Ed.), *The Cambridge companion to Weber* (pp. 42–58). Cambridge: Cambridge University Press.

Simmel, G. (1950). *The sociology of Georg Simmel*. K. Wolff (Trans. and Ed.). New York: Free Press.

Simmel, G. (1955). *Conflict and the web of group-affiliations*. K. Wolff and R. Bendix (Trans. and Eds.). New York: Free Press.

Simmel, G. (1971). *On Individuality and social forms*. D. Levine (Ed.). Chicago: University of Chicago Press.

Simmel, G. (1978). *The philosophy of money*. T. Bottomore and D. Frisby (Trans. and Eds.). London: Routledge and Kegan Paul.

Simmel, G. (1984). *Georg Simmel: On women, sexuality, and love*. Guy Oakes (Trans.). New Haven, CT: Yale University Press.

Simmel, G. (1997). *Simmel on culture*. D. Frisby and M. Featherstone (Eds.). Thousand Oaks, CA: Sage.

Smith, P. (1982). Does play matter? Functional and evolutionary aspects of animal and human play. *Behaviorial and brain science*, 5: 139–155.

Smith, P. (1986). *Children's play: Research developments and practical applications*. New York: Gordon and Breach.

Spariosu, M. (1989). *Dionysus reborn: Play and the aesthetic dimension in modern philosophical and scientific discourse*. Ithaca, NY: Cornell University Press.

Sponseller, D. (1974). *Play as a learning medium*. Washington, D.C.: National Association for the Education of Young Children.

Stone, G. (1955). American sports—play and display. *Chicago review*, 9: 83–100.

Suttles, G. (1968). *The social order of the slum*. Chicago: University of Chicago Press.

Sutton-Smith, B. (1997). *The ambiguity of play*. Cambridge: Harvard University Press.

Sutton-Smith, B. (2001). Reframing the variability of players and play. In S. Reifel (Ed.), *Theory in context and out: Play and culture studies*, 3 (pp. 27–50). Westport, CT: Ablex.

Sutton-Smith, B. (2003). Tertiary emotions and ludic nature—the ideologies and human nature. In M. Kruger (Ed.), *Menschenbilder im sport* (pp. 263–280). Berlin: Verlag Karl Hoffmann.

Sutton-Smith, B. (2004). The theory and practice of play. Address given at the Association for the Study of Play annual meeting, February 20, 2004. Atlanta, GA.

Sutton-Smith, B., and Kelly-Byrne, D. (1984a). The idealization of play. In P. Smith (Ed.), *Play in animals and humans* (pp. 305–321). London: Basil Blackwell.

Sutton-Smith, B., and Kelly-Byrne, D. (1984b). The phenomenon of bipolarity in play theories. In T. Yawkey and A. Pellegrini (Eds.), *Child's play: Development and applied* (pp. 29–47). Hillsdale, NJ: Laurence Erlbaum.

Sutton-Smith, B., Mechling, J., Johnson, T., and McMahon, F. (1995). *Children's folklore: a sourcebook*. New York: Garland.

Theberge, N. (1994). Toward a feminist alternative to sport as a male preserve. In S. Birrell and C. Cole (Eds.), *Women, sport, and culture* (pp. 181–192). Champaign, IL: Human Kinetics.

Theberge, N., and Birrell, S. (1994). The sociological study of women and sport. In D. Costa and S. Guthrie (Eds.), *Women and sport: Interdisciplinary perspectives* (pp. 323–330). Champaign, IL: Human Kinetics.

Tocqueville, A. de. (1945). *Democracy in America,* 2 vols. New York: Alfred Knopf.

Toennies, F. (1963). *Community and society.* C. Loomis (Trans. and Ed.). New York: Harper Torchbooks.

Turner, S. (2000). Introduction. In S. Turner (Ed.), *The Cambridge companion to Weber* (pp. 1–20). Cambridge: Cambridge University Press.

Turner, V. (1967). *The forest of symbols: Aspects of Ndembu ritual.* Ithaca, NY: Cornell University Press.

Turner, V. (1969). *The ritual process: Structure and anti-structure.* Chicago: Aldine.

Turner, V. (1982). *From ritual to theatre: The human seriousness of play.* New York: Performing Arts Journal Publications.

Van Gennep, A. (1960). *The rites of passage.* Chicago: University of Chicago Press.

Van Krieken, R. (1998). *Norbert Elias.* New York: Routledge.

Veblen, T. (1934). *The theory of the leisure class: An economic study of institutions.* New York: Random House.

Veblen, T. (1953). *The theory of the leisure class: An economic study of institutions.* New York: Mentor Books,

Von Neumann, J., and Morgenstern, O. (1944). *Theory of games and economic behavior.* Princeton, NJ: Princeton University Press.

Vygotsky, L. (1962). *Thought and language.* Cambridge: MIT Press.

Weber, Marianne. (1975). *Max Weber: A biography.* New York: John Wiley.

Weber, M. (1958a). *From Max Weber: Essays in sociology.* C. W. Mills and H. Gerth (Trans. and Eds.). New York: Oxford University Press.

Weber, M. (1958b). *The Protestant ethic and the spirit of capitalism.* T. Parsons (Trans.). New York: Charles Scribner's Sons.

Weber, M. (1958c). *The rational and social foundations of music.* D. Martindale et al. (Trans.). Carbondale: Southern Illinois University Press.

Weber, M. (1964). *The theory of social and economic organization.* T. Parsons (Trans. and Ed.). New York: Free Press.

Weingartner, R. (1962). *Experience and culture: The philosophy of Georg Simmel.* Middletown, CT: Wesleyan University Press.

Weinstein, D. and Weinstein, M. (1993). *Postmodern(ized) Simmel.* New York: Routledge.

Whyte, W. (1956). *The organization man.* New York: Simon and Schuster.

Williams, R. (1988). Understanding Goffman's methods. In P. Drew and A. Wootton (Eds.), *Erving Goffman: Exploring the interaction order* (pp. 64–88). Boston: Northeastern University Press.

Willis, P. (1982). Women in sport and ideology. In J. Hargreaves (Ed.), *Sport, culture, and ideology* (pp. 117–135). London: Routledge and Kegan Paul.

Wimbush, E. (1989). *Relative freedoms; Women and leisure.* New York: Taylor and Francis.

Wohl, A. (1970). Competitive sport and its social functions. *International review of sport sociology,* 5: 117–124.

Wolfenstein, M., and Leites, N. (1950). *Movies: A psychological study.* Glencoe, IL: Free Press.

Wolff, K. (1950). Introduction. In G. Simmel, *The sociology of Georg Simmel* (pp. xvii–lxiv). K. Wolff (Trans. and Ed.). New York: Free Press.

Wrong, D. (1970). Introduction: Max Weber. In M. Weber, *Max Weber* (pp. 1–76). Englewood Cliffs, NJ: Prentice-Hall.

INDEX

Adorno, T., 42–43, 91
adventure, 122–124
agon. See contests
alienation: in Marx, 31, 38–41, 52; in Marxian analysis of sport, 47–48
Alport, H., 70
amateurism, 18, 21
asceticism, 47, 66–67, 75, 93, 144, 213
athleticism, 47–48

Bateson, G., 161, 171, 190–191
Baudrillard, J., 91
Benjamin, W., 42, 91
Biesty, P., 201
Birrell, S., 171–173, 177
body-building, 179
Bohannon, P., 63
Boorstin, D., 1
Bordo, S., 179
Bourdieu, P., 91, 178, 211; on forms of capital, 141, 176–177; on habitus, 142; on social distinction, 139–145; on sports participation, 143–145
British cultural studies, 44–45, 211
Brubaker, R., 83, 86
Burckhardt, J., 18
Burns, T., 148

Caillois, R., 23, 97, 209
Carroll, L., 2
CCCS. *See* British cultural studies
Coakley, J., 75–77
Collins, R., 82, 90, 149
communitas: collective effervescence as example of, 200; compared to play, 92–93, 197–200, 206–207; compared to ritual, 197–198, 206; as conformitive and consummatory

behavior, 193 (fig.); as descending meaning, 92–93; as integrative and unpredictable interaction, 203 (fig.), 204, 206–207; love as an example of, 199–200; postmodernism and, 207; sociability as example of, 198–199; in Turner, 73, 200
Comte, A., 56, 58, 83
conspicuous leisure. *See* leisure class; Veblen, T.
contests: in Goffman, 165–168; in Huizinga, 20–21, 53, 183; relationship to play and games, 208–214; and Sutton-Smith's rhetoric of power, 3–4; in Weber, 96–97. *See also* games; play, characteristics of; sport
critical theory. *See* Frankfurt School
Csikszentmihalyi, M., 153–154
culture industry, 42–43. See also Frankfurt School

Derrida, J., 91, 107
Douglas, M., 74
Dunning, E., 103–105
Durkheim, E.: on anomie, 59; on collective conscience in, 63–64, 73; on collective effervescence, 68–69; compared to Huizinga, 53–54; criticisms of, 64, 200; on human nature, 62–63; on individuation and individualism, 59–60, 198; life, 54–55; opposition to utilitarianism, 59, 62; political philosophy, 56; on ritual and play, 64–70, 196–197; on sacred and profane, 60–64; societal integration as theme of, 57; on society as reality of its own type, 58

THOMAS S. HENRICKS is Danieley Professor and Distinguished University Professor at Elon University, where he has centered his career. He received his B.A. from North Central College and his M.A. and Ph.D. in sociology from the University of Chicago. He is the author of *Disputed Pleasures: Sport and Society in Preindustrial England* and of numerous articles in a wide range of academic journals. Much of that writing has focused on the interaction between human experience and social and cultural forms. An active member of the Association for the Study of Play, he has concentrated several years on the nature and significance of adult play.

The University of Illinois Press
is a founding member of the
Association of American University Presses.

Composed in 9.5/12.5 Trump Mediaeval
at the University of Illinois Press
Manufactured by Thomson-Shore, Inc.

University of Illinois Press
1325 South Oak Street
Champaign, IL 61820-6903
www.press.uillinois.edu